D1309433

Get Cisco Certified and Get Ahead

Anne Martinez

McGraw-Hill

New York   San Francisco   Washington, D.C.
Auckland   Bogotá   Caracas   Lisbon   London
Madrid   Mexico City   Milan   Montreal   New Delhi
San Juan   Singapore   Sydney   Tokyo   Toronto

Library of Congress Cataloging-in-Publication Data

Martinez, Anne
    Get Cisco certified and get ahead / Anne Martinez.
       p.   cm.
   ISBN 0-07-135258-9
    1. Electronic data processing personnel—Certification. 2. Cisco
Systems, Inc. I. Title
QA76.3.M3255   1999
004.6'076—dc21
                                    99-33028
                                      CIP

McGraw-Hill

A Division of The McGraw-Hill Companies

1 2 3 4 5 6 7 8 9 0 AGM/AGM 9 0 4 3 2 1 0 9

ISBN 0-07-135258-9

The sponsoring editor for this book was Steven Elliot and the production supervisor
was Clare Stanley. It was set in New Century Schoolbook by Patricia Wallenburg.

Throughout this book, trademarked names are used. Rather than put a trademark symbol
after every occurrence of a trademarked name, we use names in an editorial fashion only,
and to the benefit of the trademark owner, with no intention of infringement of the
trademark. Where such designations appear in this book, they have been printed
with initial caps.

Printed and bound by Quebecor Martinsburg.

 This book is printed on recycled, acid-free paper containing
a minimum of 50% recycled, de-inked fiber.

Contents

Contents

Part 2   How to Get (Happily) Certified   69

5   Inside Perspectives   71

6   Dollars and Sense: Financial Answers Before You Begin   89

7   Certification Mistakes You Need Not Make   117

8   Understanding Training Alternatives   133

9   Your Personal Training and Certification Road Map   157

Preface

Cisco's CCIE designations are unquestionably the most respected in the industry. Numerous magazine articles have cited CCIE certification as a ticket to a six figure paycheck for computer professionals and a source of both extreme value and no small amount of stress to their employers. The stress comes from the fact that CCIEs are in such demand that they can pretty much change jobs it will, and employers have been known to poach them from each other.

A large measure of the CCIE designations' value comes from the very high level of expertise required before someone become's eligible to put those four letters after his or her name. And then there's the Internet and the explosion of corporate internetworking technology. Cisco is the leading vendor of the equipment that makes all these network interconnections work—routers and switches. Cisco claims 85% of the market share for routers and 35% of the market share for LAN switches. And these are not simple pieces of equipment—they have multiple network interface cards, their own operating system, algorithms and tables that tell them what to forward to where, and the ability to handle a vast array of protocols and physical network topologies.

Until recently, the very guru nature that has made Cisco certification so valuable also put it out of reach of many competent computer professionals who lacked the work environment or the experience to have even a reasonable shot at obtaining CCIE status. But Cisco certification is no longer an all or nothing proposition. In late 1998 Cisco added a tiered collection of certifications that from day one benefitted from having the prestige of the Cisco name attached to them. These new designations can be used as stepping stones by professionals with the CCIE as their ultimate goal, but also handily stand on their own as verification of internetworking skills at respectably high levels. And, thanks to the certification preparation resources that have appeared for these new certifications, even the coveted CCIE has moved within reach of more individuals.

But Cisco certification isn't just a tool to achieve a higher paycheck, it's a blueprint for continued learning and professional development. To reap the pleasures of working with the latest technologies as well as to protect ourselves from becoming limited by an out-of-date skill set, computer professionals must regularly update their existing skills and add new ones. The computer profession is a learning profession. But there are so many choices, and so much knowledge to choose from, that it can be difficult to know what to undertake next. This is especially true if you want to learn any new specialty. If you don't know the field, how are you supposed to know what to need to know? Certifications solve this problem by defining a learning pathway leading to a specific competency. All you have to do is start at the beginning and work through the requirements until you reach your goal of certification. Cisco's CCNA designation provides an entry point into internetworking for people completely new to the field. A CCIE is the prize for IT professionals who have already achieved a high level of internetworking expertise but seek to advance their careers even further. Other Cisco certifications lay out paths to competency in network design and advanced support.

Get Cisco Certified and Get Ahead is designed to help both experienced and novice computer professionals harness the power of Cisco certification. It is the only book that provides a complete picture of Cisco certification options as well as specific guidance on how to choose the right certification, earn it in an efficient and cost-effective way, and really put it to work as a career advancement tool.

In *Part 1:Why Certify?* you'll find the answers to 24 of the most commonly asked questions about Cisco certifications, learn how certification has become such an important force in the IT industry, and find out in detail the opportunities and benefits Cisco that certification can bring to you. You'll also hear from six individuals who have already earned Cisco certification as they described what the process was like for them, how well it has lived up to their expectations, and what advice they have to offer those who will follow in their footsteps. And, of course, you will learn about each Cisco certification: who will benefit, the material covered, what it takes to get it, and the suggested curriculum Cisco has defined to accompany it.

Part 2: How to Get (Happily) Certified opens with a chapter covering the financial ins and outs of getting Cisco certified. You'll learn how to estimate what your total expenditure will be and how to apply the tricks and techniques that can substantially lower your out-of-pocket costs. Next you'll find out the most common certification mistakes and how you can avoid them. You will also explore the wealth of training alternatives available to you, along with the strengths and weaknesses of each, develop your personal training and certification roadmap, find out what's needed to set up a home lab, and learn the study secrets that will make your journey to certification quicker and easier. The final chapter in this section lays out the specifics of Cisco certification exams. You'll find out how many questions you can expect to encounter on each exam, what form those questions will take, how long you'll have to answer them, and how and where to register when you're ready for your first exam. You'll also find a detailed, day-by-day breakdown of the CCIE hands-on lab exam and what it takes to pass it.

Part 3: Utilize Your Certification to the Max focuses on the often overlooked topic of how to get the most benefit from your certification after you've earned it. This begins with specific advice on promoting your new, certified status. You'll also find step-by-step advice on how to utilize your certification as a key to a new job, including learning how to find that job, or, if you are happy with your current employer, how to parlay your new credentials into a raise or promotion. Part 3 also describes how to take full advantage of the perks and privileges that accompany Cisco certification, shows you how and why to keep your certification and your skills current, and looks at the pros and cons of adding additional certifications in the future.

The resource section of *Get Cisco Certified and Get Ahead* puts an extensive collection of publications, Web sites, training and equipment vendors, free online documentation, a list of Cisco's authorized training partners, and other useful Cisco certification resources at your fingertips. You'll also find a table to help you decode the most commonly used Cisco acronyms and a glossary to introduce you to internetworking terminology.

This is an exciting time in the world of certification for computer professionals: a time when the demand for people with IT skills is expected to continue to outstrip the supply, a time when companies large and small have come to rely on the expertise that computer professionals bring, a time when more and more companies are using certification as a way to identify that expertise. If you've been thinking about getting Cisco certified, now is the time.

Acknowledgments

Many individuals contributed in large and small ways to the creation of this book, and because of them it's a more valuable resource than any single individual could possibly provide. The computer professionals who were kind enough to share in extensive detail their experiences with Cisco certification include: Scott Urban, Pamela Forsyth, Terry Slattery, Ben Lovegrove, Chad Marsh, and Lou Rossi. Lou, co-owner of CCPrep.com, also provided the sample exam questions incorporated into Chapter 11. Thanks to Tom M Thomas II for answering the oft raised question: "What do I need in my home lab?" with several detailed equipment lists, and to Jennifer Kalainikas for conducting the recruiter survey.

My appreciation also goes out to Paul Borghese for hosting the excellent www.groupstudy.com mailing list—a resource that made it possible for me to connect with already certified professionals as well as those who are just beginning, and to learn from both groups, and to each of the recruiters who took the time to complete and return my survey regarding the demand for people with Cisco skills.

I'm also grateful to Cisco Systems employees Ana Rada George, Cisco Career Certifications Program Manager, Ann Merlo, Marketing Communications Manager, and Gail Carruthers, CCIE Program Coordinator, who did their best to answer my frequent questions throughout the writing of this book.

Others who were instrumental to the creation of *Get Cisco Certified and Get Ahead* include Steve Elliot of McGraw-Hill, who helped mold this project into its finished form, Patty Wallenburg, who transformed close to 400 pages of text and graphics into high quality page proofs at her usual record speed, and to Martha Kaufman, my agent for this and other books.

Last, but far from least, thanks to Evan and Rebecca for all the times they entertained themselves while I worked on this book.

PART **1**

Why Certify?

CHAPTER 1

The Quick FAQs

1. What Does Cisco Certified Mean?

In the most basic sense, being Cisco certified means that you have met the requirements that Cisco Systems has created to identify specific levels of competence in working with Cisco products. This includes demonstrating your knowledge by passing exams and meeting other requirements.

While that's the technical definition, the practical application is perhaps more pertinent: being Cisco certified can give your career a substantial boost. The Cisco designations allow you to stand out as an expert in the networking field. They are credentials that many hiring managers hold in high esteem and there are plenty of Cisco related positions waiting to be filled.

Consider that Cisco sells more than $20,000,000 worth of products every day and employs 16,700 people in its own operations. The company shipped its millionth product in 1996 and reported revenues of $8.46 billion in fiscal 1998. That is a lot of product needing qualified people to operate it. Computer networking is not likely to go away any time soon or get any easier. In fact, growth in computer positions is currently outpacing the growth in supply of qualified computer professionals.

Cisco certifications, the CCIE in particular, have a reputation for being tough to obtain, and because of that convey significant professional accomplishment and ability. Being Cisco certified means that you are identified by a party other than yourself as an accomplished, skilled internetworking professional. It means that you can command the respect and financial compensation due such a person. It means you have a significant career leg up on individuals who do not hold such a credential. It means that you will be a top candidate to fill one of the many interesting and challenging job opportunities available.

2. Who Benefits from Cisco Certification?

Certification programs can benefit people and organizations working in the computer field, selling to the computer market, or employing technical people to perform computer-related tasks. Those with the most to gain are:

* Computer professionals
* Certification sponsors
* Employers
* Clients and customers.

Virtually any IS professional can get *something* (in addition to the official piece of paper) by pursuing a well-chosen certification. Most will reap many benefits. The payoffs may come in the form of a salary increase, better job, added confidence, or additional skills that allow you to move into a new area or perform your current functions more effectively. Course work often includes hands-on exercises with up-to-the-minute software and/or equipment, exposure you might not otherwise have.

This is not to claim that every certification program is equally valuable. But there are many, and Cisco's program is one of them, that can have a potentially dramatic impact your earning and advancement potential.

Certification sponsors benefit from these programs too. In addition to revenue from training courses and materials, certification programs generate product and company recognition. Every CCIE, CCNA, CCNP, CCDA, and CCDP is a confirmation of the power and importance of Cisco Systems in the computer industry. The more people Cisco teaches to master Cisco products, the more likely it is that those products will be successfully utilized to their fullest extent.

To employers, certification serves as independent evidence that you have demonstrated the skills and abilities required to complete the program. It also offers a method for bringing employees up to speed on the latest technologies, as well as a way to provide for the continuing education computer people often crave. Certification training can reasonably be billed as an employee benefit. Research has also shown that certified employees are more satisfied and more productive than their non-certified counterparts. Customers benefit, too, because a certification gives them additional evidence of your qualifications and suitability for the task at hand.

3. What Cisco Certifications Are There?

Cisco Systems currently offers so many choices it can be difficult to sort them out. To begin with, the eleven designations available as this book goes to press are:

* Cisco Certified Network Associate (CCNA)
* Cisco Certified Network Associate (CCNA)—WAN Switching
* Cisco Certified Network Professional (CCNP)
* Cisco Certified Network Professional (CCNP)—WAN Switching
* Cisco Certified Design Associate (CCDA)
* Cisco Certified Design Professional (CCDP)
* Cisco Certified Design Professional (CCDP)—WAN Switching
* Cisco Certified Internetwork Expert (CCIE)
* Cisco Certified Internetwork Expert (CCIE)—WAN Switching
* Cisco Certified Internetwork Expert (CCIE)—ISP Dial
* Certified Cisco Systems Instructor (CCSI).

All except the CCIE designations are what Cisco calls "training certifications" or "career certifications." That means that although it would certainly help, it isn't necessary to have extensive on-the-job experience to obtain one of them. For each of these Cisco has designed a specific curriculum and corresponding exams.

The certifications that incorporate the word "Network" are considered support-oriented—i.e. for ongoing operations—while the "Design" certifications involve designing networks. The CCNA (Cisco Certified Network Associate) is for individuals who install, configure, and operate simple-routed LAN, routed WAN, and switched networks. The professional level—CCNP (Cisco Certified Network Professional)—covers more complex networks and Dial Access services.

The first certification in the design track is the CCDA. This is Cisco's entry-level internetwork design certification. It was created to certify expertise in designing simple routed LAN, routed WAN, and switched LAN networks. The professional level, the CCDP, involves more complex network designs—those that include more protocols, connections, media, and so on.

The CCIE certifications, on the other hand, rely more on sub-stantial hands-on experience. They also have the added require-ment of completing an arduous lab test. The difficulty of qualify-ing for this certification adds considerably to its value in the marketplace.

With the exception of the CCDA certification, each of the desig-nations (CCNA, CCNP, CCDP, CCIE) has a WAN switching varia-tion. According to Cisco, there is no WAN switching partner to the CCDA certification because the complexity of designing WAN switching puts it above the associate level. The CCIE also has an ISP Dial variation. This certification covers IP routing, dialup, and remote access in addition to WAN technologies.

4. What Is Internetworking?

Networking is the science of connecting multiple computers and/or other devices such as printers so that they can communi-cate with each other. A basic network is typically in one location, such as a particular office building.

Internetworking is the process of connecting these individual networks together. One network located in Japan, another in Aus-tralia, and a third in New York City may all need to communicate with each other. Or the networks might simply be on different floors of the same building. Often the individual networks will have different physical and logical structures, adding to the com-plexity of the task.

5. What Are Routers and Who Uses Them Anyway?

A router is a piece of computer hardware (and/or sometimes soft-ware) that provides a way for data from an originating host com-puter to reach a destination host computer on a different network or network segment. When a router receives data for a computer not on the local network, it will forward those data to the appro-priate destination—which might be the target computer or anoth-er router.

Routers have the ability to filter data and to forward data to different locations depending on how they are configured. They can connect networks that use different protocols and different physical and logical topologies.

The Internet uses routers to make it possible for data to reach a destination. Corporations use routers to connect remote locations into a single, large network (wide-area network or WAN). Even multiple networks within a single building use routers for efficient communication among network segments. Cisco is not the only vendor of routers but is one of the most popular.

6. How Do Cisco Certifications Compare to Other Certifications such as Microsoft's MCSE?

Cisco certifications are not the only career-boosting credentials available. There are currently over 200 computer professional certifications to choose from. Vendor certifications such as the Microsoft Certified Systems Engineer (MCSE) are also valuable routes toward professional advancement. Vendor-independent certifications can prove worthwhile too. Because context is crucial to defining the value of any credential, it is impossible definitively to place one certification above another. The key to success with certification is to match a credential with goals. A person who administers a stand-alone Novell network would find little relevance in a Cisco certification or an MCSE.

Despite this, the question of whether to pursue an MCSE or the CCIE is commonly asked. In making the decision, keep in mind that Cisco certifications are about WAN/internetworking technologies, protocols, and Cisco products. The MCSE is about supporting clients and servers on a Microsoft network. Although the delineation is not absolute, one is primarily about software, the other hardware.

That said, Cisco certifications are currently enjoying an even higher level of prestige than the MCSE. The CCIE is popularly considered to be the most difficult certification to earn. Those who hold it command a high level of respect from others in the computer industry, both peers and employers. This is partly because one cannot earn it without significant work experience. The Cisco career certifications are more directly comparable to those of Microsoft, Novell, and other vendors, as they are still challenging, but obtainable by mere mortals who don't have a great deal of internetworking experience to draw upon.

Cisco-certified individuals are also in shorter supply than are Microsoft certified professionals. As this book went to press, 3,508 CCIEs had been granted, compared to 116,825 MCSEs. A recent search of a computer job board turned up 153 openings seeking CCIEs and 1,305 seeking MCSEs. The ratio of CCIEs to open positions on this single job board was 23 to 1. For MCSEs it was 90 to 1. And as a rule, the CCIE openings specified the highest pay rates, with numerous positions promising over $100,000 a year.

7. Will Cisco Certification Help Me Earn More?

Although nothing in life and especially in work is guaranteed, it is hard to imagine that getting Cisco certified would not boost your salary or consulting rate. Cisco certifications are simply some of the hottest, most prestigious computer credentials currently available. This is a time when certification programs in general are experiencing an explosion of popularity and recognition, a time when any respectable certification can serve as a career booster at least to some extent.

Cisco-certified individuals command especially impressive salaries. In its November 20, 1998 issue, *Smart Reseller News* reported that CCIEs regularly receive starting salaries of over $100,000 a year and that "high end CCIEs make $200k without breaking into a sweat."

The newer Cisco certifications, which include CCNA, CCNP, CCDA, and CCDP, have less of a track record to draw on when attempting to identify pay rates. Because these certifications are not as demanding as the CCIEs, pay rates are lower, although still substantial. Word on the street is that newly minted CCNAs with a computer background can expect $45,000–$55,000. Add in a network operating system certification, and the pay shoots up to between $60,000 and $80,000. As with most employment, pay rates vary substantially based on geographic area.

Even if you somehow do not parlay your Cisco certification into an immediate pay increase, it will, nonetheless, add to your base of knowledge and qualifications, which should pay off in the long term.

8. How Will Cisco Certification Affect My Marketability?

Cisco certification is likely to send your marketability off the charts. People with any sort of professional certification are enjoying increased visibility in the computer job market, and of all certifications available, the Cisco certifications enjoy one of the best reputations.

Individuals with Cisco certification report receiving recruiting calls almost a soon as they complete the final exam. In fact, publications such as *Smart Reseller News* report that retaining a Cisco certified employee can be challenging because other employers are constantly trying to lure them away. This is the kind of marketability that spawns articles such as "Cisco Certified Experts: A Headhunter's Paradise" (*Computer Reseller News* May 15, 1998). Although rumors suggest that newly minted CCIEs are heavily recruited by Cisco, most Cisco certified individuals, including CCIEs, are employed by other companies.

Even being in the process of earning Cisco certification often boosts marketability! Certification training listed on your resume demonstrates your ability and your desire to stay current; this is no small task in an industry where skills can become obsolete as quickly as they became cutting edge. It also shows that you take initiative and care about your career, traits many employers find attractive. Cisco certification will have a significant positive impact on your marketability.

9. Can Certification Compensate for Inexperience?

Certification cannot replace experience; it can to some degree compensate for lack of experience. It is certainly far preferable than offering neither experience nor credentials. The ideal combination is to have both certification and extensive work experience. When starting out, nobody has experience. Think about the new college graduate with a bachelor's in computer science but no on-the-job experience. When it comes to landing a job, or even an interview, in the information technology department of a good-sized company, she's light years ahead of an equally inexperienced non-college grad counterpart, because she has a credential. Professional certifications are credentials that operate in the same way that college degrees do—to open doors.

Hands-on experience is still a key criterion in determining qualifications for a particular position. Its importance depends upon the level of the job you're after. For the lower-level certifications, it is acceptable to have less experience. A CCIE with no experience probably would not get the job. But then, an individual without some WAN experience is not going to earn the CCIE in the first place.

The thing about experience is that it takes time, often a lot of it. And there is not much you can do to accelerate the process. Certification, on the other hand, is something you can add to your resume in the more immediate future. Even for newcomers to Cisco technology, the process of obtaining a Cisco certification helps you gain experience. Certifications provide a path for learning, and as you work through that path you will gain some of that oh-so-valuable experience. When pursued with the proper spirit, the knowledge you gain while earning Cisco certification will help you do your job better.

Although some certification programs have a problem with a reputation for producing individuals who look good on paper, but fail in real-world environments, Cisco certifications have so far managed to avoid being tarred with that brush. Due to the difficulty of obtaining the premier CCIE certifications, the "paper CCIE" is rare if not non-existent.

The bottom line is that although Cisco certification cannot completely substitute for hands-on experience, it will still increase expertise, marketability, and most likely, salary.

10. Which Cisco Certification Is Best for Me?

It may seem obvious, but many people underestimate the importance of matching choice of professional credentials with career goals. Part of the problem arises because career plans are sometimes vague and ill-defined, such as "to earn more money." Other times confusion occurs because there are multiple routes to achieving a particular goal, and there is not enough information available to help you choose. This book will help you past both of those potential road blocks. With Cisco certifications, the CCIE choices are basically for people with strong Cisco experience. The rest of the certifications can benefit both experienced professionals and relative newcomers to networking with Cisco. Chapter 4 will walk you through the process of selecting the specific Cisco certification that will work best for you.

11. How Much Will Getting Certified Cost?

The total cost of certification can be tricky to calculate beforehand, yet that is exactly what you should do. It is important to develop a reasonable estimate so that you know exactly what you are getting into financially. Your estimate will also help you budget accordingly, so that your plans do not get put on hold due to unexpected certification-related expenses.

During the course of obtaining certification, there are several kinds of expenses you are likely to incur: exam fees, training materials (sometimes including hardware), training instruction, and travel to training and testing sites. Cisco certification exams cost from $100 to $200 each. Since classes are not required in order to take the exams, you could, theoretically, simply take and pass the exam to become a Cisco Certified Design Associate (CCDA) or Cisco Certified Network Associate (CCNA) for $100 or less. Exam fees for the Cisco Certified Design Professional (CCDP) or the Cisco Certified Network Professional (CCNP) range from $300 to $400. In each case, before becoming a candidate for the "professional" certification you must first earn the "associate" level. The two-day hands-on lab exam for the CCIE designations comes with a price tag of $1,000, plus the cost of traveling to the lab site.

Additionally, for some certifications, you will need access to Cisco routers to practice on. You may have to borrow, buy, or rent equipment for this purpose.

In reality, it is nearly impossible (maybe someone, somewhere has done it) to pass these exams without putting in the requisite study time first, and purchasing some kind of class or material to help you prepare. How much your training expenses will total depends upon which preparation methods you choose and how much you need to learn. The price of training materials varies widely. To give you an idea of the costs, during the writing of this book:

* Bad Dog Computer (**www.baddogcomputer.com**) was selling two CCNA training bundles—one for $395 and the other for $1395.
* Subscribing to a popular CCIE preparation site (**www.ccprep.com**) cost $20 per month.
* A five day Introduction to Cisco Router Configuration (ICRC) course from Geo Train (**www.geotrain.com**) was going for $1895.

Monetary expenses are not the only costs of earning certification. You will also have to devote time and effort, often a substantial amount.

Although this has given you a general idea of the kinds of expenses you will incur; you will still want to develop an actual estimate. Chapter 6 will walk you through doing that. It includes a simple worksheet to help you total up the various types of expenses. It will also reveal a number of ways to reduce your total outlay and still achieve your goal.

The costs of obtaining certification can obviously become quite substantial. It is important to put that in perspective by considering how quickly you will recoup your investment once you take your new certification to the job market.

12. Is Financial Assistance Available for Certification Training?

As professional certification has become an increasingly popular career choice, the number of ways to obtain funding to pay for it have multiplied. Employers and even recruiting firms are beginning to recognize that certification is important to their employees/clients and is good for their own bottom line. For that reason, it is often possible to obtain direct reimbursements for certification training and/or testing costs. The money may come from the training budget or from the tuition reimbursement program.

If you are an American citizen, the U.S. Government is also interested in seeing you advance your career. Although training expenses have been to some extent deductible for many years, the Tax Act of 1997 makes it even easier to regain some of your training costs through your Federal income tax return. If you are using the training to advance in your current profession (rather than to change professions) you will want to explore Form 2106, Employee Business Expenses, or, if you are self-employed, Schedule C, Profit or Loss from Business.

The 1997 Tax Act created two credits you may be able to take advantage of: the Lifetime Learning Credit and the Hope Scholarship Credit. Credits are dollar-for-dollar reductions of your tax bill. Chapter 6 includes specific advice explaining how to take advantage of education-related tax breaks like these.

If you do not have the cash on hand to fund your certification efforts, and you do not have an employer willing to foot the bill, there are several loan programs specifically designed for computer professional certification candidates. You will find out about those later in this book.

Besides using financing, tax breaks, and third-party funding, there are many ways you can cut your certification bill to make the total more manageable. Judicious selection of training and preparation materials is the first place to trim expenses. You can also save money by doing little things such as through your selection of exam options. For example, the Foundation R/S exam is a conglomeration of three other exams. Passing it in place of the other three will save you $100. You'll learn more tricks like this later in this book.

13. How Long Does Earning Certification Take?

The time span varies considerably depending on your choice of certification, current experience level, and the learning methods you employ. The biggest portion of your time will go to preparing for exams. For some of the certifications it is possible to compress preparation time into a few weeks—if you are willing and able to put just about everything else aside. It is more common, and more practical for professionals who are earning certification on their own time, to start with one exam, determine the requirements, study, and then take the exam. The process is repeated for the next exam for that certification.

Several Cisco certifications offer the unique option to take a kind of mega-exam (the Foundation R/S exam) that combines three other exams into a single test session. If you manage to go this route, you can save time and money. The combination exam lasts 2.75 hours while the individual exams combined last 4 hours. It also costs $100 less.

The higher-end certifications will take more time to earn than the entry level choices. It is important to note that you do NOT have to go through the CCNA/CCDP path in order to earn CCIE certification, although you might choose to do so for various reasons.

14. Where Will I Have to Go for Certification Training and Testing?

For some tests you will be able to study largely from books and/or software preparation materials—which means you can study from home or at work. These materials are available directly from Cisco as well as through third-party outlets. Cisco's master list of self-study materials is on the Web at **www.cisco.com/warp/ public/10/wwtraining/cust/course_selfp_main.shtml**.

If you choose to take instructor-led training, which may be just what you need in order to best meet a particular requirement, you will have to travel to the class site. If you are lucky, that will be nearby, perhaps even through a local college, but you may have to travel to find the class you want when you want it. Cisco maintains a list of approved "training partners." You can locate the one closest to you by using the Cisco Training Locator (**www.cisco.com/ pcgi-bin/front.x/wwtraining/locator.pl**). The list can also be found in the reference section at the end of this book. Keep in mind that "unofficial" training is often as good as or better than its "authorized" counterpart, and can cost substantially less.

There is another alternative for individuals who find self study inadequate and travel to instructor-led courses too expensive and/or time consuming: online learning. It is possible to study for Cisco certifications using courseware over the Internet. These online classes can take a variety of forms, and you will learn all about them in the training alternatives chapter of this book.

As many other certification programs, Cisco certification testing is administered through Sylvan Prometric testing centers. There are over 1,200 of these testing centers serving 80 countries, so there is probably one not too far away from you. You can find the closest one using the online test center locator available through **www.2test.com**.

If you decide to pursue one of the CCIE certifications, you will need to pass a hands-on lab examination. Lab exams are much less widely available. As this book was going to press, the following Cisco labs were open:

WAN Switching Labs

* San Jose, California, USA
* Stockley Park, England

ISP-Dial Labs

* Halifax, Nova Scotia, Canada
* San Jose, California, USA

Routing and Switching Labs

* Beijing, China
* Brussels, Belgium
* Capetown, South Africa
* Chatswood, Australia
* Halifax, Nova Scotia, Canada
* Raleigh, North Carolina
* San Jose, California
* Tokyo, Japan

15. What Will I Receive from Cisco When I Get Certified?

When you have completed the requirements for a particular certification, including signing the certification agreement, you will be sent a "graduation kit." The kits for associate and professional level graduates include a graduation letter, wallet card, T-shirt, and information on using the proper designation on your business cards. CCIEs receive a graduation letter, certification, and framed CCIE medallion, as well as priority access to technical support. CCIEs also receive access to special Cisco tools and resources through Cisco's Web site.

16. Is Passing Exams the Only Thing I Have to Do to Become Certified?

Passing the tests alone will not qualify you as Cisco certified. You must also sign and submit a document called a certification agreement. This document, which ran six pages as this book was being written, lays out the terms of the agreement between Cisco and the candidate wishing to be certified. Most professional certification programs require a similar type of agreement. The Cisco agreement specifies what an individual must do to become and remain certified. Topics covered include:

* Allowed usage of "marks" which include the designations themselves (CCNA, CCIE, etc) and logos
* A promise to keep exam details confidential
* Agreement that Cisco can revoke your certification if they think you are acting in a way that damages Cisco's reputation or if you otherwise violate the terms of the agreement
* Acknowledgment that Cisco can change the terms of the program at any time
* Clarification that certification does not convey any licensing rights to Cisco software, and other items along similar lines. The agreement can be downloaded from Cisco's web site (**www.cisco.com/warp/public/10/wwtraining/certprog/testing/agreement.htm**). Alternatively, you can submit an electronic version through a Sylvan Prometric testing site.

17. Do I Need a College Degree to Get Cisco Certified?

You don't even need a high school diploma. What you do need is an urge to excel, along with large amounts of self motivation, determination, and persistence. If you can learn the material, you can pass the exams and become certified.

That is not to claim that a college degree would not do good things for your career. Adding Cisco certification on top of a college degree will open more doors for you than Cisco certification alone, but you do not have to have the degree too—the certifications are valuable career boosters in and of themselves.

18. What if I Don't Remember How to Study?

The prospect of going back to studying after a long hiatus can be intimidating, but if it is, that is probably because you did not develop efficient and effective study skills the first time around. If so, you are not alone. It is amazing how many people manage to make it through formal schooling without learning the techniques that make studying easy. It is never too late to learn how to learn. In fact, you may be among the many people who find studying much easier this time around simply because there are specific reasons and personal goals driving your effort. Whether your study brain cells never developed much muscle, or if they are simply a little dusty, the tips and techniques in this book will help you brush up on efficient and effective study habits.

19. What Resources Are Available to Help Me Achieve Certification?

You will find information to help you pass Cisco certification tests all over the Internet and on the shelves of your nearest megabookstore. Available resources include:

* Internet forums and discussion groups
* Study guides and text books

* Self-assessment tests and computer programs
* Expert instructors
* Documentation and preparation materials available through Cisco
* World Wide Web sites
* And, of course, this book.

Thanks largely to the Internet, you will be able to access many powerful and useful learning aids right from your computer. If you are not already set up with an Internet connection, this is a good reason to get yourself a modem and sign up for service. You will be giving yourself virtually 24-hour access to others who have obtained your certification already, are in the process of doing so, or who write or teach about it or about related technologies.

There are plenty of offline resources, too. Because Cisco certifications have a good reputation in the industry you can expect continued growth in the variety and depth of preparation assistance available.

20. Do I Need Access to Cisco Routers to Get Cisco Certified?

Although it is possible to earn the lower-level certifications through studying without actually practicing on Cisco routers, it is best if you can work with the real thing. At the higher levels, particularly for the CCIE certifications, it is virtually imperative. That does not mean you have to lay out a boat-load of money to build a Cisco router lab in your basement. Many Cisco certification candidates manage to borrow a Cisco router from somewhere. It is also fairly easy to buy an affordable used router to work on during your preparation period and then resell it (probably to another certification candidate). Another possibility is to rent the equipment, or to travel to one of the Cisco labs for a practice session or two. It is also possible to subscribe to one of several services that provide access by the Internet to a bank of Cisco routers.

21. What Are the Certification Tests Like?

Cisco certification exams are administered through Sylvan Prometric testing centers. Candidates can register by phone (800-204-EXAM) or online (**www.2test.com**). You must register in advance. On the day of the test you go to the center, present two forms of identification, and sign in. You will be escorted to a quiet room with one or more testing stations. You will not be allowed to bring anything into the room with you but your wits, and either a few blank pieces of paper or a wipe-off note board. You will sign onto the computer using your social security number and the test will begin. You may be required to complete an agreement promising not to reveal the contents of the test before you receive any actual questions. The questions themselves are mostly variations of multiple choice formats. Most Cisco certification exams last one to two hours. Passing scores vary depending on the exam but hover around 70%. The CCIE written exam consists of approximately 100 questions and candidates have up to two hours to complete it.

Passing score on the CCIE written exam is 70% or better. CCIE lab exams, on the other hand, are NOT proctored by Sylvan. You will have to go to a Cisco testing lab and build a network to specifications you are given. Then, the proctor will insert faults and you will have to find and fix them. This is not for the faint of heart! The lab exam lasts two days. A score of 80% or better is required to pass.

22. How Can I (or Anyone Else) Verify That Someone Is Really a CCIE?

To confirm CCIE status, send an e-mail containing the individual's name and CCIE number to the CCIE program at the addresses listed below. Don't ask for any test score or other contact or personal information in your message, because it will not be released.

* North and South America: ccie_ucsa@cisco.com
* Europe, Middle East and Africa: ccie_emea@cisco.com
* Australia and Pacific Rim: ccie_apt@cisco.com

CCNA, CCNP, CCDA, and CCDP individuals wishing to have the credentials verified must fax a letter to the career certification program manager indicating to whom the information is to be released.

23. How Can I Promote Myself and My Certification?

Professional certification has the power to boost your career and increase your job opportunities, but only if you use it! To make the most of your certification, you will want to learn how to maximize its value as a career tool. Filing it away in a cabinet won't do that. The most obvious thing to do is advertise your new status by adding it to your resume, business cards, and e-mail signature, but don't stop there. You can also learn to be your own PR person. With a little effort you can get your name out into the world as an expert in your field. The Internet is an excellent tool for this purpose. Through well-planned use of Web pages, forums, and other Internet resources, you can get your name to pop up in association with your area of Cisco certification. But be careful to abide by Internet etiquette (often called netiquette); indiscriminate self-promotion will annoy other Internet users and ultimately work against you. You can also establish expert status by providing useful information to media outlets such as newspapers and television.

There are also techniques you can use to move up in the ranks at your current company or in billing rates if you are an independent. These include finding ways to demonstrate your enhanced value, and making an airtight case for a raise or promotion. After you obtain a certification, you might also decide that it is time to move on to a new company or perhaps become an independent contractor or consultant. Because it is so important, you will find specific advice on how to get the most oomph from your new credential in several chapters of this book.

24. What Is the Future of Cisco Certification?

The computer certification marketplace is in the midst of explosive growth. Consider that there are currently over 200 professional certifications available and that number will probably continue to expand rapidly. Among all the certifications, there are some that garner little respect and others that are very well regarded and potentially extremely valuable. Cisco certifications are in the latter group. Although Cisco may modify its certification offerings—adding new ones and fine-tuning those already in place, this program is one that is poised to provide enduring value to the professionals who participate in it.

CHAPTER 2

The Evolution
of Cisco Certification

Cisco Systems was not the first organization to sponsor a computer professional certification program. Certification has been a part of the computer industry since before ASCII (American Standard Code for Information Interchange) was invented to allow computers to exchange data. Today, the array of certification sponsors includes numerous computer organizations and a list of industry vendors that reads like a who's who of computing, but when interest first began to stir, the only participant was a single professional society.

The First Certification

The year was 1962. Vacuum tube computers had given way to machines built with individual transistors, and the integrated circuit was new on the scene. The COBOL programming language, which seems to have been around forever, was entering its tender second year. Such was the state of the industry when, in New York, the first computer professional certification exam was conducted, and the certification marketplace was born.

That exam, called the Certificate in Data Processing, or CDP, was developed and administered by the National Machine Accountants Association (NMAA). Later that same year, the NMAA changed its name to the Data Processing Management Association (DPMA). The DPMA underwent another name change and is currently called the Association of Information Technology Professionals (AITP).

For eight years, the CDP was the only certification for computer professionals. Then, in 1970, the DPMA added a second exam and professional designation: Registered Business Programmer (RBP).

The DPMA's experience with certification led them to believe that an organization other than their own was needed; an independent group focused solely on the definition of computing knowledge and skills. In 1973, the DPMA joined with seven other professional associations to establish the Institute for Certification of Computer Professionals (ICCP). The other founding organizations included such well-known groups as the Association for Computing Machinery (ACM) and the Canadian Information Processing Society (CIPS). According to plan, the ICCP took over administration of the CDP program in early 1974.

From 1974 to 1989 the computer certification marketplace idled. Professional societies and organizations added a few additional certifications, but not much else happened until commercial powerhouse Novell Corporation jumped in with both feet.

Novell Dives In

Seizing upon certification as a business growth strategy, Novell launched its CNE (Certified Novell Engineer) program in January 1989. At the time, local-area networking was catching on like wildfire. Because of the early stage of the technology, Novell found itself with overloaded customer support lines and resellers with limited technical knowledge. The company, on its own, could not supply all the expertise needed to use its products. This was a condition that threatened to seriously hamper the company's potential for continued growth. The answer proved to be a variation of what today, we call outsourcing.

Novell's initial intention was to train its resellers to handle many technical support issues on their own. At first, the CNE was aimed not at computer systems professionals but at computer sales people. Novell provided the training through its own education centers.

The company's success soon began to get in its way again. Resellers were not the only ones signing up for CNE training; staff who supported Novell networks within individual companies found the training valuable, too. And they signed up in droves. As Novell's technical support people before them, the education centers were quickly overwhelmed. So they again off-loaded the burden to resources outside the company.

Because certification worked so well, it must have made sense to use it again, because the company created an international network of authorized (that is, certified) training centers. Before a training company could become a Novell Authorized Education Center (NAEC), it had to meet Novell's curriculum requirements, which set standards for equipment, facilities, and instruction. To ensure qualified instructors, Novell launched its second professional designation: the Certified Novell Instructor (CNI), which went live in April 1989.

There is little doubt that Novell's pioneering efforts in the certification marketplace were strictly devoted to its own commercial goals. The first training classes reflected that, but as the certifications evolved, and criticisms were leveled, the focus of Novell certification training steadily shifted from sales aspects to technical support issues.

Today, the question of tainted certifications still lingers in the marketplace, especially when a certification is sponsored by an industry vendor. That is one reason why it is important to evaluate the quality *and* reputation of individual training programs before enrolling in them. The Cisco certification program passes this "smell test" with flying colors. The sponsor has invested the time and effort to create a program with real value to certification candidates and to those who might employ them.

Cisco Participates as Certification Takes Off

As recently as the early nineties, even though the ICCP and other professional groups had been promoting certification-based designations for years, many in the business community had never heard of them. Awareness barely stretched beyond the individuals who belonged to the sponsoring societies. Employers presented with evidence of certification were likely to shrug their shoulders and say: "So?" Certification's minimal track record and poor recognition severely limited its value. All this meant that although certification might have value and meaning to the individuals who went through the process, broad-based career and employment boosting power just wasn't there.

That began to change shortly after Novell joined in. Recognizing the tremendous potential of certification to boost the company's presence in the marketplace, Novell put its marketing might behind certification. Suddenly, everyone in the computer field had heard of the CNE program, and so had much of the business community. A Novell certification became a hot ticket for IT professionals.

The Company Behind the Certifications

Cisco Systems was founded in 1984, at a time when there were only 1,000 host computers on the Internet. It was two years before their first router shipped. Even then, there were just 4 employees.

Cisco's initial public offering took place on February 20, 1990, under the NAS-DAQ symbol CSCO. Its reported revenues that year were $69.8 million, with a net income of $1.4 million. A year later revenues had more than doubled, and net income was up to $43.2 million. That was just the beginning.

In 1996 Cisco shipped its millionth product and hired its 7,500th employee. Revenues that year exceeded $4 billion. For 1998 revenues hit $8.46 billion and the number of employees topped 15,000. In December 1998 Cisco completed its 30th acquisition of another company.

Today, according to Hoover's Online, Cisco holds 85% of the market for routers and 35% of the market for LAN switches. On February 9, 1999, its stock was trading at around $100 a share, having split seven times since the initial offering in 1990. The IPO price was $18 per share.

Cisco Systems is currently headquartered in San Jose, California, and has additional major operations in Research Triangle Park, North Carolina and Chelmsford, Massachusetts. Sales and support offices exist in 54 countries. As of early 1999 it was number 253 in the FORTUNE 500 and employed 17,000 people in its operations.

However, all was not rosy in CNE land. Although the designation was proving wildly successful for Novell, and for companies operating Novell networks, its shortcomings became apparent. Not only was it product-specific, it was version-specific. It promoted Novell products and solutions, which annoyed many potential candidates. To professionals and organizations operating a non-Novell environment, it was worthless.

Waiting in the wings were those other certifications, those platform-independent designations that had been slowly gathering strength since 1962. They began to emerge from the shadows. Novell's efforts to gain acceptance for its certifications were working, and not just for Novell. As the concept of certification for computer professionals became more widely known and accepted, other certification sponsors received a boost. They were perfectly positioned to market themselves as an alternative to the product-centric certifications from industry vendors. They could promote their features of product and platform independence, while still promising the other professional benefits of certification that Novell's programs offered.

Novell did a great deal to advance professional certification in the computer industry. The company's development of a network of independent training centers opened up the certification marketplace to other industry vendors. They also discovered the big problem areas, specifically the problem of diluting the value of a certification by making it too easy to get and too vendor focused.

Cisco Systems officially jumped into the certification marketplace on September 27, 1993, when it launched the first incarnation of the Cisco Certified Internetwork Expert (CCIE) program. Figure 2.1 shows the original press release, available on the Cisco Web site.

FIGURE 2.1

Cisco Launches
CCIE Program

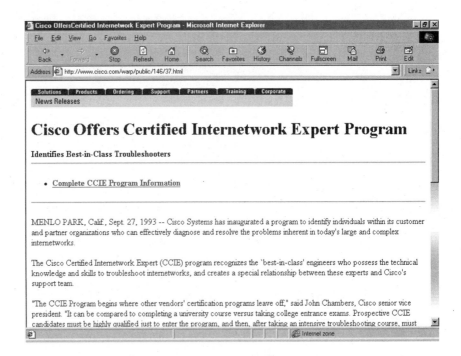

From the beginning Cisco must have paid attention to the pitfalls encountered by other certification programs, because the CCIE program was structured to overcome them. The CCIE became a high-level, difficult-to-obtain qualification. The CCIE also managed to some degree to combine the strengths of vendor-sponsored and vendor-independent certifications. This means that although it centers around Cisco products, it does so in the context of broad internetworking expertise.

The original release cited three steps to becoming a CCIE instead of the current two: a written CCIE Qualification Test, a four-day 'hands-on' network troubleshooting class, and a two-day Cisco Certified Internetwork Expert certification lab. Costs of the program were $100 for the CCIE Qualification Test ($150 outside the U.S. and Canada), $1700 for the network troubleshooting class, and $1000 for the Lab. According to Cisco officials, the class requirement was never really implemented, because it was unpopular with certification candidates.

Each CCIE is assigned a unique identification number. The numbers are given out sequentially, but there is no CCIE #1. The lab where the first certification test was administered was identified as facility #1024, and based upon that, the first CCIE was assigned #1025. The second became CCIE #1026. By the end of 1998, CCIE #4151 had been given out.

The first person to earn the CCIE title was a Cisco employee. The second person was Terry Slattery, who was doing consulting work for Cisco at the time. Slattery is currently President of Chesapeake Computer Consultants, Inc. and coauthor of *Advanced IP Routing in Cisco Networks* (McGraw-Hill 1999). It took a while for the CCIE program to gain momentum. In September of 1995, two years into the program, there were only 613 CCIEs. It was not until 1997 and 1998 that the CCIE program began to receive widespread recognition and popularity. By the end of January 1999, there were about 3,390 CCIEs, and the demand for the certification was high.

The CCIE is so difficult to obtain that it was until recently rather an all-or-nothing program. There was no training path identified for individuals who wanted to become CCIEs but did not have the on-the-job experience necessary to have a chance at passing the lab exam. This was not really a problem until the CCIE became a coveted certification and it became clear that there was a demand for Cisco certifications that signified competence, but did not demand a guru level of expertise. Cisco responded to this need by creating a new family of certifications dubbed "career certifications," which were launched in April 1998. The initial announcement of the new certifications is shown in Figure 2.2. The newly created career certifications are being welcomed by computer professionals worldwide. By February 1999 there were over 4,000 CCNAs certified, nearly 4,000 CCDAs, approximately 200 CCNPs and nearly 100 CCDPs.

FIGURE 2.2
Cisco Adds Career
Certifications

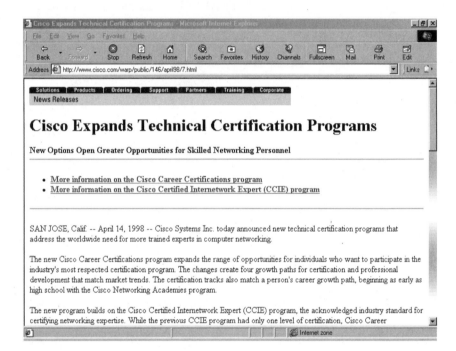

In a departure from the CCIE program, which is experience based, each of the four career certifications is accompanied by a suggested training path. A network of official training partners teaches the necessary classes (see Appendix for a list of training partners), and self-study materials following the identified curricula are also available.

At approximately the same time as the new career certifications were announced, the CCIE program was modified. The single CCIE certification was expanded into three certifications:

1. CCIE—Routing and Switching
2. CCIE—WAN Switching
3. CCIE—ISP Dial.

Cisco appears to be determined to keep the two certification programs (CCIE and career) distinct. Although it seems inevitable that management of the two programs will eventually be combined, for now they are largely managed as separate entities within Cisco.

Figure 2.3 provides a time line of IT certification to date.

FIGURE 2.3
IT Certification
Time Line

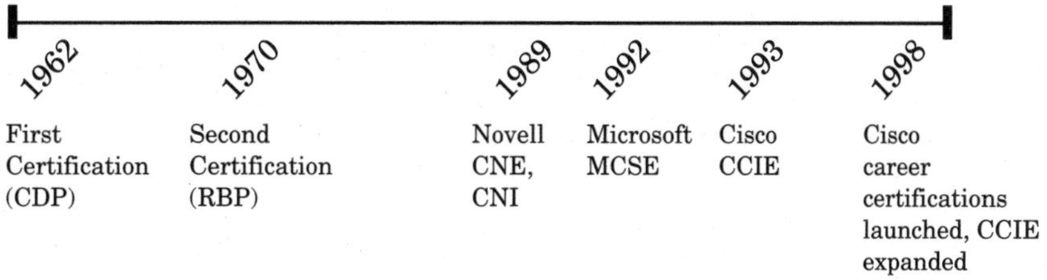

1962	1970	1989	1992	1993	1998
First Certification (CDP)	Second Certification (RBP)	Novell CNE, CNI	Microsoft MCSE	Cisco CCIE	Cisco career certifications launched, CCIE expanded

CHAPTER 3

Opportunities and Benefits

A major attraction of certification is its flexibility of purpose and application. If you want to move on to a new and better job, certification can help you. If a new specialty has caught your eye, certification can simplify the transition. If you want to become more of an expert at what you already do, certification can serve that purpose as well. As one of the top certification programs going, Cisco's is especially valuable for accomplishing these tasks.

That is not to say that professional certification is a career cure-all. What it *does* do is offer a powerful set of tools you can use to make significant, positive changes in your work life.

More Options, Better Pay

When you become Cisco certified, you open doors to new and different career options, increase your professional credibility, learn where your knowledge gaps are and how to plug them, and receive an objective measure of your technical accomplishments. Whether you stay where you are or move on to another employer, these benefits will give you a leg up the career ladder.

Jobs, Jobs, Jobs

A recent search of a Web site that caters to job hunting computer professionals turned up well over 1500 positions that either require or desire applicants with Cisco training and certification (one of the results pages is shown in Figure 3.1). The site is an electronic repository of open positions posted by technical recruiters and is only one site among many that includes job opportunities for certified professionals. The openings were quite diverse and included:

* Network Architect
* Cisco Trainer
* Senior Network Consultant
* Router Specialist
* Network Engineer
* Cisco Internet Expert
* Cisco Specialist

FIGURE 3.1
Internet Job
Postings Seeking
Cisco Skilled
Applicants

Back to search page

Jobs 1-10 of 1664 matching your query

Select position title for additional information about job listing.

1 - 10 ▶

Position Title: Network Specialist - Cabletron & Cisco

Skills required:	Cabletron, Cisco, LAN		
Location:	NY		
State:	NY	Pay Rate:	Experience related
Area:	914	Term:	CON W2ONLY
Start Date:	ASAP	Length:	3 - 6 months

Position Title: Strong CISCO and NT Server Engineer

Skills required:	Cisco Router Networking + FireWaLL Experience		
Location:	New York City		
State:	NY	Pay Rate:	open
Area:	212	Term:	CON INDOK
Start Date:	asap	Length:	12+ months

Position Title: Network Engineer

Skills required:	Cisco, token ring, ethernet, general sniffer		
Location:	Torrance		
State:	CA	Pay Rate:	DOE
Area:	310	Term:	FTE PERM
Start Date:	Immed.	Length:	perm

Position Title: Cisco Engineer

Skills required:	LAN/WAN CISCO		
Location:	Irvine		
State:	CA	Pay Rate:	Open
Area:	909	Term:	CON W2ONLY
Start Date:	Asap	Length:	Temp to Perm

Position Title: WAN Engineer

Skills required:	Cisco, ATM, Firewall, Cisco PIX, TCP/IP, WAN, telecom		
Location:	Roseville		
State:	CA	Pay Rate:	DOE
Area:	916	Term:	FTE PERM
Start Date:	ASAP	Length:	Full-time

* WAN Engineer
* Project Leader
* Project Marketing Engineer
* Network Measurement and Tuning
* Network Administrator
* And others

Why are so many employers beginning to seek people with Cisco expertise? They are recognizing the value of an objective measurement of applicant skills and expertise. Hiring the wrong person is an expensive mistake that employers strive to avoid. When you present yourself with a Cisco certification, you are making it easier (and less risky) for the hiring manager to assess your technical qualifications.

Training to Train

Besides improving your chances for the "standard" mix of technical jobs, you can take advantage of an interesting and potentially lucrative outgrowth of the certification explosion. People are needed to teach the necessary classes, write exam questions, and develop certificate curriculums.

Firms hiring technical trainers like to see people with related certifications and experience. Because training requires a high level of expertise in both the technology at hand *and* the ability to teach and communicate well, salaries can be impressive.

You must know what you are doing to be able to handle the questions and problems that arise during a training session, but it is often possible to land such a position without a trainer certification. Based on a review of advertised openings for trainers, it appears possible to break into this field based on nontraining-related technical certifications coupled with other technical skills you hold. Once hired, you will be put through trainer certification, *at the employer's expense*. In fact, you cannot become a Certified Cisco Systems Instructor (CCSI) unless you are sponsored by a Cisco training partner!

QUICKTIP

Cisco training partners are required to use Cisco certified instructors to teach Cisco courses.

Employers who hire trainers this way pay less than those who want a certified trainer to start with, but the salary is still likely to be quite reasonable. Once you demonstrate your capabilities and go through the new certification, you're golden. If you leave the training partner, your CCSI will lapse, but you can renew it if you become employed with another authorized training partner.

You need not hold any of the other Cisco certifications to become a CCSI because instructors are certified on a course-by-course basis. You only need to be an expert in one course (and a good trainer) to become a CCSI.

Adding to Your Bottom Line

If one of the main reasons you are considering Cisco certification is because you want to increase your earnings, you will be encouraged to hear what International Data Corporation (IDC) found when it investigated that question. A 1996 study (conducted before certification's current boom) revealed that, on average, certified employees earn 12 percent higher salaries than noncertified employees. That is probably directly related to another statistic from the same study. Seventy-eight percent of IS managers believe that certified employees are more productive.

Honing in on the value of Cisco certifications, I conducted a survey of IT recruiters and found the following results:

* While most recruiters have heard of the CCIE, the newer Cisco certifications are just beginning to gain recognition (Figure 3.2 shows recruiter recognition rate for each certification).
* As might be expected, pay rates vary widely, depending upon certification and experience. The lowest hourly pay rate reported for CCIEs was $50+, the highest $150+. Annual income for CCIEs ranged from $70k–$125k+. The big differentiator was experience.

* Less salary data were available for the other Cisco certifications. Only one recruiter ventured an opinion: $35+ an hour and $65k and up per year.

* Forty percent of respondents reported that clients have specified Cisco certification as required or desirable for a particular position.

* Eighty percent of responding recruiters report growing demand for Cisco certified individuals.

* Most respondents agree that Cisco-focused certifications offered by sponsors other than Cisco itself are valuable, but probably less so than the ones created directly by Cisco.

FIGURE 3.2
Recruiter
Familiarity with
Specific Cisco
Certifications

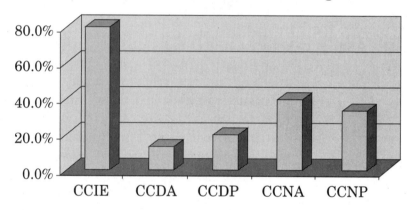

Recruiter Certification Recognition

Large Demand Plus a Short Supply
Equals a Higher Market Price

According to the Information Technology Association of America (ITAA), 190,000 information technology jobs are *currently open* in mid- to large-sized companies in the United States. Employers need skilled workers, and, for many, certification rates a premium.

Articles in trade publications confirm the power of certification to boost income. A May 1998 article in *Smart Reseller News*, titled "Cisco Certified Experts: A Headhunter's Paradise," reported that "Every network engineer wants to add this cash-cow credential to their resume. However, resellers are reluctant to fund this expensive endeavor and risk losing the employee to a deep-pocketed competitor."

In its February 1998 issue, *Inside Technology Training* revealed that "another name for 'certified employees' may be 'former employee'". Newly certified workers have been known to bolt from their employer to take advantage of their dramatically increased marketability (to get paid more). From the employer's viewpoint, that's a problem; from yours, it's evidence of the value of certification. The same article suggests that "a manager budgeting for certification should include the cost of the raises certified employees have come to demand—to keep them from leaving." This is fundamental economics in action.

Leading the Crowd

Although we have not reached that point yet, it is reasonable to predict that the increasing popularity of this type of credentialing will make it more universal. When and if that eventually happens, people who have ignored the trend will have to play catch-up. Certifying now or in the near future will place you near the leading edge of the trade, at least in the perception of potential employers. Wait too long and certification may become a requirement for basic success rather than a springboard for career advancement.

QUOTE

One Recruiter's Perspective

They [Cisco certifications] are all valuable...especially the CCIE. Up until recently the CCIE was the only Cisco certification I was familiar with. The others that have recently come along provide "stepping-stones" to the CCIE. They too are valuable to me as a recruiter. In the past two weeks I've found two individuals...one with the CCDA working to get his CCDP and the other with the CCNA working to get his CCNP. They will both be EXTREMELY placeable.

—Anna Helen Breckinridge, Technical Recruiter, Consultis of Richmond

Career Shifting

Are you feeling a bit bored and restless within your current computer specialty? Perhaps it isn't as hot as it once was, and you like to work with more cutting edge technology. Maybe you have reached a plateau where you are and would like to move on to something new—like the highly popular and lucrative area of WANs and internetworking. A Cisco certification (or three) may be just what the career counselor ordered.

If you want to switch your career focus, then, by definition, you already have one big thing going for you: experience. It probably isn't in WANs and internetworking, but at least it is there, and that is very valuable. Nevertheless, you still face a resume and training gap that stretches between where you are and where you want to be. The Cisco career certifications (which include all but the CCIE designations), include training paths to help you bridge that gap. In fact, one of the more prevalent uses of certification is as a springboard to a new job. That makes employers anxious about the subject. They like to hire certified people, but when their current workers get on a certification track, managers may lose a little sleep. They probably wonder if you are planning to leave for greener pastures or if another company will attempt to lure you away.

Although some people (but surely not you) might find the idea of stressing out their boss appealing, the point is that managers recognize the meaning of certification, and the value of Cisco certification. People who get certified are pursuing something more than they already have—something better, something different.

The person who gives you your first job in your new, postcertification area of specialty is likely to be a manager. Remember, managers like to hire people who are already certified, as you will be. By getting this training, you have demonstrated that you take initiative and are serious about this career move. Perhaps, more importantly, you will have gained knowledge and skills relevant to your new domain; *and* you have added a credential directly related to the position you are seeking. If you get asked technical questions during interviews, you will be able to field them fairly competently.

This is not to say that obtaining a Cisco certification will automatically enable you to jump from one computer field to another at the same or higher level of pay and responsibility. But it is likely significantly to ease that leap, and to enable you to start in your new field at a higher level than you might otherwise. Who wants to go back to square one?

Power Perks

As an added incentive to professionals and employers contemplating certification, Cisco Systems bestows a range of perks on those who complete their programs (Cisco's perks list is shown in Figure 3.3). The best perks incorporate elements that help you to perform your job at a higher level. They address your reasons for pursuing the certification and add value to the program for you and for your clients/employer.

FIGURE 3.3
Cisco Certification
Perks FAQ

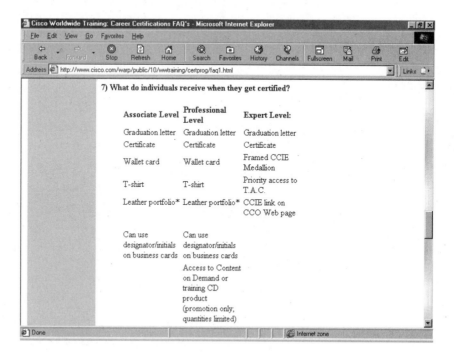

Priority Technical Support

Think about the last time you placed a call to a technical support line. Did you spend upward of half an hour listening to tinny music in a phone queue? Perhaps you had to leave your phone on automatic redial all morning just to make it into the queue. Such delays are especially frustrating when your project is on hold until you get the answers you need from tech support. You don't feel good, and you certainly don't look good.

But once you are certified by Cisco, your success or failure is a direct reflection on them. To put it bluntly, if you look bad, they look bad, and vice versa. Therefore, your calls for technical support will be treated more expeditiously. For some reason Cisco does not offer priority tech support to any of its certified people except for CCIEs. Perhaps this will change (it should), but meanwhile, CCIEs do get to enjoy "automatic routing of TAC [technical assistance center] calls to second-level support."

What a relief not to spend 45 minutes on hold when you run into a snag or obscurity in the documentation. Your redial finger might miss the workout, though.

Exclusive Forum

Cisco CCIEs gain access to a CCIE-only Internet forum. When you want to hash over an idea, glean some arcane advice, or discuss the pros and cons of a new release, these forums can serve as a valuable resource. Because only individuals with the same certification as yourself can post and respond to questions, there is a much higher signal-to-noise ratio than in unrestricted discussion forums. That means you will not have to wade through dozens of off-topic postings, as you would in a typical Usenet newsgroup. In addition, Cisco employees usually maintain a presence in the forum, so you may even get your feedback straight from the horse's mouth. Typical of the certification dichotomy at Cisco, there is no similar forum for the other Cisco certifications.

Training and Conference Admission

Once you are certified, you cannot (and probably will not want to) rest on your laurels. Because of the same rapid pace of change that makes your certification valuable, you will need to keep updating your skills. Many sponsors recognize this, and require that you complete continuing education each year to retain your designation. Cisco requires CCIEs periodically to attend a technical update conference held every year.

Even when retaining your certification is not the issue, you may want to take advantage of free and reduced-cost training offered by Cisco. In some cases the training will be for certified individuals only. It can be an inexpensive way to expand your technical skills and network with others in the computer industry.

Free Subscriptions

CCIE Central, a quarterly publication put out by Cisco, contains interviews with senior Cisco engineers, discussion of emerging networking issues, and of course, program information. A recent issue included an interview with Cisco's Chief Network Architect about network design, information on new Cisco practice labs, changes to the recertification cycle, a call for technical articles, and a profile of a CCIE. CCIE Central is available online at **www.cisco.com/go/cciecentral**.

Use of Logos and Marketing Materials

Cisco is interested in helping you promote your new status (and, along with it, their program). To that end, they take advantage of a useful product recognition tool—the logo. A Web page featuring the CCIE logo is shown in Figure 3.4. When you obtain certification, you will be granted permission, and even encouraged, to use the logo to advertise your status. You will be able to place it on your business cards, stationery, Web site, and in other places. The sponsor's advertising experts expend time and money promoting logo recognition, and you reap the benefits.

QUICK TIP

Although for a long time the only Cisco designation with its own logo was the CCIE, as this book was going to press logos for all of the Cisco certifications were in the works.

Independents, especially, may appreciate the ability to include the logos on marketing materials. The sight of a professional logo increases customer confidence in your abilities. Suddenly you are not an unknown or a risky proposition anymore. You are Cisco certified after all.

If you work for an employer, you may have less use for these logos. On the other hand, your employer may wish to place the logos on company materials in association with your name, which can work out well for both of you. This is especially true for Cisco resellers.

You can expect to receive specific instructions on the proper use of the logos. Although this might seem a bit controlling at first, it's actually in your best interest. If the logos are misused, their value may be diminished.

FIGURE 3.4
A Certification Logo on the Cisco Web Site

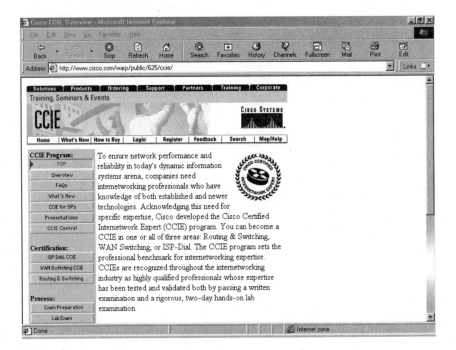

Other Payoffs

The benefits and opportunities mentioned so far are largely concrete and directly related to income or career advancement. As we all know by now, there are other, less tangible, aspects of career satisfaction that are equally important.

Study Dividends

If you get certified simply by taking a test, you will not expand your knowledge of the subject area. In most cases, you will attend one or more classes, participate in a hands-on lab session, or at the minimum, work through a self-study guide. In doing so, you are virtually assured of gaining exposure to new areas in your field and to different ways of doing things.

You already know how to perform the duties required by your current position, but do you know the most efficient ways to do them? How do you learn about what could or should be done in the near future? Through the certification process you will achieve added exposure to the issues related to your area of expertise and answers to these questions. This has the potential to make your work life easier by:

* Augmenting your level of proficiency
* Increasing your personal productivity
* Decreasing downtime
* Familiarizing you with product and technology advances.

Peace of Mind

Serenity is probably beyond what any of us can hope to achieve in the workplace and may not even be desirable. Freedom from various job-related fears and anxieties is another story. How can certification bring you increased peace of mind? As you probably have already guessed, it does this in several ways.

Let's start with that most basic of workplace concerns: the possibility of getting downsized, rightsized, released, phased out, riffed (subjected to a reduction in force), or just plain laid off.

Whatever your company calls it, it comes down to two little
words: job security.

Cisco certification has the potential to address job security in
two key ways. It does this

1. By increasing your value to the company
2. By increasing your value to *other* companies.

By keeping in tiptop technical shape through certification, you
multiply your value to your employer, enabling you to keep your
employer's customers satisfied. In fact, the more integral you are
to smooth daily operations, the more painful it would be for your
employer to let you go. Why would they want to discharge a valuable employee? In addition, an employer who helped finance your
certification has invested in you and has added incentive to keep
you on board.

By demonstrating your desire to excel at your current duties
(through earning certification) you simultaneously communicate
your ability to take on new or different tasks (for increased compensation, you hope), should the need arise. Transfer within the
company then becomes a distinct possibility when layoffs threaten.

In reality, you only have control over your own actions, not
those of "the boss." That is what makes job security key number
two so critical. Suppose that one day the dreaded pink slip does
land in your mail slot. If you have chosen your certification wisely, it will not be as big a deal as it might be otherwise. Yes, losing
your job would still be stressful (unless you are lucky enough to
receive a generous severance package). But by adding to your
technical credentials, you will have secured a competitive advantage over many other job seekers; you will have greater marketability.

During a time in which companies are hungry for the latest
technical expertise, recent training and certification is likely to
translate into quicker and more lucrative job offers. If you are any
good at all, you are not likely to be idle for long. Since changing
jobs is one of the most effective ways to obtain a significant salary
boost, you may actually find yourself thanking your employer for
pushing you out the door.

Food for Your Ego

Last but not least, is an extremely personal benefit of professional certification: self-satisfaction. Individuals often report a feeling of pleasure and accomplishment after achieving certification. This arises from the professional recognition conferred by your peers within the industry, from the knowledge that your skills and expertise have been assessed by someone (Cisco) other than yourself, and from the fact that you have successfully measured up to professional standards.

CHAPTER 4

The Certifications

To get the most benefit from professional certification, it is important to take the time to choose the certification that best matches your goals, current skill level, and the amount of time and effort you are willing to invest. Choosing a certification because it's the one everyone is currently talking about will not serve you as well as making your selection based on your background and future goals. It's also important to balance the cost, time, and effort required to earn a particular certification with the benefits you hope to obtain and the time span that you find acceptable. If you decide to aim for a top of the line Cisco CCIE certification, you will also have consider whether it makes sense to earn some of the lower-level designations along the way. To help you make these decisions, this chapter discusses each Cisco certification in detail, and includes tables to help you compare various paths.

QUICK TIP

It might surprise you to learn that Cisco is not the only source of certification on Cisco products. Learning Tree International offers a Cisco Router Certification as well. Details of the Learning Tree Certification are provided later in this chapter.

The way Cisco Systems certifications are organized can be confusing. To begin with, Cisco Systems certifications are primarily divided into two categories: support and design. The support certifications are for individuals who work at installations that use Cisco routers and related technologies. They primarily involve implementing, troubleshooting, configuring, and operating a network or networks already in place. The CCNA and CCNP certifications fall into this category. Although CCIE's have quite a bit of design knowledge, Cisco includes them in this category as well.

The design certifications are for individuals who are responsible for the architecture of network solutions before they are installed. These are the people who will work with a client to determine the necessary specifications, and who are able to understand and explain the tradeoffs involved with different configurations. Design experts start with a blank piece of paper and end with a detailed network implementation specification. Two Cisco certifications fall into this category: CCDA and CCDP.

There is one Cisco certification that does not fit neatly into either category: Certified Cisco Systems Instructor (CCSI).

Instructors are certified on a course-by-course basis. Table 4.1 summarizes these categories.

TABLE 4.I
Cisco Certification
Categories

Support	Design	Instructor
CCNA	CCDA	CCSI
CCNP	CCDP	
CCIE—ISP Dial		
CCIE—Routing and Switching		
CCIE—WAN Switching		

The support and design categories include an entry-level (associate) and an advanced-level (professional) certification. In order to earn the professional certification, you must first earn the associate level. It is important to note that although many aspiring CCIEs choose to start with the CCNA and work their way up, that is not required. People who are capable of doing so can go directly to the CCIE certifications. Interestingly, although Cisco has tagged the CCNA as a support certification, it is also a prerequisite to earning the CCDP, a design certification.

Once you have decided whether you are interested in a support or design role (or both), you will need to choose a track. This further customizes the certification to a particular technology. Table 4.2 shows the tracks for each certification. Cisco certifications have three primary tracks to choose from: Routing and Switching, WAN Switching, and ISP-Dial. For all the certifications the routing and switching track is the "default" track i.e., a routing and switching CCNA is simply referred to as a CCNA while a WAN switching CCNA would use the designation CCNA – WAN Sw. Similarly, a CCIE in routing and switching would refer to herself simply as a CCIE, while graduates of the other tracks would call themselves CCIE – WAN Sw and CCIE – ISP Dial respectively.

The exams and material you will be expected to know are specific to the track you choose: the CCNA Routing and Switching exam is different from the CCNA WAN Switching exam. To further complicate matters, some certification tracks offer several alternate testing paths. This is one case where you are better off looking at the trees instead of the forest—i.e. don't worry too much about completely understanding the organization of Cisco's program, just hone in on the section you have identified as your target.

TABLE 4.2
Cisco's
Certification Tracks

	Routing and Switching	Wan Switching	ISP-Dial
Support			
CCNA	x	x	
CCNP	x	x	
CCIE	x	x	x
Design			
CCDA	x		
CCDP	x	x	
Instructor			
CCSI	course specific		

Now that you understand how Cisco certifications are structured, let's look at each certification individually.

Cisco Certified Network Associate (CCNA)

If you are in doubt on where to start, this is the place. This entry-level certification is a prerequisite for both the CCNP and the CCDP. It's also a good tool to help you land a job that will give you the hands-on experience necessary to become a CCIE at some point in the future. To obtain this certification you will need to pass one computer-based exam. See Figures 4.1 and 4.2

FIGURE 4.1
CCNA

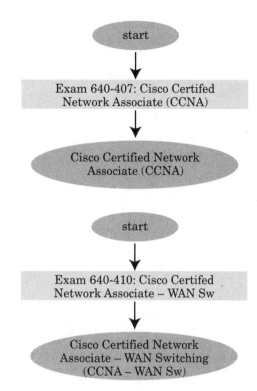

FIGURE 4.2
CCNA – WAN
Switching

As shown in Table 4.2, this certification is available in two tracks: routing and switching, and WAN switching. Cisco identifies its exams by number. The CCNA exam for the routing and switching track is exam #640-407. The WAN switching CCNA exam is #640-410. Cisco has defined a suggested training curriculum for each of these tracks as follows:

CCNA Suggested Curriculum

CCNAs are expected to understand "simple" routed and switched LANs and WANs. By Cisco's definition, simple routed networks utilize the following protocols and technologies: IP, IGRP, IPX, Serial, AppleTalk, Frame Relay, IP RIP, VLANs, IPX RIP, ethernet, and access lists. Two training paths have been defined:

For individuals familiar with internetworking, but unfamiliar with Cisco equipment:

1. Internetworking Technologies Multimedia (ITM) (CD-ROM)

2. Cisco Routing and LAN Switching (CRLS) (5-day class).

For individuals new to internetworking:

1. Internetworking Technologies Multimedia (ITM) (CD ROM)
2. Introduction to Cisco Router Configuration (ICRC) (5-day class)
3. High Performance Solutions for Desktop Connectivity (HPSDC) (self-study guide).

QUICK TIP

It's important to remember that you do not have to take these specific courses in order to achieve certification—they are simply available as learning options. You may choose to learn the information another way, such as through third-party materials.

CCNA–WAN Switching Suggested Curriculum

CCNA–WAN Switching individuals must be comfortable with installing WAN switches, IPX, IGX, BPX, AXIS Shelf, and modems. The following training path has been defined:

1. WAN Quick Start (WQS) (self-study guide)
2. Installation of Cisco WAN Switches (ICWS) (4-day class).

Cisco Certified Network Professional (CCNP)

The CCNP is the next step up from the CCNA. You must earn the CCNA before you can obtain the CCNP. The main difference between the two is the complexity of the networks you will be expected to understand.

As shown in Table 4.2, there are two CCNP tracks to choose from: Routing and Switching, and WAN Switching. To earn the CCNP–Routing and Switching (see Figure 4.3) you will have to pass the CCNA–Routing and Switching exam, plus four more: Advanced Cisco Router Configuration (ACRC) exam #640-403, Cisco LAN Switch Configuration (CLSC) exam #640-404, Configuring, Monitoring, Troubleshooting, and Dial up Services (CMTD) exam #640-405, and Cisco Internetworking Troubleshooting (CIT) exam #640-406. If you prefer, you can take a single, composite exam called the Foundation R/S exam in place of the ACRC, CLSC, and CMTD exams. The Foundation R/S exam lasts 2.75 hours while the total time for the other three exams is 4 hours. You can also save $100 by taking the Foundation R/S exam.

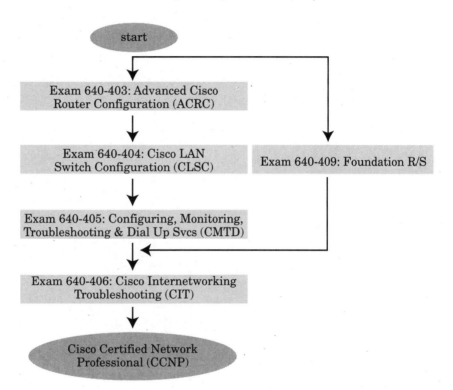

FIGURE 4.3
CCNP–Routing
and Switching

To become a CCNP–WAN Switching (shown in Figure 4.4), you'll have to pass the CCNA–WAN Switching exam plus four additional exams.

The CCNP–WAN Switching exams are: Multiband Switch and Service Configuration (MSSC) exam #640-419, BPX Switch and Service Configuration (BSSC) exam #640-425, MGX ATM Concentrator Configuration (MACC) exam #640-411, and either StrataView Installation and Operation (SVIO) exam #640-451 or exam #640-422, Cisco Strata View Plus (CSVP).

FIGURE 4.4
CCNP–WAN
Switching

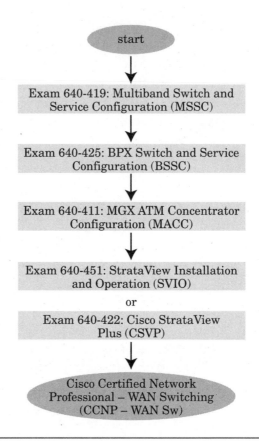

start

Exam 640-419: Multiband Switch and
Service Configuration (MSSC)

Exam 640-425: BPX Switch and Service
Configuration (BSSC)

Exam 640-411: MGX ATM Concentrator
Configuration (MACC)

Exam 640-451: StrataView Installation
and Operation (SVIO)

or

Exam 640-422: Cisco StrataView
Plus (CSVP)

Cisco Certified Network
Professional – WAN Switching
(CCNP – WAN Sw)

If you encounter an acronym or term you don't understand, check the glossary
section of this book for a definition.

QUICK TIP

CCNP Suggested Curriculum

Cisco specifies that CCNPs must be comfortable with IP, IGRP,
IPX, async routing, AppleTalk, extended access lists, IP RIP, route
redistribution, IPX RIP, route summarization, OSPF, VLSM,
BGP, Serial, IGRP, frame relay, ISDN, ISL, X.25, DDR, PSTN,
PPP, VLANs, ethernet, access lists, 802.10, FDDI, and transpar-
ent and translational bridging. The following suggested training
path has been identified:

1. Advanced Cisco Router Configuration (ACRC) (5 day class)
2. Cisco LAN Switch Configuration (CLSC) (5 day class)

3. Configuring, Monitoring, Troubleshooting, and Dial Up Services (CMTD) (5 day class)
4. Cisco Internetworking Troubleshooting (CIT) (5 day class).

CCNP–WAN Switching Suggested Curriculum

If you choose the WAN Switching track, you will be expected to demonstrate the skills needed to configure, operate, troubleshoot, and manage WAN switched networks. Cisco has created two training paths to help you accomplish this:

Path 1

1. Multiband Switch and Service Configuration (MSSC) (5-day class)
2. BPX Switch and Service Configuration (BSSC) (4-day class)
3. MGX ATM Concentrator Configuration (MACC) (5-day class)
4. StrataView Installation and Operation (SVIO) (4-day class)

Path 2

1. WAN Switch and Services Configuration (WSSC) (7-day class)
2. MGX ATM Concentrator Configuration (MACC) (5-day class)
3. StrataView Installation and Operation (SVIO) (4-day class).

CCNP Specialties

Those who achieve CCNP status, can add a specialty to their certification. This requires passing one or two additional exams, depending on the specialty chosen. Each exam has a corresponding suggested Cisco course. These exams are still being developed and many were not acutally available as this book was being written. The specialties are:

Security

Course: Managing Cisco Network Security (MCNS) (5-day class)
Exam#: 640-442 (MCNS)

Network Management

Courses: Managing Cisco Routed Internetworks (MCRI) (5-day class)
Managing Cisco Switched Internetworks (MCSI) (4-day class)
Exam#s: 640-442 (MCRI) and 640-443 (MCSI)

LAN ATM

Course: Cisco Campus ATM Solutions (CATM) (5-day class)
Exam#: 640-446 (CATM)

Voice Access

Course: Cisco Voice Over Frame Relay, ATM, and IP (CVOICE) (4-day class)
Exam#: 640-447 (CVOICE)

SNA Solutions

Courses: SNA Configuration for Multiprotocol Administrators (SNAM) (5-day class)
Data Link Switching Plus (DLSWP) (4-day class)
Exam#s: 640-445 (SNAM) and 640-450 (DLSWP).

Cisco Certified Design Associate (CCDA)

The CCDA, shown in Figure 4.5, is the first Cisco certification in the network design category. It's also the most straightforward—there is one exam (Designing Cisco Networks [DCN] exam #640-441) and one suggested training class. Although the CCNA is not a prerequisite for this certification, you will be expected to have the skills to support types of networks that CCDAs design. CCNPs may also find this a logical next step in training/professional credentialing.

There is no CCDA–WAN Switching certification. According to Cisco, this is because WAN switching technology is too complex to have an associate level design certification.

FIGURE 4.5
CCDA

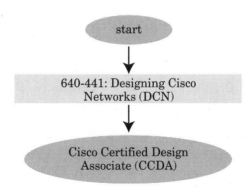

CCDA Suggested Curriculum

CCDA skills include designing simple routed LAN, routed WAN, and switched LAN networks. The suggested, but not required, course is Designing Cisco Networks (DCN), which is a self-paced training kit available from Cisco. It covers designing a topology, selecting hardware and software for WANs and LANs, routing and bridging protocols, design documentation, network management strategies, and implementation strategies.

Cisco Certified Design Professional (CCDP)

The CCDP is for individuals who design more complex routed and switched networks. It is the next step for CCDAs who want to advance their technical credentials. As shown in Table 4.2, there are both Routing and Switching and WAN Switching tracks for this certification. The track requirements are very different.

To earn the CCDP (routing and switching), candidates must first earn the CCDA and CCNA certifications. Candidates must then pass Advanced Cisco Router Configuration (ACRC) exam #640-403, Cisco LAN Switch Configuration (CLSC) exam #640-404, Configuring, Monitoring, Troubleshooting, and Dial up Services (CMTD) exam #640-405, and Cisco Internetwork Design (CID) exam #640-025. As with the CCNP, candidates have the option of taking a single, composite exam called the Foundation R/S exam (#640-409) in place of the ACRC, CLSC, and CMTD exams. The Foundation R/S exam lasts 2.75 hours while the total time for the other three exams is 4 hours. You can also save $100 by taking the Foundation R/S exam. Figure 4.6 shows this certification.

FIGURE 4.6
CCDP

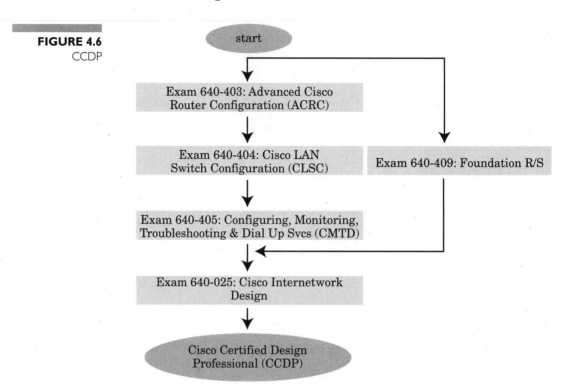

Requirements for the CCDP–Wan Switching, shown in Figure 4.7, are quite different. Candidates must earn the CCNA–WAN Switching and CCNP–WAN Switching plus pass one additional exam: Designing Switched WAN and Voice Solutions (DSWVS) exam #640-413. Each CCDP track has a matching curriculum.

CCDP Suggested Curriculum

Routing and switching CCDPs are expected to design complex routed LAN, routed WAN, and switched LAN networks. It is assumed that candidates already have the knowledge and skills to install, configure, and operate such networks. The following courses are recommended to help you prepare:

FIGURE 4.7
CCDP–WAN
Switching

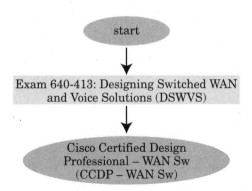

1. Advanced Cisco Router Configuration (ACRC) (5-day class)
2. Cisco LAN Switch Configuration (CLSC) (5-day class)
3. Configuring, Monitoring, Troubleshooting, and Dial Up Services (CMTD) (5-day class)
4. Cisco Internet Design (CID) (5-day class).

There is substantial overlap between the CCNP and CCDP curriculums.

QUICKTIP

CCDP–WAN Switching Suggested Curriculum

According to Cisco, CCDP–WAN Switching professionals are able to design and implement an ATM network (with CBR, ABR, and VBR traffic) and a Frame Relay network (using CIR and MIR traffic parameters), as well as troubleshoot an existing WAN switched network and manage traffic and voice technologies. They also know how to install WAN switches. There is only one suggested class for this track: Designing Switched WAN and Voice Solutions (DSWVS), which is a self-study CD ROM available from Cisco.

The details of Cisco tests, including lab facility locations, and resources to help you prepare, are covered in depth in Chapter 11.

QUICKTIP

Cisco Certified Internetwork Expert (CCIE)

The CCIE certifications are not on the same plane as Cisco's other certifications. First, the requirements are much more demanding. Second, although some training suggestions are made, the CCIE designations have never been intended to provide a training path as the others do. Candidates are expected to have a high level of expertise and significant hands-on experience before even undertaking these certifications. If you do not have this experience, you are better off setting your sights a bit lower, and working your way up through the certifications already discussed before attempting a CCIE.

There are three CCIE tracks to choose from: the basic routing and switching CCIE, CCIE–WAN Switching, and CCIE ISP Dial. Whichever one you choose, you will have to pass a two-hour CCIE qualification test, followed by a two-day hands on lab exam. Candidates must pass the qualification test before they are allowed to register for the lab exam (see Figure 4.8). As this book was being written, the routing/switching test was a two-hour multiple choice exam consisting of about 100 questions, administered through Sylvan Prometric. The WAN Switching test had 123 questions. But at press time the routing and switching written exam was also being revised, with the new version in beta, so check the Cisco CCIE routing and switching Web site (**www.cisco.com/warp/public/625/ccie/routing.html**) for the latest details on this particular exam.

FIGURE 4.8
CCIE

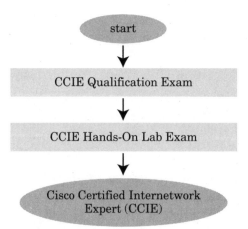

For the lab exam you will have to travel to a Cisco lab facility. Some of these offer preparatory labs—a place to practice before you take the official lab exam.

To keep their credentials, CCIEs are required to pass a recertification exam every two years, and must attend technical update seminars.

CCIE–R/S

Routing and Switching CCIEs must demonstrate the ability to install, configure, operate, and troubleshoot complex routed LAN, routed WAN, switched LAN and ATM LANE networks, and Dial Access services. They must also be able to diagnose and resolve network faults and use packet/frame analysis and Cisco debugging tools. The routing and switching qualification exam is #350-001.

As stated earlier, there is no specified curriculum for this certification. However, Cisco does recommend the following classes to help you prepare:

* Introduction to Cisco Router Configuration (ICRC) (5-day class)
* Installation and Maintenance of Cisco Routers (IMCR) (4-day class)
* Advanced Cisco Router Configuration (ACRC) (5 day class)
* Cisco Internet Design (CID) (5 day class)
* Cisco Internetworking Troubleshooting (CIT) (5 day class)
* SNA Configuration for Multiprotocol Administrators (SNAM) (5-day class).

CCIE–WAN Switching

WAN Switching CCIEs must demonstrate the skills to implement an ATM network (with CBR, ABR, and VBR traffic) and a frame relay network (using CIR and MIR traffic parameters) as well as troubleshoot an existing WAN switched network and manage traffic and voice technologies. The CCIE WAN Switching qualification exam is #350-007. Cisco's recommended (not required) preparation classes are:

* Installing Cisco WAN Switches (ICWS) (4-day class)
* BPX Switch and Service Configuration (BSSC) (4-day class)
* AXIS Switch and Service Configuration (ASSC) (details not available)
* Network Operations for BPX/AXIS Products (details not available)
* Multiservice Concentrator 3810 Configuration and Monitoring (MCCM) (5-day class)
* Multiband Switch and Service Configuration (MSSC) (5-day class)
* StrataView Installation and Maintenance (SVIM) (2-day class)
* StrataView Installation and Operation (SVIO) (4-day class).

CCIE–ISP Dial

This certification is focused on networks that use dial up network services, such as those operated by Internet service providers (ISPs). CCIE–ISP Dial individuals must demonstrate expertise in IP routing, dialup, remote access and WAN technologies. The qualification exam is #350-004. Suggested preparation courses largely overlap those for the routing and switching CCIE. They include:

* Introduction to Cisco Router Configuration (ICRC) (5-day class)
* Installation and Maintenance of Cisco Routers (IMCR) (4-day class)
* Advanced Cisco Router Configuration (ACRC) (5-day class)
* Cisco Internet Design (CID) (5-day class)
* Cisco Internetworking Troubleshooting (CIT) (5-day class)
* Cisco AS5200 Installation and Configuration (AS5200) (2-day class)
* Configuring, Monitoring, Troubleshooting, and Dial Up Services (CMTD) (5–day class).

QUICK TIP

> It is important to recognize that you may not need to attend instructor-led training to prepare adequately. You may be able to meet many of your training needs through self-study options, such as purchasing third-party books on individual topics and on the job training.

Figure 4.9 shows how the support and design certifications interrelate, including the prerequisites for each.

FIGURE 4.9
Cisco Design and Support Certifications and Prerequisites

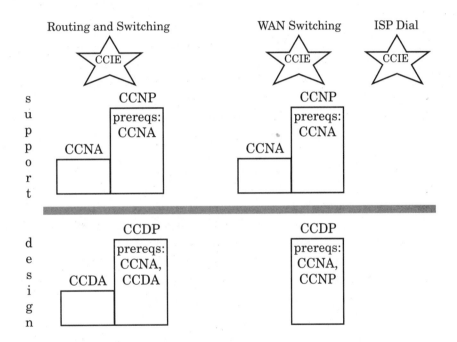

Certified Cisco Systems Instructor (CCSI)

The CCSI differs from the other Cisco certifications in a number of important ways. First of all, it matters who your employer is. You must be employed by a Cisco training partner or be a training partner yourself. The minute you leave that training partner, your certification lapses.

The second major difference is that there is no series of exams, but rather, candidates must attend the course they want to teach, then pass the related exam. Once that has been accomplished, candidates must attend a two-day Instructor Certification Process (ICP) at Cisco. During this session instructors will have to teach parts of the class they wish to be certified on, as well as assemble and troubleshoot a Cisco training lab. Obtaining certification to teach additional courses is simpler. CCSIs must attend the course, pass the related exam, and submit a request to extend their certification to include the new course.

CCSI candidates must have hands-on technical experience in bridging and routing, switching, and/or WAN environments, plus at least a year of technical teaching experience in order to be considered for certification.

CCSIs can lose their certification for many reasons, such as teaching with photocopies instead of original Cisco materials, leaving employment with the Cisco Training Partner, missing administrative deadlines, or not maintaining at least 4.0 out of a possible 5.0 on student critiques.

Learning Tree International Cisco Router Certification

With the addition of the career certifications, alternative, non-Cisco sponsored certifications on Cisco equipment are less attractive than they once were. However, it is important to note that they do exist, and to consider them as an alternative. Learning Tree International sponsors one such program, the Cisco Router Certified Professional. Obtaining it requires attending four core courses plus an elective course and passing associated exams. The total cost of tuition plus exams is about $10,900. The core courses are:

* Introduction to Internetworking: Bridges, Switches and Routers (4 days/$2,495)
* Cisco Routers: A Comprehensive Hands-On Introduction (4 days/$1,995)
* Configuring Cisco Routers: Advanced Hands-On Workshop (4 days/$1,995)
* IP Routing with OSPF and BGP: Hands-On (4 days/$1,995).

Electives include:

* Hands-On Internetworking with TCP/IP (4 days/$1,995)
* Migrating to IPv6: Hands-On (4 days/$1,995)
* Hands-On SNMP: From Workgroup to Enterprise Networks

(4 days/$1,995),

* Hands-On Introduction to TCP/IP (4 days/$1,995)

* Data Network Design and Performance Optimization (4 days/$1,995)

* Deploying Internet and Intranet Firewalls: Hands-On (4 days/$1,995)

* Internet and System Security: Attacks and Countermeasures (4 days/$1,995)

* Fast LAN Technologies (4 days/$1,995)

* Hands-On High-Performance Ethernet: Switched, Fast and Traditional (4 days/$1,995)

Even if the complete certification does not interest you, you might find some of the courses valuable as preparation tools for the Cisco exams.

As you can see, there are quite a few certifications to choose from. Cisco plans to add additional certifications in the future, so a periodic check of the Cisco certification Web pages at **www.cisco.com/warp/public/10/wwtraining/certprog/index. html** for the latest information is a good idea.

PART 2

How to Get (Happily) Certified

CHAPTER 5

Inside Perspectives

Six professionals who have earned Cisco certifications report: the view from inside is rosy.

The Way In

No matter which Cisco certification you choose to pursue, the process of achieving certification is straightforward. The basic steps are:

1. Choose a certification
2. Identify gaps between what you know and what you need to know
3. Determine what you will do to fill those gaps
4. Choose an exam and prepare for it
5. Take the exam
6. Repeat steps 4 and 5 until all requirements are met
7. Put your certification to work for you.

Each of these seven steps can be further broken down and will be later, but this is the basic process for obtaining a certification. Depending on your choice of certification and your current level of experience and skills, the commitment needed to go through this process will vary considerably. Significant time and expense may be involved, and self-motivation is an absolute must. You should know what you are getting into.

Reports from the Field

If you wanted to find out what skydiving is like, you might begin by asking someone you know who has seen parachutists in action. That would only give you a partial picture—the pieces that a spectator can observe and convey. To fill in the details, you would also want to ask a participant, perhaps a parachutist or the pilot of a jump plane. Better yet, ask more than one.

In the same way, when it comes to getting a good sense of the roles certification can play in the careers of computer professionals, statistics, study, and trend observations can provide only part of the story. The most meaningful insights come from people who've been through the certification process and/or encounter it on a daily basis.

The interviews that follow offer the inside scoop on Cisco certification. Six computer professionals who have taken the plunge share their personal perspectives on these certifications and the process of obtaining them.

Scott Urban, CCIE, CCNA

Job title: Systems Engineer–US Channels, Cisco Systems
Certifications Held: CCIE #3977, CCNA, MCNE, 3Com Wizard
Years of experience in computer field: 6

When did you obtain your Cisco certifications?
I received my CCNA in July 1998 and my CCIE in August 1998. I am working toward the CCIE–WAN switching.

What made you decide to pursue Cisco certifications?
Several reasons made me decide to get my certifications. First, the information and knowledge that you gain from the studying required for a certification like the CCIE is extremely valuable. I wanted in-depth knowledge of the protocols and technologies that are fundamental in this industry, and the CCIE provided that to me. Next, the CCIE gives you instant credibility in the industry. Most people are familiar with what it takes to achieve such a certification and recognize that to pass the CCIE you have to demonstrate a certain level of proficiency. The CCNA and other Cisco certifications are similar, but to a lesser degree. They progressively require you to know more as you move from the CCNA to the CCIE.

How did you do to prepare?
Study, study, study! I spent many hours reading and even more hours in the lab.

Who paid for your training and testing?
I funded the first part of my CCIE (the written), but was fortunate enough to work for a company that supported and even pushed for CCIE certification and they paid for the lab portion.

How has being Cisco certified affected your career?
Cisco certification makes you instantly marketable. Many lucrative job opportunities today state CCIE certification as a requirement. With around 3,000 CCIEs worldwide, supply is limited. I have received many inquiries about other positions both internal and external to Cisco.

What do you think of the Cisco career certifications?
I think the certifications are excellent. Before, the CCIE was an extremely lofty goal that could take years to attain. With the new certifications, a person can have "stepping stones" towards the CCIE, which provides a sense of accomplishment. Also, some certifications specialize in certain areas. This was done because some people do different things (i.e.—WAN switching, ISP dial, security, IBM, etc.) The different CCIE certifications and CCNP specializations allow users to become certified in their area of expertise.

What do you feel is the best way to prepare for certification exams?
Hands-on time and access to equipment are critical to passing the lab. You can read all day long, but until you've sat down and done route redistribution or VLSM, you won't know it well enough to pass. For the written portion, I usually tell the candidate to fork over the $200 and take the test cold. It will give them an idea of what the test is like and enable them to focus their studies. This industry is full of information, and a candidate can study for hours and hours and not be in the right ballpark. To invest 100 hours studying and then find out you were going in the wrong direction can be discouraging.

What do you think is the biggest misconception about Cisco certifications?
The biggest misconception is that having a CCIE means you know everything. The CCIE is extremely hard to pass, but the industry is so big and so many different technologies are in use today that no one certification can teach you everything. What the CCIE does give you is a detailed knowledge of the fundamental concepts needed to succeed in this industry. It shows to cus-

tomers, employers, and co-workers that you understand *and can implement* the concepts that drive data communications.

What do you think is the most common mistake people make when pursuing Cisco certification?
Underestimating the amount of work needed to attain a particular certification.

What advice do you have for anyone who is considering earning a Cisco certification?
Study hard, very hard. To pass the CCIE lab is as much strategic as it is technical. Reading the entire exam and understanding it before any configuration is done is critical. Documentation is critical. Time allocation is critical. Many factors go into creating a successful environment to help you pass your CCIE lab. Did you get enough sleep the night before? Did you eat a good breakfast? People react to stressful situations in different ways, and a timed test like the CCIE can certainly be a stressful situation. Deciding what makes you comfortable and relaxes you the most is just as important as knowing the correct commands.

Pamela Forsyth, CCIE, former CCSI

Job title: Internetworking Expert, Force 3, Inc.
Certifications Held: CCIE #3439, CCSI, CNX, Master CNE, MCSE, CBS (Certified Banyan Specialist), plus a few more
Years of experience in computer field: 25

When did you obtain your Cisco certifications?
CCIE–WAN Switching—in progress
CCIE Routing & Switching—February 1998
CCSI (Certified Cisco Systems Instructor)—1997–1998. CCSI certifications lapse when the instructor severs her relationship with her sponsoring training partner, and that's what happened in this case. I quit being a full-time instructor to get more hands-on experience.

What made you decide to pursue Cisco certification?

Back in 1994–95 I was a CNE with several solid years of experience, and worked with a fellow who was one exam away from CNE who literally didn't know how to attach a PC to the LAN after two years in his LAN support position. I had long felt that the CNE would have benefited by having just a simple certification lab. Then I learned that Cisco had a certification that required a two-day lab, and decided it was for me—simply because the stringent lab requirement meant that most people would not have the persistence to pass it, and that those who achieved it would be able to do the job.

For the instructor certification, I was hired by a training partner to be a Cisco instructor, and couldn't do the work unless I got certified. Fortunately, it's a lot easier to get the instructor certification than the CCIE. I hadn't actually been seeking that sort of work, but the opportunity seemed attractive when it arose so I decided to do it.

What did you do to prepare and what was the process like?

The first thing I had to do was find a job in which I could get some console time on the routers. After that it was a struggle to get some interesting console time on the routers! My employers, seeing that I was really good at the applications and servers, wanted to keep me in support roles in which I could be maximally productive (if bored and discouraged), not roles in which I could grow professionally. I had several quick job changes as a result.

Getting instructor-certified actually helped my CCIE preparation quite a lot. The course I taught the most was Advanced Cisco Router Configuration (ACRC), which has a lot of material that is directly relevant to the CCIE lab. Just learning that material to the depth necessary to do a good job of teaching it, then going over it again and again, was valuable. Not to speak of all the troubleshooting I had to do for the students' misconfigured classroom networks!

Who paid for your training?

It was a long, tough road to CCIE. I was able to get employers to pay for almost all of the training I needed as well as the first of my three lab attempts, but it was a struggle all the way. I paid for the second two labs myself because my employer at the time required that such expenses be repaid anyway if an employee quit before two years, and I thought it likely that I might do just that. I didn't want it to be an issue.

My employer paid for the instructor certification—it was a necessary business expense for them. I had already had the applicable training when I went to work there.

How has being Cisco certified affected your career?

Having the CCIE has opened a lot of doors for me, but the additional potential opportunities have forced me to think carefully about what sort of work I really prefer doing and where I prefer doing it. I know I am making a lot less money than I could if I wanted to travel constantly, for instance.

Also, it's great to have the sort of credibility the CCIE provides. Networking is still 98% a man's world, and the CCIE certification proves I am as good as anyone at this business.

What do you think of the Cisco career certifications?

The new career certification programs certainly have created a huge market for training materials and study guides! But seriously, they are good and bad, just as all certification programs are. They are good in that they establish objective knowledge standards that a candidate must meet in order to be certified. This is a great boon to employers, who may not have senior technical people on board to evaluate potential employees' credentials. On the other hand, I believe some employers have more faith in the certifications as a means of identifying competent employees than they should, and forget to take other considerations into account.

What do you feel is the best way to prepare for certification exams?

Very simply, study the exam objectives on the Cisco certification pages, then study about those topics in depth and learn what commands to use to configure the routers and switches for them. If you can, create some configuration problems to try out on some actual equipment. When your immediate goal is passing the CCIE lab you must spend enough time with the routers and switches to become fluent at the basic commands, and then become familiar with everything that can be configured.

What is the biggest misconception about Cisco certifications?
That you will immediately be worth a six-figure salary! Your compensation depends a great deal on the other qualities and experience you bring to the table.

What advice do you have for anyone who is considering earning a Cisco certification?
Strive for in-depth understanding. Don't rely only on the Cisco documentation—you'll never learn enough from it. You need to be well-grounded in the underlying technologies before configuring the routers will make sense.

Terry Slattery, CCIE, CCSI

Job title: President of Chesapeake Computer Consultants, Inc
Certifications Held: CCIE #1026, CCSI
Years of experience in computer field: 23

When did you obtain your Cisco certification?
CCIE, 1993—the second CCIE world-wide and the first one outside Cisco. CCSI, 1993.

What made you decide to obtain it?
I heard about the program while doing consulting work for Cisco and the program developers thought I'd make a good first candidate.

How did you prepare?
I took the Cisco Internetwork Troubleshooting class, which is almost a requirement for checking that you know what you're doing. I had a lot of hands-on experience with Cisco equipment and commands, since we had just finished writing the new user interface for Cisco (this is the user interface that allows command line editing, command history, command completion, and interactive help). We were forced to learn every command in the IOS through the conversion process.

Who paid for your training and testing?
It was OJT, so there was no direct cost.

How has being Cisco certified affected your career?
It has helped obtain consulting engagements because people recognize the knowledge and experience that are required to pass the test. It has also brought some name recognition since I'm the first non-Cisco CCIE. It has also helped Chesapeake Computer Consultants too, since we have been able to build a staff of 14 CCIEs.

What do you think of the Cisco career certifications?
The career certifications provide internetworking professionals a range of certifications that grow as their knowledge and skills grow. Obtaining the CCIE is a great challenge. Having lower level certifications increases people's motivation by providing easier-to-obtain goals along the path to the CCIE certification.

What do you think is the best way to prepare for certification exams?
There are two things that are needed:

1. Learn the basic protocols and how they operate and how they fail. Learn how to configure Cisco equipment for proper operation with these protocols.
2. Get hands-on experience with the configurations. Chesapeake is now selling a product called "vLab" which is from Mentor-Labs (**www.mentorlabs.com**). It is hands-on access to real hardware over the Internet. Through this mechanism, there is no reason why someone cannot gain the necessary hands-on experience to pass the CCIE test.

What do you think are the most common mistakes people make when pursuing Cisco certification?
Not getting enough hands-on time with the equipment. The CCIE test is very much a hands-on test. The time constraints make the test very difficult. If you have to take time to look up very much configuration information, you'll run out of time.

What advice do you have for anyone who is considering earning a Cisco certification?

Learn the protocols. Learn how they work. Learn how they fail. Learn what symptoms are exhibited when they fail. Learn how to troubleshoot them when they fail. Learn the Cisco configurations for each protocol. And practice, practice, practice. Just like the master musician that practices each day, the master network professional must spend time practicing configurations.

Additional comments:

The Cisco certifications, particularly the CCIE, have really set the level of expectations for future certifications by all vendors. It is now comparable to advanced degrees, but with practical experience also required. It is almost like a medical doctor degree, where time must be spent in a hospital, learning the real-world experiences that cannot be learned in the classroom or from a book.

Ben Lovegrove, CCNA

Job title: Senior Network Engineer, NTL Incorporated
Certifications Held: CCNA, NVQ National Vocational Qualification) Level II, Webmaster diploma
Years of experience in computer field: $5\frac{1}{2}$

When did you obtain your Cisco certifications?
CCNA (January 1999). CCNP in progress.

What made you decide to pursue Cisco certifications?
* A desire for a measure of my knowledge—a sort of benchmark of what I had absorbed after a few years' experience.
* The ambition to become a CCIE, and by choosing the "slow" route, believing that I will absorb the knowledge more thoroughly.
* Knowing that gaining these accreditations would give a boost to my self confidence.
* Being able to add the accreditation to my CV (resume) would make my skills more marketable.

How did you prepare and what was the most difficult aspect of the process?
Having obtained an updated list of the exam objectives from the Cisco Web site, I reviewed the ICRC manual once, then read and reread the Syngress CCNA study guide. I explored the Cisco Web site, read choice threads in the **groupstudy.com** mailing list, explored other Web sites of related material, etc.

The most difficult aspect was not being able to match what I was reading with hands-on examples. I have practical experience of live networks consisting of mostly Cisco routers, but not as much as I would prefer to have. Also, at this early stage, there is an unavoidable amount of theory.

Who paid for your training and testing?
My employer, IBM UK at the time, paid for the courses and the exam fee. I bought the study guides. I will buy the next four study guides and, if required, I will pay for the next exams. I might even stretch to the CMTD course if my employer does not sponsor me.

How has being Cisco certified affected your career?
It has enhanced my visibility and improved my CV. Since registering with some employment agencies, the CCNA has been referred to many times, and obviously counts for something. It opens doors.

Overall, what do you think of the Cisco career certifications?
I'm sure that from Cisco's point of view there are sound business reasons for launching them. From my point of view (and although CCNA and CCNP are not prerequisites for CCIE) they provide a graded career path that employers have not so far supplied, that will lead to CCIE status. They have motivated me to study more and learn new skills. They give a structured approach to learning sections of the vast and complex fields of networking and inter-networking. They are a map through the jungle.

What do you feel is the best way to prepare for certification exams?
Ideally, attend the required course(s), make good use of the hands-on time during the course, review the course materials, make use of the study guides that are now becoming available. Use the Internet for "second opinions" or someone else's explana-

tion of a subject if you get stuck or fail to understand. Ask your employer to allow your team to set up a practice lab using spare routers and experiment and practice in that lab. Use the **www.groupstudy.com** mailing list.

What do you think is the most common mistake people make when pursuing Cisco certification?

Perhaps they underestimate what is involved in gaining them. The CCIE lab is one of the toughest in the industry. Perhaps they rush in eager to add another "paper" certification to their collection. I view these certifications as practical, not theoretical.

What advice do you have for anyone who is considering earning a Cisco certification?

Don't skimp on hands-on time if you truly want to be a networking professional. Don't give up if you fail any exam. Learn from it, do some more work, then try again.

Do share your knowledge. Talking to others often clarifies your own misconceptions or hazy understanding of an area. Do keep training. You should allocate time and money for training for most of your working life in IT.

Additional comments:

Some people have argued that as more people gain these accreditations, they will attract less kudos and their value will be lessened. Obviously there will be many more CCNAs, more CCNPs and a few more CCIEs in 1999/2000 and beyond, but this is why your other skills are so important, and this why you should continue to add to your skill set with further training and study. You cannot afford to rest on your laurels in an industry that is progressing and changing as fast as networking and in which new technology, new products, and new software are launched every week.

Chad Marsh, CCNA

Job title: Communications/Networking Technician, Tacoma School District #10, Tacoma, WA
Certifications Held: CCNA, numerous Fujitsu certifications
Years of experience in computer field: 7

When did you obtain your Cisco certifications?
CCNA—December 1998. Currently working toward CCNP, planning completion by August 1999 (2 months per test/course).

What made you decide to pursue Cisco certifications?
I am at the top of my field in voice communications, and I was looking for something to further my career and salary level, as well as keep my mind challenged.

How did you prepare?
I took a 5-day custom course from GeoTrain, that was a composite of the ICRC and ACRC courses. I then thoroughly studied everything pertaining to CCNA that I could get my hands on in the next 5 weeks. This included: the ICRC student course book, the Sybex and Syngress CCNA Study Guides, the **CCIEPrep.com** book—chapters 1 and 2, the **CCNAPrep.com** Web site, and the book *Virtual LANs* by Gilbert Held (for the switching info). I also borrowed a Cisco 2522 router from an associate to practice Cisco IOS commands.

CCIEPrep.com and CCNAPrep.com have combined into **CCprep.com**.

Obtaining CCNA was about as difficult as I expected; I went from zero Cisco knowledge and very little OSI/internetworking knowledge, to CCNA in six weeks. It was not too difficult; the exams I have taken since then have been more difficult.

Who paid for your training and testing?
The course was paid for by the State of Washington K-20 Cooperative, to train staff for support within their school district. All other resources I paid for myself.

How has being Cisco certified affected your career?
It has not yet, but I am just getting started.

Overall, what do you think of the Cisco career certifications?
Excellent idea. I believe they are beneficial to everyone involved.
They give Cisco more revenue and recognition, they give would-be
CCIEs a stepping-stone type approach that gives recognition and
satisfaction at various stages in their professional development,
and they give employers a way to gauge prospective employees.

What do you feel is the best way to prepare for certification exams?
The best way is to know the material, period. You can pass by
memorizing and cramming, but you're only kidding yourself if you
get the certification and don't really know the material.

*What advice would you give someone who is considering earning a
Cisco certification?*
Go for it.

Lou Rossi, CCIE, CCSI, CCNA

Job title: Senior Network Engineer, Andrews Rossi Inc., co-
owner, CCprep.com
Certifications Held: CCIE, CCSI, CCNA, CNE3, CNE4,
MCNE, MCP
Years of experience in computer field: 7

When did you obtain your Cisco certifications?
CCSI–August 1996; CCIE–October 1997; CCNA–June 1998. I will
probably take the CCNP, CCDA, and CCDP exams this year.

What made you decide to pursue Cisco certifications?
I was working with Novell and Microsoft network operating systems and noticed that I enjoyed working on infrastructure and
the lower layers of the OSI model; I also noticed that there was
more money to be made. I talked with a friend who suggested I
teach Cisco classes rather than the Novell and Microsoft classes. I
took several of the Cisco classes and thought "This is great! And I
get paid more!" I have been consulting, writing, and teaching
Cisco ever since. I am convinced that Cisco has the best products
available and will continue to dominate the marketplace in the
future.

How did you prepare and what was the most difficult aspect of the process?

I prepared for my certifications by taking the classes and having a two-year hands-on background working with Cisco products off and on. I thought the most difficult part was taking the classes and learning those little things I never got to see in the real world, like BGP or DLSW. I don't work with these features that often.

Who paid for your training and testing?

I was going to teach for a company called American Research Group, so they picked up all my expenses, however I was not being paid for my first several classes. After I was certified to teach I could take classes for a small daily rate. They also only paid for the first attempt on any given test. This was great incentive to pass the first time.

How has being Cisco certified affected your career?

Being a CCIE has opened many doors I never thought possible. It has improved my financial situation, and has given me the confidence to do a lot of things I never thought I would be able to do.

I have received generous offers from Cisco Systems to be an SE and have had many calls from VARs, all with salaries in the $100,000–$150,000 range, depending on position and location.

Overall, what do you think of the Cisco career certifications?

I think the new certifications are great! When there was only the CCIE it was an all-or-nothing approach. I actually remember people putting on their resume that they had passed the CCIE written. This was not a certification but they would put it on anyway. Now there are certifications to let employers know just how experienced a engineer is with Cisco equipment.

What do you feel is the best way to prepare for certification exams?

Use a combination of classes and real-world experience as well as help from books and Web sites such as my **CCprep.com** that will give a student an idea of what is involved in taking and passing the exams.

What do you think is the biggest misconception about Cisco certifications?

I really don't see too many students who have a misconception. Most understand that is a combination of written and practical tests that when passed will help one's career tremendously. Sometimes students may think that the practical [lab exam] is too difficult for them because of horror stories they have heard, but books and Web sites have dispelled most of those rumors.

What do you think is the most common mistake people make when pursuing Cisco certification?

The most common mistake is studying the wrong material. A candidate needs to understand the objectives given by Cisco. To do this, one will need guidance from somewhere other than Cisco. Cisco is not in the business of teaching students how to pass the exams. Companies like CCprep.com, McGraw-Hill Publishing, Macmillan Publishing, and the Cisco training partners are where one needs to look for guidance. If one tries to read the recommended reading list from Cisco they will go insane and fail the exam.

What advice would you give someone who is considering earning a Cisco certification?

Study hard! Don't make a half-hearted attempt. Set your mind to it and do it. It will be well worth the effort both mentally and financially.

Additional comments:

Cisco certification has had the biggest impact on my career and I am looking forward to the challenges of recertification and the new technologies that it will introduce me to.

Putting the Pieces Together

As you can see, these professionals agree that Cisco certification is a valuable career tool. At the CCIE level, it can rocket your income up to the six figures. At the lower levels, it can add valuable credentials to your resume as well as provide a learning path to help you achieve internetworking expertise. While these reports show that the certifications are not easy to obtain, the people who have invested the time, effort, and money to gain Cisco certification have found the return on their investment to be very satisfactory.

It is important to note that these certification will open doors for you, but it is up to you to keep them open, which is a good sign of effective and reasonable use of credentialing in any industry. Those extra letters on your business card or resume signify that you have (or once had) particular expertise. Although that will get you a quicker and closer look, you will still be required to provide evidence of your accomplishments in additional ways. That is as it should be, and if you have pursued certification in the proper spirit, backing up your credentials should be no problem. Strive to learn the material as thoroughly as possible instead of attempting to cram in just enough knowledge to pass the next exam.

Certification processes provide a method and motivation for keeping up on the latest products and technologies, a key to career success in the computer field. Although a few computer professionals have been disappointed by their efforts in the certification marketplace, the Cisco program is one of the strongest going. By and large, individuals who have obtained one or more Cisco certifications report that the experience has been both personally and professionally satisfying. So much so that they rarely stop at one.

CHAPTER 6

Dollars and Sense: Financial Answers Before You Begin

Depending upon the program and training methods you choose, obtaining a professional certification can entail a substantial investment. Because there are numerous possible routes to a single certification, it can be difficult to make an accurate assessment of what your actual cost will be. However, it is worthwhile to work up an estimate in advance so you won't be blindsided by unexpected expenses.

A detailed expense estimate can also help convince your employer to pay for part or all of your certification costs. When you itemize the figures on paper, you demonstrate that this is not just a whim; you have carefully considered the path to your goal, its costs, and its consequences. You'll also be better able to compare certification to other career-boosting alternatives, such as earning a traditional degree.

QUICK TIP

As certification continues to gain popularity, the number of ways to pay for it are increasing. Don't assume your own bank account is the only source of certification funding.

Once you have developed your initial estimate, you'll also be able to create alternate scenarios. This will enable you to compare the costs of various approaches. With that information, you will be able to decide, for example, whether the classroom training classes are worth X dollars more to you than the self-guided CBT course covering the same material. You will also be able to identify potential savings points, which can prove very useful if your funds are in short supply.

Throughout the process of estimating your expenditure, it is important to remember that while you may be laying out a substantial chunk of change today, you are doing so in expectation of an even larger payback in the future. That payback comes in the form of increased income, a better job, and increased personal and professional satisfaction.

Total Expenditure

Standard certification expenses include study materials, training costs, testing fees, and application fees. Depending upon the certification, you may also find yourself paying for travel to a training site or lab test, purchasing equipment or software, or incurring other charges.

Another expense you will encounter is opportunity cost. Opportunity cost addresses the value of what, besides money, you will be giving up in order to pursue certification. If you will be studying during your usual work hours, then you will not be producing the income you otherwise would. If that will be the case, then your opportunity cost is measurable in dollars.

Some might argue that another opportunity cost is time out from other career advancement or networking activities. But focusing on certification is really a shift in method rather than a replacement for such activities; the time is still being dedicated to the same purpose but in a different way. In fact, you will most likely be spending more time (or at least more effective time) on career enhancement activities than you would otherwise.

If you plan to do the majority of your studying outside your usual business hours, then you will not be trading income for study time, but you will still be taking time from somewhere else, such as family time or other areas of personal life, and dedicating it to your professional goals. That opportunity cost is more difficult to quantify but still important to keep in mind.

Table 6.1 lists both the monetary and opportunity costs of certification.

TABLE 6.1
Certification Costs

Out-of-Pocket Expenses	Opportunity Costs
Training tuition	Foregone earnings
Study materials	Reduced personal/family time
Test/lab fees	
Practice equipment	
Application fee	
Travel to testing/training facilities	

Creating a Worksheet

In estimating your total expenditure, it is helpful to use a spreadsheet like the one in Figure 6.1, or you can develop your own. You can make it the old-fashioned way—with paper and pencil—but a spreadsheet generated using Excel, Quattro Pro, or other programs will be quicker and more versatile. An electronic version of the spreadsheet in Figure 6.1 can be found at **www.gocertify.com**.

FIGURE 6.1

Expenditure Worksheet

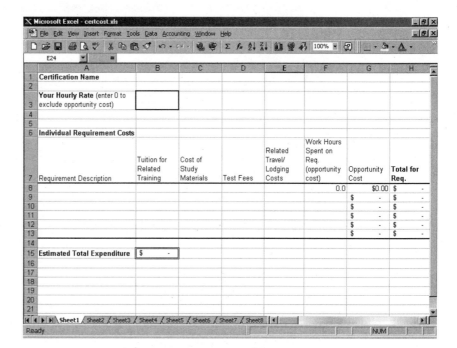

To calculate your total expenditure using the worksheet in Figure 6.1, first enter the certification name at the top of the sheet. If you prepare multiple worksheets (to compare various certifications), the name will make it easy to identify which worksheet goes to which certification program.

Next, enter your hourly pay rate. This is needed to calculate your opportunity cost. If you do not wish to include opportunity cost in your estimate, simply enter 0 (zero) for hourly rate.

The next section contains the meat of the worksheet. Beginning with the first requirement needed to obtain the certification, enter a brief description of the requirement. Then go across the row, filling in estimated tuition, cost of study materials you will need to meet the requirement, any test fee related to the requirement, associated travel costs if you will need to attend training elsewhere, and, last, the number of hours you will take from work and apply to meeting this requirement. If you are using the electronic spreadsheet from the **gocertify.com** Web site, the opportunity cost and total cost for meeting the requirement will calculate and fill in automatically. If not, you will need to perform the calculations and fill in the blanks by hand.

To determine the opportunity cost manually, multiply your hourly rate by the number in the "Work Hours Spent On Req." column. The total cost of the requirement is calculated by summing all numbers in the requirement row *except* the entry in the "Work Hours Spent On Req." column.

For each requirement you need to meet, fill in another row. Don't be afraid to make an educated guess at figures you do not know. You can dig up the actual numbers by calling vendors, surfing the Internet for course listings, or asking friends.

The estimate of your total certification expenditure will appear at the bottom of the spreadsheet. If you are completing the worksheet manually, add up the requirement expenses to obtain the same number. Figure 6.2 shows a worksheet completed by a CCNA candidate.

Save the completed worksheet, or print it out. Then you can go back and play with the numbers to create "what if" scenarios. If you complete the necessary training through CBT self study instead of instructor-led training, how will the total expenditure be affected? If you work on certification strictly outside your regular business hours, how much will you save in opportunity cost? To go back to your beginning worksheet, you can simply reload the version you originally saved. Additional scenarios you want to keep should be stored under other file names or printed out.

How to Cut Your Costs

You can significantly cut your certification expenditures in a number of ways. Some of them will come with one or more tradeoffs that you will have to measure against your savings. As we all know, cheaper is not always better and sometimes may not even be adequate. Which cuts make sense in a particular situation is a highly personal decision that involves factors such as your available free time, your individual learning strengths and weaknesses, your financial situation, the extent of your employer's support, time pressures, and so on. With that in mind, the basic ways you can make certification more affordable are:

* Convince an employer to shoulder part or all of the cost
* Cut your training costs
* Spread out your expenses over time
* Take any related tax deductions you qualify for
* Consider taking out an education loan.

FIGURE 6.2
Completed
Worksheet

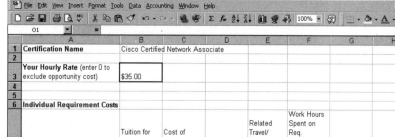

Getting Subsidized

As part of its third annual salary survey of professionals who have obtained or are in the process of obtaining one of the Microsoft Certified Professional (MCP) designations, *MCP Magazine* asked respondents who paid for the last certification/training program they attended. Well over half (67%) of respondents reported receiving financial support for their training from their employer. Of those, more than half (57%) of respondents said that their employers footed the entire bill, while 10% shared the expense with an employer. A third of respondents paid for their own training. Although there is no comparable study available about Cisco certification, it is likely the numbers are at least as good. Give the strict channel partner requirements Cisco has, the numbers are likely to be even more in your favor. Clearly, the odds are good that you will be able to convince an employer to subsidize your training, at least to some extent. But, first, you have to know where the available money is.

Tapping the Company Budget

At least two areas of the company budget are potential contributors of certification funding, especially at larger organizations: the departmental training budget and the company-wide tuition reimbursement program. Your employer's department training budget is likely to cover a broader variety of training options than the tuition reimbursement plan. Still, it may have been created largely with manager-selected and in-house training in mind, so you will have to approach your manager (or the appropriate human resources person) and convince him or her that certification training and/or testing is an appropriate use of the funds. Be prepared to explain how your certification training would provide value to the company and why the company should fund it. Think of this as a business presentation, and prepare for it by collecting the necessary facts and practicing beforehand in private.

QUICKTIP

When taking your case for certification to your boss, it often helps to present independent verification of the value of certification. Even though they are not Cisco specific, the following sources can be used to argue the benefits of certification:

The IDC (International Data Corp.) white paper *Benefits and Productivity Gains Realized Through IT Certification* **www.ibm.com/Education/certify/news/ proidc.phtml**). Figure 6.3 shows the online version.

Microsoft Corporation's *Microsoft Certified Professional Program Corporate Backgrounder* and several certification case studies (**www.microsoft.com/mcp/ mktg/bus_bene.htm**).

Novell's *Novell Certification: A Strategic Investment; An Executive Brief for Employers* throws some pretty impressive numbers your way too. (**education.novell.com/ general/stratinv.htm**)

FIGURE 6.3

Benefits of
Certification
White Paper

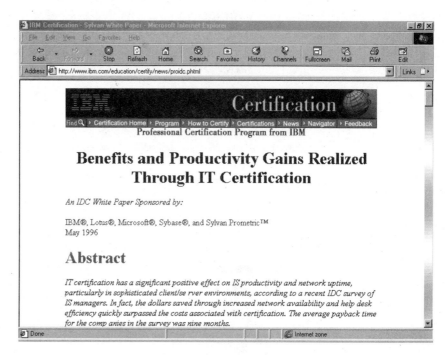

A tuition reimbursement plan is typically more narrowly defined than a training budget; it is often limited to courses that qualify toward a traditional degree. That does not mean it cannot fund certification training. If you are working toward a degree of some kind, many certification courses and programs are accepted by colleges as transfer credits and applied toward your degree. If you can demonstrate to your company that the programs will count toward your degree and the company has a tuition reimbursement policy, there is a good chance you will be able to get certification training coverage.

If you hope to receive funding from your employer, it is important to investigate both the tuition reimbursement and training budget possibilities *before* you begin your program. There may be steps you will have to take to qualify for the funds, and you will want to find out just how much of which kinds of training will be covered.

Questions to Ask the Budget Minders

At a large corporation, there is usually a human resources department, and within it, an individual who is in charge of employee benefits. That person is the one to whom to bring your questions. In smaller companies, start with your manager or supervisor. If that person cannot answer your reimbursement questions, there will be someone who can. Here are the important questions to ask:

* If you take certification courses that are recommended for college credit, will the company cover the tuition?
* If the certification and/or training will benefit your job, will the company cover your costs?
* Besides tuition itself, will the company reimburse you for related expenses such as books and travel? If so, which expenses are covered?
* Do you need to obtain official advance approval in order for your curriculum to qualify? From whom?
* What evidence will you need to provide in order to obtain reimbursement?
* Are there limits on the total reimbursement you can receive?

In addition to the above questions, take care to clarify any reimbursement-related concerns you have. It is a good idea to present your queries in the form of a memo, and to request the answers in writing, signed by the person who provided them. Then, if a difference of opinion arises later over just what was promised, you will have indisputable evidence to support your side.

The Payback Plan

When you cannot obtain funding as part of an existing budget category, consider working out an arrangement with your employer. One reason that employers may be reluctant to finance certification is the fear that the newly qualified employee will jump ship. You can understand how, from the employer's perspective, spending money on an employee to enable that person to leave (taking their expensive training with them) for another job would be counterproductive. This fear is especially intense around the CCIE certifications. So you may have to offer some reassurance.

One of the more common methods of overcoming this impediment is to form an agreement with your employer that insures the company against your departure. Basically, you agree in writing that if you leave the company within a certain period of time after receiving company-financed certification training, you will reimburse the company for its expense. If you decide to move on after the end of the specified period, you will not owe the company anything.

An arrangement like this often allows for prorating the amount of refund you would owe the company, based on how long you remain with your employer after training. Recruiting companies may also agree to an arrangement like this in return for your promise to continue to use them as your placement agency.

Look ahead. If you are very dissatisfied with your current position (or recruiting company) and expect to leave in the near future, this probably is not a good way to pay for certification.

Hitting the Road

Your current employer is not the only potential source of certification funds. Another route used by computer professionals is to begin training on their own and then look for a new position. Some employers consider an individual who has already embarked on the road to certification to be a superior job candidate. As an incentive for you to switch jobs, a new employer may well agree to pay for the rest of your certification program, as part of your new employment contract.

To follow this route, go ahead and complete your first requirement and test. Then begin searching online databases and elsewhere for job opportunities that appeal to you. Your resume should note that you are in the process of obtaining certification. When you reach the negotiating table, work to include funding for continuing training as part of your employment contract.

QUICK TIP

Cisco resellers are required to have Cisco-certified individuals on staff. This translates into job opportunities that include certification training. Your chances are especially good if you already have one Cisco certification under your belt or are well on your way to the higher levels. Resellers will also have access to equipment you can practice on. To find a reseller go to Cisco's partner locator Web page at **www.cisco.com/public/partnerlocator.shtml**.

Training on the Cheap

One of the most effective ways to cut your certification expenditure is also perhaps one of the simplest: be budget conscious when selecting and purchasing training for your certification. Because of the popularity of certification, there are many vendors and an extensive array of training options to choose from. A few rules of thumb to keep in mind are:

* Self study is less expensive than instructor-led training
* A training package is often cheaper than purchasing the components separately
* Special discounts are frequently available, if you ask for them
* Training time span affects costs
* Prices vary significantly among training vendors.

Training Methods and Costs

Self study is radically cheaper than instructor-led training. Although the 5-day Introduction to Cisco Router Configuration (ICRC) course taken through a Cisco training partner runs around $1795, you can purchase a self-study book such as the *Cisco Certified Associate Study Guide* by Syngress (Osborne 1998) for $39.95. Depending on your learning style, abilities, existing knowledge, and access to other resources, you may be able to get by with a study guide or even just studying the manuals that accompany Cisco hardware and other free papers available through the Cisco Web site.

You will also find "study kits" and CBT software on the market. The kits incorporate several training media, such as videotaped presentations, text material, and self tests, into one package. Baddog Computer, for example, offers a $1395 3 CD-ROM CCNA kit that includes the ICRC, High Performance Solutions for Desktop Connectivity (HPSDC), and Internetworking Technology Multimedia (ITM) curricula. You can find this kit at (**www.baddogcomputer.com/training/html/cisco_training.html**).

The price and quality of training products vary widely, so do not commit to any of them without a solid preview. This book's companion Web site contains links to CBT programs and training materials, but you will find even more by searching the Internet and reading trade magazine advertisements.

Professionals who have taken the self-study track often recommend study materials that include practice tests, so that may be an important feature to look for. You will also find that some companies actually guarantee that if you use their materials (or take their classes) that you will pass the associated test, but don't be misled; the best guarantee in the world is not as meaningful as your personal determination—you are in this to get certified, not to get your money back.

If you do not feel confident that self study will work for you, the next level up is facilitated training online. Courses offered via the Internet are cheaper than their classroom cousins and offer some of the same benefits. You will have access to an instructor and interaction with other students, but you will not have to travel to a training center or follow as rigid a schedule. CyberState University (**www.cyberstateu.com**) offers two different online CCNA packages.

Step up another price level and you will encounter another option that may prove just the ticket if time is not in short supply: college classes. Increasingly, the same certification classes offered by authorized training companies are available as college courses. The major difference is the time span; instead of blasting through requirements with several intense, sequential days of training, you will complete them at a more leisurely pace. For some people, the pace is a bit too leisurely. But when instructor-led training appears to be what you need, colleges will save you money over commercial training centers. Cisco has an entire program called "Cisco Networking Academies" that is increasing the availability of these classes around the world. Some of these are in high schools. To locate the one nearest you, visit **www.cisco.com/edu/academies/index.html** (shown in Figure 6.4).

The top tier of certification preparation, in cost, is the authorized training center class. For some people and for some requirements, it can be irreplaceable. You will have the equipment, trained and certified instructors, and other resources at hand. But you will pay for it. This type of class may be the way to go for requirements you find especially daunting, but in other cases, lower-cost options will do the job handily. Table 6.2 illustrates the comparative costs of the various options. The table provides a general expense assessment based upon typical market prices, but individual products may sometimes fall outside their category.

Of course, price is neither the only consideration in choosing a training method, nor necessarily the most important one. Additional pros, cons, and characteristics of available training options, including resources that are free, are discussed in detail in Chapter 8.

FIGURE 6.4

Training at Cisco Networking Academies

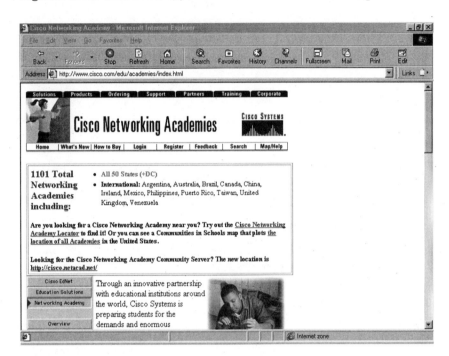

TABLE 6.2

Comparing Training Costs

Method	Standard Price
Self-study book/manual	$
Single CBT program	$$
Online class	$$$
Self-study kit	$$$
College course	$$$$
"Unauthorized" training vendor	$$$$$
Authorized training vendor	$$$$$$

Package Deals

Just as stocking up in a supermarket can pay off, bulk purchasing training can, too. If you are preparing for one of the more complex certifications, there will be multiple requirements and corresponding exams. Training vendors want to keep your business, and one way to do that is to hook you in for an extended period. In exchange for customer loyalty, they offer substantial savings.

Consider Learning Tree International's Alumni Gold Tuition Discount. Everyone who attends a Learning Tree course receives the discount card, which entitles the holder to a significant discount on the tuition for additional courses you take in the following 12 months. Many training providers offer similar bulk purchase discounts.

QUICK TIP

Make any bulk certification training purchase with extra care. It's a good idea to try a single course first to make sure the training style and materials are a good fit with your needs. Ask for the names of satisfied customers and talk to them about what they did and did not like in their dealings with the company. Signing up for a package training deal only to discover afterwards that you do not like that certification, training company, or learning method can be a costly error.

You may come across deals, especially with the newer "online universities," where you pay one fee in return for all the classes you can or care to complete within a given period of time. These sound like a great deal, and for some people, they may be. If this is an option you are considering, carefully assess:

* The quality of the classes
* The selection of classes offered
* How many you will realistically complete within the stated time period.

You may find a great deal or, instead, discover that although the offer sounds like a bargain, the quality of the courses or your ability to utilize them makes it much less so.

Another type of package deal is one that your employer can enter into, especially if yours is a medium- to large-sized company. Your employer agrees to use the vendor as the company's trainer of choice, and employees receive discounted tuition in return. Ask your employer if there is a similar arrangement with a training organization. If not, suggest the employer consider implementing one.

Special Discounts

Make sure you ask about any available discounts. You may find that government employees or other specific groups that you may belong to are eligible for reduced rates at a particular vendor.

Shop Around for the Best Deals

In contrast to purchasing the entire package from a single vendor, you can also purchase a piece here and a course there. This method requires a greater investment of your time and legwork (or keyboardwork), but will allow you to purchase each training item at the lowest price you can uncover.

To locate training vendors in your area, you can contact the sponsor of the certification you are pursuing. That is only a starting point because the listing is likely to be limited to authorized trainers. Internet search engines are a powerful tool for uncovering training vendors. A few places to start your search are:

* **www.yahoo.com/Business_and_Economy/Companies/ Computers/Software/Training/**—Yahoo's indexed compilation of software training companies.
* **www.nerdworld.com/nw190.html**—Nerd World Media's list of computer training companies. Each entry contains a brief summary and link to a related Web page.

Part of effective price shopping is to ask others who have pursued the same credentials where they obtained training and materials, how much they paid, and how they rate the vendor they purchased from. In this way, you can gather tips that will spare you both search time and quality problems.

Make Your Funds Do Double Duty

If you cannot trim your training costs appreciably, perhaps you may be able to get double mileage for your money. A certification training course may qualify for college credits toward a degree program, so be sure to check with your academic institution beforehand to see if and how you can get your training applied toward your degree.

QUICK TIP

As valuable as certifications are, do not overlook the importance of college degrees. For better or worse, many employers use a college degree as a break point for getting an interview. You may be able to get around this with a combination of certification and experience, but you will face greater challenges than if you have that college degree. This means it is really worth checking into the possibility of applying certification training towards a traditional four year diploma.

Condense Training

Getting back to opportunity cost, one of the simplest ways to cut your expenses is to reduce the amount of time you spend earning certification. When work time is being devoted to certification, it is not being used to generate income. That is the age-old time-equals-money equation.

Correspondingly, less time equals less money. That is, reducing the amount of time away from work can drastically reduce total certification costs. For example, if your income works out to an hourly rate of $35 per hour, and you cut 20 hours off your certification training time, you've trimmed $700 from your certification bill (or conversely, returned that 20 hours to the income side of your budget resulting in an additional $700 to your bank account).

Another way to compress certification time is to take intense, condensed courses or sequences of courses which are often called boot camps. Because the vendor need not repeatedly set up the training environment, coordinate staff and facilities, or lay out other one-time costs, the vendor's cost is lower if the same material were offered over a more extended period of time. The savings are often passed on to the students.

Stretch It Out

If paying for certification will just put too much of a squeeze on your budget, you may be able to manage it more easily by meeting the requirements over time. Your overall cost may well be higher than if you did not follow this route, but it will be spread out into more manageable outlays. You may even find that once your certification is under way, you will be able to boost your billing rate, and financing your education will no longer be a problem.

QUICKTIP

It is important to remember that, other than death and taxes, nothing in life is guaranteed, including an income boost from certification. So if you are considering relying on your credit cards (with their high interest rates) to pay for certification, look for another way. Perhaps a loan at a more reasonable rate from a bank or family member will tide you over. Otherwise, seriously consider putting off certification until your financial picture improves.

Join the Exchange

Certification training materials (software and printed matter), especially "authorized" materials, do not come cheap. A price tag of $75 to $100 or more is not unusual. After the exam, the materials become like last semester's college textbooks; an expensive reminder of courses gone by. College students cope with the issue by selling used textbooks to each other, and, now, certified professionals have begun doing the same thing. In **gocertify.com**'s swapshop, you can buy, sell, or swap Cisco or any other certification preparation course materials. The site does this strictly as a public service, at no charge to participants. The swapshop is shown in Figure 6.5.

Taking Advantage of Tax Breaks

Although taxes may be an inevitable price of life in the United States and elsewhere, that does not mean you have to pay more than your fair share. Luckily for Americans pursuing professional training, Uncle Sam smiles on citizens who work to improve themselves and their economic position. A strong worker makes for a strong economy, and all that. So employees who pay out of pocket for certain types of education get to deduct their expenses from their federal tax return. The available deductions apply whether you are self employed or on the payroll of a national conglomerate. If you're not self employed, you will need to itemize your deductions in order to claim these, too, and the amount will be subject to the two percent limitation.

This section details federal tax deductions in force at the time this book was written. Tax consequences vary depending on individual situations and circumstances, and although I am not qualified, nor do I intend to advise you on your personal tax position, this book can provide a good overview of some potential deductions. Because of the ever-shifting nature of the tax landscape, it is a good idea to consult a tax professional or study up, using publications from the IRS for the latest details and tax laws.

FIGURE 6.5
The gocertify.com Swapshop

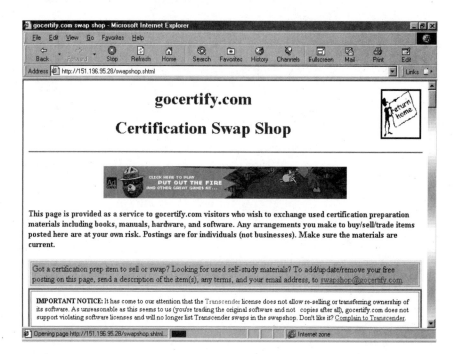

Do You Qualify?

To calculate your deduction(s), the first thing you must determine is whether your courses are considered "qualifying education" according to the IRS definition. Specifically, the education must either:

1. Be required by your employer or the law to keep your present salary, status, or job (and serve a business purpose of your employer) **or**
2. Maintain or improve skills needed in your present work.

That sounds pretty straightforward, and as long as you already work in the computer field, your certification training is likely to fall squarely under number 2, which, according to the IRS, includes refresher courses, courses on current development, and academic or vocational courses.

But, the tax code being what it is, there are complicating exceptions—namely, education is not "qualifying" if it:

1. Is needed to meet the minimum educational requirements of your present trade or business, **or**
2. Is part of a program of study that can qualify you for a new trade or business, even if you have no plans to enter that trade or business.

Again, assuming that you are already a computer professional, neither of these is likely to invalidate your certification expenses as qualifying education. If this seems confusing, look at Figure 6.6, which contains a reproduction of a handy decision flowchart included in IRS Publication 17 to clarify the definition of qualifying education.

What You Can Deduct

Once you have determined that your training qualifies, you will need to know which expenses are deductible. They are:

* Tuition, books, supplies, lab fees, and similar items
* Certain transportation and travel costs
* Other educational expenses, such as costs of research and typing when writing a paper as part of an educational program.

You cannot deduct personal or capital expenses (which include opportunity expense).

The IRS further defines "certain transportation and travel costs." Basically, you can deduct your transportation from work to school and then school to home, as long as you are attending school on a temporary basis (defined as a matter of days or weeks). If you go to school from home, again, on a temporary basis, you can probably deduct your transportation both ways. Longer-term educational engagements may only be eligible for mileage from work to school.

FIGURE 6.6

IRS Flowchart:
Are Your
Educational
Expenses
Deductible?

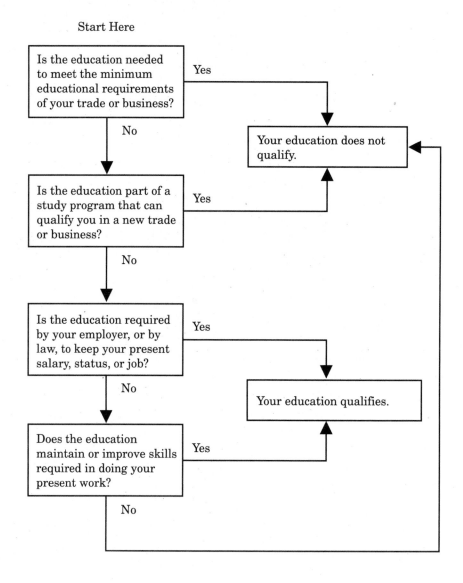

Cab, subway, and bus fares; car expenses; and parking fees and tolls are all transportation costs. Car expenses can be either your actual expenses or at the standard mileage rate (32.5 cents/mile in 1999).

If your training takes you away from home overnight, then you have moved into the realm of travel expenses. As far as education-related travel expenses, the IRS says that you can deduct expenses for travel, up to 50 percent of the cost of your meals and lodging, if you travel overnight to obtain qualified education and the main purpose of the trip is a work-related course or seminar.

Claiming Your Deductions

If you are self employed, your qualifying education expenses can be deducted on your Schedule C Profit or Loss from Business or Schedule C-EZ Net Profit from Business. When using Schedule C (see Figure 6.7) your tuition, lab fees, books, and similar items will fall under Part V, Other Expenses. Other amounts should go under their matching headings elsewhere on the form.

If you are an employee, the form you need will be 2106, Unreimbursed Employee Business Expenses (or its shorter cousin 2106-EZ). Form 2106 is shown in Figure 6.8. Note the word Unreimbursed in the form title; if an employer already refunded your expenses, you are not allowed to double-dip. Especially if you file a Schedule C, you might find it more financially beneficial to utilize these pre-1997 Tax Act methods of claiming education expenses.

FIGURE 6.7

Schedule C
Profit or Loss
from Business

SCHEDULE C (Form 1040)	**Profit or Loss From Business** (Sole Proprietorship)	OMB No. 1545-0074

Department of the Treasury
Internal Revenue Service (99)

▶ Partnerships, joint ventures, etc., must file Form 1065 or Form 1065-B.

▶ Attach to Form 1040 or Form 1041.   ▶ See Instructions for Schedule C (Form 1040).

1998   Attachment Sequence No. 09

Name of proprietor   Social security number (SSN)

A   Principal business or profession, including product or service (see page C-1)   **B** Enter NEW code from pages C-8 & 9 ▶

C   Business name. If no separate business name, leave blank.   **D** Employer ID number (EIN), if any

E   Business address (including suite or room no.) ▶ ....
City, town or post office, state, and ZIP code

F   Accounting method: **(1)** ☐ Cash   **(2)** ☐ Accrual   **(3)** ☐ Other (specify) ▶ ....

G   Did you "materially participate" in the operation of this business during 1998? If "No," see page C-2 for limit on losses   ☐ Yes   ☐ No

H   If you started or acquired this business during 1998, check here . . . . ▶ ☐

Part I   **Income**

1	Gross receipts or sales. **Caution:** *If this income was reported to you on Form W-2 and the "Statutory employee" box on that form was checked, see page C-3 and check here* . . . . . . ▶ ☐	1	
2	Returns and allowances	2	
3	Subtract line 2 from line 1	3	
4	Cost of goods sold (from line 42 on page 2)	4	
5	**Gross profit.** Subtract line 4 from line 3	5	
6	Other income, including Federal and state gasoline or fuel tax credit or refund (see page C-3) . . .	6	
7	**Gross income.** Add lines 5 and 6 . . . . ▶	7	

Part II   **Expenses.** Enter expenses for business use of your home **only** on line 30.

8	Advertising	8			19	Pension and profit-sharing plans	19	
9	Bad debts from sales or services (see page C-3) . .	9			20	Rent or lease (see page C-5):		
					a	Vehicles, machinery, and equipment . .	20a	
10	Car and truck expenses (see page C-3)	10			b	Other business property . .	20b	
11	Commissions and fees . .	11			21	Repairs and maintenance . .	21	
12	Depletion	12			22	Supplies (not included in Part III) .	22	
13	Depreciation and section 179 expense deduction (not included in Part III) (see page C-4) . .	13			23	Taxes and licenses	23	
					24	Travel, meals, and entertainment:		
					a	Travel	24a	
14	Employee benefit programs (other than on line 19) . . .	14			b	Meals and entertainment .		
15	Insurance (other than health) .	15			c	Enter 50% of line 24b subject to limitations (see page C-6) .		
16	Interest:				d	Subtract line 24c from line 24b	24d	
a	Mortgage (paid to banks, etc.) .	16a			25	Utilities	25	
b	Other	16b			26	Wages (less employment credits) .	26	
17	Legal and professional services	17			27	Other expenses (from line 48 on page 2)	27	
18	Office expense	18						

28	**Total expenses** before expenses for business use of home. Add lines 8 through 27 in columns . ▶	28	
29	Tentative profit (loss). Subtract line 28 from line 7	29	
30	Expenses for business use of your home. Attach **Form 8829**	30	
31	**Net profit or (loss).** Subtract line 30 from line 29.		

• If a profit, enter on **Form 1040, line 12,** and ALSO on **Schedule SE, line 2** (statutory employees, see page C-6). Estates and trusts, enter on Form 1041, line 3.   }   31

• If a loss, you MUST go on to line 32.

32   If you have a loss, check the box that describes your investment in this activity (see page C-6).

• If you checked 32a, enter the loss on **Form 1040, line 12,** and ALSO on **Schedule SE, line 2** (statutory employees, see page C-6). Estates and trusts, enter on Form 1041, line 3.   }

• If you checked 32b, you MUST attach **Form 6198.**

32a ☐ All investment is at risk.
32b ☐ Some investment is not at risk.

For Paperwork Reduction Act Notice, see Form 1040 instructions.   Cat. No. 11334P   Schedule C (Form 1040) 1998

FIGURE 6.8

Form 2106
Employee Business
Expenses

Form **2106**

Department of the Treasury
Internal Revenue Service (99)

Employee Business Expenses

▶ See separate instructions.

▶ Attach to Form 1040.

OMB No. 1545-0139

19**98**

Attachment
Sequence No. **54**

Your name	Social security number	Occupation in which you incurred expenses

Part I **Employee Business Expenses and Reimbursements**

STEP 1   Enter Your Expenses

		Column A Other Than Meals and Entertainment		Column B Meals and Entertainment
1	Vehicle expense from line 22 or line 29. (Rural mail carriers: See instructions.)	1		
2	Parking fees, tolls, and transportation, including train, bus, etc., that **did not** involve overnight travel or commuting to and from work . .	2		
3	Travel expense while away from home overnight, including lodging, airplane, car rental, etc. **Do not** include meals and entertainment	3		
4	Business expenses not included on lines 1 through 3. **Do not** include meals and entertainment	4		
5	Meals and entertainment expenses (see instructions)	5		
6	**Total expenses.** In Column A, add lines 1 through 4 and enter the result. In Column B, enter the amount from line 5	6		

Note: If you were not reimbursed for any expenses in Step 1, skip line 7 and enter the amount from line 6 on line 8.

STEP 2   Enter Reimbursements Received From Your Employer for Expenses Listed in STEP 1

7	Enter reimbursements received from your employer that were **not** reported to you in box 1 of Form W-2. Include any reimbursements reported under code "L" in box 13 of your Form W-2 (see instructions)	7		

STEP 3   Figure Expenses To Deduct on Schedule A (Form 1040)

8	Subtract line 7 from line 6	8		
	Note: If **both columns** of line 8 are zero, **stop here.** If Column A is less than zero, report the amount as income on Form 1040, line 7.			
9	In Column A, enter the amount from line 8. In Column B, multiply the amount on line 8 by 50% (.50). If either column is zero or less, enter -0- in that column. (Employees subject to Department of Transportation (DOT) hours of service limits: Multiply meal expenses by 55% (.55) instead of 50%. For more details, see instructions.)	9		
10	Add the amounts on line 9 of both columns and enter the total here. **Also, enter the total on Schedule A (Form 1040), line 20.** (Fee-basis state or local government officials, qualified performing artists, and individuals with disabilities: See the instructions for special rules on where to enter the total.) . . . . ▶	10		

For Paperwork Reduction Act Notice, see instructions.   Cat. No. 11700N   Form **2106** (1998)

The Tax Act of 1997

The Tax Act of 1997 contained several education provisions that change how much and in what ways you can claim tax breaks for education expenses. The provision most relevant to computer professionals obtaining certification is the one called the Lifetime Learning tax credit.

Unlike a deduction, which reduces the amount of income you pay taxes on, a credit is a dollar for dollar reduction of your tax bill. The Lifetime Learning credit equals 20 percent of the first $5,000 of your qualifying education expenses (a $1,000 maximum per family per year). That amount will increase to 20 percent of the first $10,000 in expenses (or a $2,000 maximum), after the year 2002. The amount of the credit is reduced for filers with higher incomes. The actual amount of the credit depends on your family's income, the amount of qualified tuition and fees paid, and the amount of certain scholarships and allowances subtracted from tuition.

The Hope Scholarship credit is an option you will want to explore if you will be enrolled at least half time in an eligible program leading to an undergraduate or graduate degree at an eligible school during the calendar year or enrolled at any enrollment level in any course of instruction at an eligible school to acquire/improve job skills during the calendar year. This credit has a maximum limit of $1,500 a year per qualifying student, and begins to phase out at an modified adjusted gross income of $40,000 ($80,000 if married filing jointly). If your modified AGI is over $50,000, ($100,000 if married filing jointly) you will not be eligible for this credit. Current law specifies that schools will supply this information in the form of a "return" to individual taxpayers and to the IRS. More information about the return will be available after the Treasury Department issues regulations to implement this law. The definition of qualifying expenses for the credits is different than for the deductions. Check with the IRS or your tax preparer for the details.

QUOTE

Qualifying for Credits vs. Deductions

There are entirely different requirements for the education credits than for the deductible education expenses. The deductible education expenses are considered "business expenses," and so need not be from a school that meets the IRS' requirements. A wider range of expenses can be included. The IRS' requirements focus on the *purpose* of the education.

On the other hand, the new credits are designed to encourage education in general. Virtually all accredited public, nonprofit, and proprietary post-secondary institutions are eligible under the education credits. The credits can be taken for education used to meet the minimum requirements of your trade or business, or to qualify you in a new trade or business. Many people either do not itemize their deductions, or have education expenses totaling less than 2% of their AGI, and as a result are unable to use them at all on the Schedule A.

—Sally Rothenhaus-Faulkner, Certified Financial Planner

There may be additional provisions of the 1997 act that you qualify for, so be sure to check with your tax advisor before filing your return for any year in which you spent money on professional education. It may be your duty as an American citizen to pay taxes, but there is no reason to pay more than you are legally obligated to.

As always, when dealing with tax matters, document, document, document. Collect and keep all receipts related to your education expenses, whether they're for $2,000 worth of tuition or a $1.20 highway toll, and keep an expense log that includes mileage records. Store the documents with your personal copy of your return. You will probably never have to look at them again; but should the need arise, they will be there.

Related IRS Forms Publications

The following forms and publications pertain to various aspects of deducting education expenses. If you don't care to wade through them all, start with the bible of individual tax returns, Publication 17; (fondly referred to by tax professionals as Pub 17). It may adequately answer your questions.

You can retrieve the most recent versions of any of these items (and a vast quantity more) from the IRS Web site at **www.irs.ustreas.gov/prod/cover.html**. Or call 1-800-TAX-FORM and ask for them to be mailed to you.

Publication 17 Your Federal Income Tax

Publication 334 Tax Guide for Small Business (C or C-EZ filers)

Publication 508 Educational Expenses

Publication 529 Miscellaneous Expenses

Publication 535 Business Expenses

Publication 552 Recordkeeping for Individuals

Publication 553 Highlights of 1997 Tax Act Changes

Publication 970 Tax Benefits for Higher Education

Form 1040 U.S. Individual Income Tax Return

Schedule A Itemized Deductions

Schedule C Profit or Loss from Business

Schedule C-EZ Net Profit from Business

Form 2106 Employee Business Expenses

Form 2106-EZ Unreimbursed Employee Business Expenses

Taking Out a Loan

Although using your credit cards to fund certification is an iffy proposition, there are lower-cost alternatives for financing your certification program. You may be able to obtain a low-interest loan, grant, or scholarship. If you attend training at a professional school or college, you may qualify for a student loan from the Federal government. To find out more about federal student loans, call 800-557-7395 or visit the Direct Loan Web site at **www.ed.gov/offices/OPE/DirectLoan/index.html**. For information about other federal financial aid programs, call 800-4-FED-AID.

There are a number of loan programs popping up that cater specifically to IT professionals and cover certification training:

* CCLC (**www.techloan.com**) provides loans for all technology training
* The Key CareerLoan (**www.key.com**)
* National Association of Communication Systems Engineers (NACSE) has a training loan program for its members (**www.nacse.com**).

There are many other educational financial aid options open to you. Visit your local library for help uncovering them. If you have Internet access, you will find the Financial Aid Information Page

at **www.finaid.org** a tremendous resource (see Figure 6.9).
Remember, if you do take out a loan for education purposes, the
interest may be tax deductible.

FIGURE 6.9

Using the Web to
Find Financial Aid

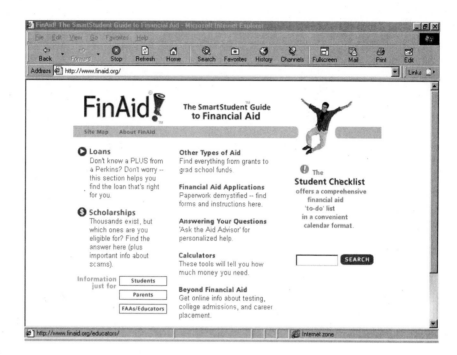

CHAPTER 7

Certification Mistakes You Need Not Make

The amount of time, money, and effort you put into achieving certification will depend upon the certification you choose and how much it is a natural extension of your current skill set. It will also depend on if and how far you stray from the direct path to your goal: certification. Although few computer professionals think of themselves as one of the herd, this is one time when staying on the beaten path is usually the best choice.

Fortunately, that path has been blazed for you by computer professionals who have been embracing certification since early on. This is especially true of the CCIE designations, but even though the Cisco career certifications haven't been around as long, plenty of professionals have gone before you. By understanding where earlier certification candidates have gone astray, you can avoid making the same mistakes. What follows is an exploration of the certification errors most commonly made, and how to steer clear of them.

The errors are grouped into three categories:

* Choosing the wrong certification
* Mistakes made while working toward a chosen certification
* Mistakes made after achieving certification.

Each of these areas contributes to your overall success and satisfaction. While a small misjudgment here or there will not cancel out all your hard work, you might as well benefit from other people's hindsight, the one type of vision that is always 20/20.

Choosing the Wrong Certification

Choosing the wrong program is one of the more common mistakes people make when pursuing certification. What makes a certification a bad choice? Either it's chosen for wrong reasons, or it's lacking in some way that could easily have been detected with a little research. This type of mistake is easier to make than you might suspect. Here is why it happens:

Error: Choosing a Certification Because It's "Hot"

The CCIE is one of the most popular certifications available today. Although reports of salaries that start at $100,000 a year may make it seem like a no-brainer, it may well be the wrong certification for you. First, if you do not have the experience to draw on, pursuing this certification will be an exercise in frustration. You would be better off choosing one of the career certifications, earning that, and using that to help you get the hands-on experience needed for a CCIE.

Cisco's non-CCIE certifications are also popular. Just because you have heard great things about them does not mean they will do great things for you. These certifications deal with internetworking. If you are a programmer, you are probably better off with a different certification. If you administer a Novell Network, this certification will not do as much for a you as a Novell MCNE. Pursuing a certification is making a choice of career direction. Choose it because it is something you enjoy doing and learning about. Find one that fits your long-term plans and success will follow.

Error: Unrealistic Expectations

Do you anticipate a significant career boost will result from gaining the certification of your choice? Are you planning on earning more money, incrementing your level of expertise, moving into a new specialty, switching to a different (and better) job?

All these goals are indeed possible outcomes of certification. However, it is important to remember that certification is not a guaranteed cure-all for what ails your career. If your boss is a jerk, getting certified will not change him. It may, however, enable you to find employment somewhere with a boss who has more positive attributes. Or it might serve as an impetus to go independent and become your own boss. (Of course then, if the boss is still a jerk, what are you going to do?)

Similarly, the skills you add in the course of earning a Cisco Certified Network Associate certification will improve your ability to keep a large network up and running, but will not transform it into a stress-free job.

QUOTE

Not a Career Panacea

Some people may believe that gaining certification is enough to warrant a job and better pay. But gaining certification does not teach you how to work as part of a team, how to communicate effectively both verbally and in writing, how to shoulder responsibility, how to motivate others, how to talk to customers, nor many other skills that are required of a person working in a busy environment with other people of a variety of abilities and management levels.

Employers are looking for more than just certification.

—Ben Lovegrove, CCNA

Certification can be a powerful career tool, as long as you take care to select the proper tool for the particular career goal.

Error: Underestimating Cost

There are so many variables to consider when estimating how much certification will cost, that it is not surprising that the calculation is often done wrong. Sometimes, it isn't done at all.

Why is underestimating the cost of certification such a problem? Consider these potential scenarios:

* You run out of funds before you are done. If you end up taking an extended break from your certification program, some of your qualifications may expire and you will have to meet them again. At best, you will need to spend time reviewing to get back up to speed once your budget gets back on track. At worst, you will never pick it up again and your efforts will have been largely wasted.
* Based on ball-park figures you described, your employer agrees to pay for certification training and testing. Then you submit a bill double what you initially suggested. How will that go over?
* You decide that a particular certification will more than pay for itself. But as the bills mount up you realize you have grossly miscalculated the figure in question. What will you do if it is not still worth it at the "new" price, yet you've already committed significant time and resources?

As you can see, miscalculating the cost or failing to calculate it at all can be a big mistake. It is a mistake that happens because naming a figure is not always a simple process. Part of the confusion arises because there are usually several different routes to achieving any particular certification. The largest variance comes under the heading of training expenses. Whether you self study from manuals or attend instructor-led, sponsor-approved training, can make thousands of dollars of difference in your total tab.

Then there is the somewhat nebulous question of opportunity cost. To some people, an estimate that does not include it is meaningless. Others consider adding opportunity cost an inaccurate inflation of price. Either way, coming up with a reasonable figure for it requires a little math.

But given the potential consequences of underestimating the price tag of a particular certification path, it is worthwhile to work out a few figures. The worksheet in Chapter 6 will walk you through the steps. When in doubt, guess a little high. Having extra money left over is a problem you can no doubt live with.

Mistakes While Working Toward Certification

When you are undertaking something new and exciting like professional certification, it can be tempting to rush ahead full speed. After all, you want to see results as soon as possible, don't you? But haste has its costs. People in a hurry tend to make assumptions in order to save time. While these assumptions may feel reasonable at the time, they sometimes turn out to be wrong, and end up disrupting your plans.

The following mistakes often result from eagerness and the desire to get on with it as much as anything else. Although these errors have less dire consequences than choosing the wrong certification, they can still cost you time, money, and frustration. Happily, forewarned is forearmed. Once you read about the pitfalls that other professionals have encountered, you can easily dodge them.

Error: Purchasing a Complete Certification Package Right Away

When you are offered a significant discount to purchase a package deal, it's tempting to leap at it. You will get all your arrangements taken care of with one vendor and grab a discount besides. But—and this is a big but—it is a good idea to hold off making such a major investment until after you pass your first exam, at the earliest. Only then can you be fairly confident that the certification you have chosen is one you can work with. There is always a chance that you will discover you have bitten off more than you care to chew or have a sudden change of heart over the direction you want to pursue.

If you buy a package up front, there is another risk: if this is your first foray into certification, how can you know which learning alternatives will become your favorites? What if you invest in a series of computer-based, self-preparation programs only to discover that you cannot bear to sit down and face your PC each evening after doing the same all day at work? If it's instructor-led training that you have purchased in bulk and you discover that you don't need such a degree of support and instruction, you will be faced with thousands of dollars of training you don't need but have already contracted for—a truly costly mistake.

QUICK TIP

Don't overlook product documentation and information available on the Cisco Web site as study tools. They are free and contain many, if not all, of the intricacies you will need to master.

It is fairly simple to protect yourself from this particular pitfall. Start with one test and one preparation package. In fact, it isn't a bad idea to see how you feel working strictly from free study guides and product manuals. Then if you want to escalate to third-party preparation materials, such as workbooks computer-based training Web-based instruction or a classroom staffed by a living, breathing technical trainer, you can easily do so. And if you discover that the resources that are free will serve your purposes adequately, you won't have expended a single extra penny.

Error: Assuming Your Employer Will Pay for Your Training

This is a big oops and a totally avoidable mistake that happens when people recall that educational incentives were mentioned somewhere in the slew of paperwork the received as part of new employee orientation, but don't spend the time to pin down the details. Perhaps you don't just think so, you *know* that the company pays for continuing education, making it unnecessary to research further.

The problem is, even if your employer does as a rule pay for continuing education, the definition of just what that encompasses may be limited. Some companies only reimburse for courses completed as part of a degree program. Others require that the degree be related to your job functions.

It also occurs when a coworker mentions in passing that the company paid for his certification training. But perhaps he neglected to mention that it was through a special arrangement, or that a dollar limit was imposed. Or maybe he really meant that the company paid his certification test fees, but you missed that clarification.

The bottom line is that what another employee got is not necessarily something that you will receive too, and vice versa. It is important to check into employer funding/reimbursement before you begin. If the purse strings do open, which they often will, you will still need to be aware of which paperwork needs to be submitted when, time limits, restrictions, and so on. Before you can comply with any guidelines, you need to know about them. To know about them, all you need to do is ask.

Error: Assuming Your Employer Won't Pay for Your Training

Just because it is not in the employee handbook doesn't mean your employer cannot be persuaded to share the expense of continuing education with you. Chapter 6 offers advice on how to bring this about. Why spend your own money on professional training if someone else is perfectly willing to foot the bill for you?

Error: Failing to Shop Around

Don't you hate it when you buy something at what you think is a good price only to see it advertised a week later somewhere else for a third less? It happens all the time with consumer purchases and it can happen with training purchases too.

You might not be willing to expend much effort to save three dollars on a pair of shoes, but when it comes to training packages, your potential savings are much higher. For a time investment of an hour or less, you may save $50, $100, or even $1000. In addition to financial dividends, when you give yourself more training options to choose from, it's more likely you will find one that closely matches your learning preferences and style.

Why then, do so many people neglect to shop certification training? Often because they:

* Are not aware that drastic price differences exist
* Do not know where to look
* Are unsure of how to compare vendors and products.

Since each of these items is addressed in this book, you can avoid this mistake. Chapter 8 explores the wide selection of learning alternatives you can choose from. Chapter 9 explains how to find certification preparation training and tools, such as through the Internet, telephone book, and Cisco itself. It also describes what to look for in a training center, and how to assess the quality of an instructor.

If you were in the market for a new television or lawn mower, you would not purchase the first one you came across. Give your selection of certification training at least as much attention, and preferably more. Pay attention to the features each option has to offer, and weigh benefits against cost. Because prices vary widely among vendors, your dollar savings alone will make it worth your while, unless, of course, money is no object.

Error: Ignoring/Missing Time Constraints

When you begin your program, inquire up front if there are any time limits specifying how long you have to complete the entire program or any element of it. As of this writing, there was only one time limit for any of the Cisco certifications, and that applied to the CCIE designations. Once a CCIE candidate passes the written exam, the lab exam must be completed within a year. Failure to do so means the written exam, which is often referred to as the qualification exam, will have to be retaken.

Another time limit does not come into play until after you have achieved certification, but it is still important: recertification. As this book was going to press only the CCIE designations had a recertification requirement, but it is likely these requirements will appear for the other certifications as well. Recertification may involve passing an update exam, attending specific educational events, or meeting other requirements. The important thing to note is that if you do not complete the specified activities before the recertification deadline, you lose your certification and must start over again from the beginning. CCIE recertification currently runs on a two-year cycle.

Error: Failing to Get Certified After Your Employer Agrees to Pay for It

Once you have announced your intentions, failure to deliver is not going to reflect well on you. This is especially true if you have approached your supervisor or boss and secured a promise of financial reimbursement. Fortunately, changing one's mind after starting a certification program is a rare occurrence.

Your goal in pursuing certification is to use it as a tool to further your career. It would be ironic if you end up damaging your image instead. If you find yourself faced with completing a certification that you have changed your mind about, one that your employer already approved, consider completing it anyway to avoid risking a reputation as someone who does not follow through.

The best course of action for this potential mistake is prevention. Develop a solid feel for the program before you enter it, including how much time you will have to put in and what benefits you hope to achieve. If you have done your homework in advance, it is unlikely that you will find yourself pursuing a certification that is not what you had hoped for, and highly probable you will obtain a credential that will be worth much more than the time and effort you spent earning it.

Error: Neglecting Your Job in Order to Study for Certification

Even if your employer has agreed to let you study during regular working hours, it's important not to allow your normal duties go unattended. This can be a difficult balancing act, especially if you have a demanding schedule. But it can be done.

Keep in mind that there is nothing like hands-on, on-the-job training for learning how to perform specific tasks. Try to apply the technology you are studying to your duties at work. If you do not have access to the equipment or software in question, but a coworker does, take him to lunch and explain your situation. Ask if you can shadow him during your lunch hour or at other times. Once you have learned how a particular task is done, try to get a chance to do it yourself.

When taking this approach, it's important to recognize that the person you are learning from may feel threatened. If you are after his job, then this plan is a bad idea. But most likely, you are not, in which case it is a good idea to explain clearly what you are after, to reassure him. Try to offer something in return, perhaps sharing skills you have with him.

Even if you get plenty of hands-on practice, you are going to have to hit the books to pass exams. Even in the busiest schedule, there is room for study time. You just have to find it. The time management guidelines in Chapter 10 can help you with that. Another trick to keep study time from encroaching on work time is to study less. Learning efficient and effective study habits will drastically reduce the quantity of time you will need to prepare. Chapter 10 can help you on that front, as well.

The key to keeping your certification plans from interfering with your current job duties is to pay attention. In your eagerness to get certified, you may devote more time to preparation than you realize. Setting up a schedule will help you keep study and work hours in the proportion you want them. With the world being the unpredictable place that it is, you can expect to find your schedule disrupted at one time or another. When that happens, simply get back on track as soon as you can.

Throughout the process keep your goals in sharp focus. The purpose of certification is to enhance your career. If you irritate your employer in the process, getting ahead is going to be that much harder. If you manage to juggle work and study effectively, you will create the impression of a capable professional who takes initiative and follows through.

Error: Assuming You Don't Need to Study

Obtaining certification requires two forms of competency: knowing what to do, and being able to prove this. These are really two separate skills. The first has to do with the extent of your experience and understanding. The second reflects your ability to perform well on a test. A shortfall in either area will hinder your success.

The person who makes the mistake of assuming there is no need to study is likely be someone quite masterful in handling the technology in question, as demonstrated by performance at a current job. Consider a WAN administrator pursuing a CCNP. As the person who manages a company WAN day in and day out, this individual certainly has an excellent grasp of the skills required to keep the WAN operating smoothly. But what would happen if this administrator arrived at work one morning to find a WAN with twice as many interfaces to other networks, a modem pool, a dedicated link to the Internet, and running an application that led to twice as much traffic load as usual? Probably, she would feel a lot less expert.

Although this WAN administrator's network would never change so dramatically overnight, she could easily face the same situation in written format, on a certification exam. And she would not be familiar with it. Don't assume that a certification test you will be taking will be limited to the environment in which you are an expert. In fact, expect it not to be.

The second component of successful certification is the ability to recall information in a test setting. You will need to respond in theory instead of in practice. A situation you may handle easily when you have your router at your fingertips can suddenly seem foreign when it's presented as words on an exam. Spend time studying, and the written version will become second nature too.

Error: Assuming You Know the Best Way to Study

Effective study techniques enable you to learn new information and recall it as needed. Studying doesn't consist of opening a book or manual and reading it through, perhaps several times. It is a lot more than that; and a lot less.

Reading skills are the foundation of much of learning. You already know how to read, but do you know how to read to learn? A skilled learner knows the tricks that make it possible to read faster and remember more.

There are many techniques you can apply to make test preparation fairly painless. These methods will serve you well for certification tests, as well as for future tasks that involve learning and remembering technical information. Even if you already know how to study effectively, you will probably benefit from brushing up on your skills. Doing so is as easy as reading Chapter 10.

Error: Failure to Set Deadlines for Yourself

You have no doubt heard the saying, "the squeaky wheel gets the grease." If you have multiple priorities competing for your time, you may well find yourself playing the role of grease monkey and running from project to project, applying the lubrication that will keep things going. Meanwhile, projects that are not in crisis go untended, until they begin to squeak, too, or are completely forgotten. Certification preparation is rarely one of the squeaky wheels. Because of that, it often falls low on the scale of daily priorities. Unless you take action to keep this from happening, your certification plans will languish and your goals will go unmet.

The best way to avoid the pitfall of inaction is to create deadlines for yourself. This should occur as part of the process of creating your personal certification plan. Each requirement should have a deadline date. If the requirement is that you pass a test, go ahead and schedule the test. As each deadline approaches, the urgency of finding time to train and prepare will grow until, like the proverbial squeaky wheel, it demands your attention. Tending to these artificially induced squeaks will keep your "certification wheel" turning.

A second challenge to your progress is the big P: procrastination. If you are the type of person who does not get things done until the last minute, then deadlines will generate time pressure to keep you on track.

Mistakes After Certification Is Achieved

Once you have completed all the requirements for a certification, it may be tempting to sit back and enjoy your accomplishment. If you do that, you will not be taking full advantage of your new status. It would be like buying a new sports car and leaving it in the garage most of the time. To get the most benefit from certification, you need to use it at every opportunity and maintain it in tiptop condition. Correspondingly, the mistakes that occur after certification is achieved are largely due to inaction or inattention. Consider the following:

Error: Forgetting about Continuing Requirements

Don't count on Cisco to remind you when updates to your certification are due. Although they may do so, that is a bonus, not a given. It is up to you to track how often professional development activities or update exams are required and to fill those requirements.

Record professional development deadlines on your calendar, allowing plenty of time to complete them and for the accompanying paperwork. Once you have completed a recertification requirement, such as attending a CCIE technical seminar, immediately collect and submit the necessary information to Cisco and verify that it has been properly recorded.

Error: Failing to Take Advantage of Perks and Privileges

Some of the benefits of certification will accrue to you even if you do nothing else once you have your certification in hand. Free subscriptions and early product news, for example, will arrive in your mailbox whether or not you request them. But other perks and privileges are provided to you on an as needed basis. To benefit from them, you have to access them. Suppose someone offered you free valuable services such as:

✳ Priority technical support
✳ Access to special forums
✳ Marketing tools and assistance
✳ A certificate.

Wouldn't it be an incredible waste to ignore them? That is exactly the mistake that newly-certified people make. Although the specifics vary depending on the certification, perks like these come with every Cisco certification. Figure 7.1 shows Cisco's list of perks you can expect to receive. These are tools to which you have earned access. They are (or should have been) part of the reason you chose the certification in the first place. Use them.

FIGURE 7.1
The Perks List

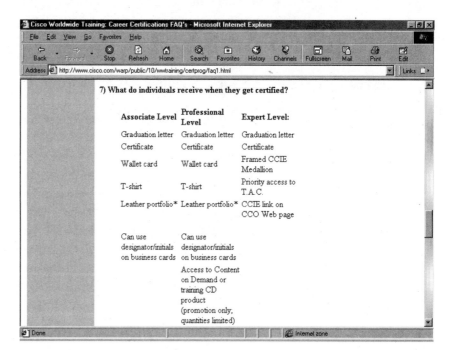

Error: Failing to Advertise Your New Status

The first thing to do with your certification is add it to your resume, but that is not the only way you can promote your new status. Certification is a marketing tool that can be applied in a variety of ways. Don't neglect to put it to work.

The simplest methods are as basic as redesigning your business cards and stationery to incorporate the certification logo. Although only the CCIE came with a logo as this book was being written, other logos for the other certifications were in the works. Include logos on your Web site too. If you don't have one, create one. Basic Web page design tools are available for all levels of site developers, from beginners through expert, and at affordable prices too. Some, such as AOLpress (**www.aolpress.com/press/**) can be downloaded via the Internet free. The AOLpress Web site is shown in Figure 7.2. Advice on these and other methods for marketing yourself as a certified expert is provided in Chapter 12.

FIGURE 7.2
AOLpress
Web Site

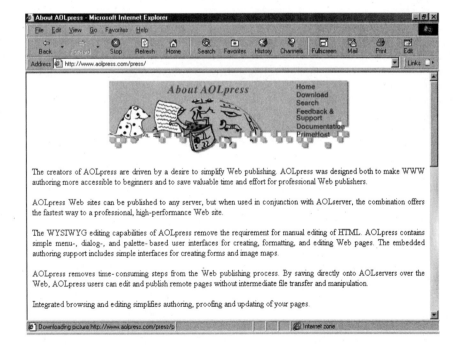

Completing the requirements for certification is 90% of the job, but the remaining 10% is important too. With a little effort, you can use certification as a launching pad to develop a reputation as an expert on the related technology, or simply to add to your credibility. You can bet that your competitors will be doing just that.

Plan, Perform, and Follow Through

If there is one key to successful use of certification as a career booster, it is attention. You control each stage, starting with how carefully you develop your personal certification plan, continuing through how closely you follow it, your application of certification as a marketing tool, and whether or not you devote attention and effort to staying current over time.

A mistake here and there will not keep you from reaching your certification goal. Individuals eager to earn their certification may experience some of these errors through simple haste. The most useful step you can take to avoid wasting time and money is to plan ahead. Each time you move on to a new step in the certification process remember the mistakes you read about here, and make sure you don't repeat them. If you do find yourself making one of these mistakes, correct your error and get back on track as quickly as possible. Above all, keep moving forward toward your goal of certification.

CHAPTER 8

Understanding Training Alternatives

Although it is possible to obtain the Cisco certifications solely on the basis of exam scores and signing the certification agreement, few people can walk in, take the tests cold, and walk out certified. This is especially true of the CCIE certifications, which require a lab exam in addition to the written exam. If you feel confident about your skills after reviewing the objectives for a particular exam, you can consider taking the exam with only your existing experience to draw upon, but it is unlikely you will be successful. This can be a mistake that costs you money and time; you won't get your money back if you fail and you may have to wait before you can get rescheduled to try again.

It is difficult to pass a certification exam without studying because an individual's knowledge is usually limited by job function. Imagine for a moment that your current job is to keep your company's intranet in tiptop shape. You may be quite the wizard when it comes to managing that intranet, but if you were suddenly placed in charge of an intranet at Company B instead, you would likely find yourself stumbling around a bit, at least at first, because every organization's computing environment is unique. Hardware and software are combined in different ways and configured to serve specific purposes. Company B's intranet architecture may be completely different from the one you are used to working with.

In the above scenario, you would probably pick up what you needed to know by turning to documentation and technical coworkers, but certification tests do not offer the same opportunities. They are not open book, and you cannot bounce ideas off the person at the next desk. Questions will not be limited to one company's computing environment, either.

This does not automatically mean that you need to sign up for thousands of dollars of intensive training before you can pass certification exams, but you do need to prepare in one way or another. Fortunately, you have many options to choose from.

Thanks in large part to the computer industry, the classroom and textbook are no longer the only, or even the primary, education venues. Current alternatives include:

* Computer Based Training (CBT) prepared by the certification sponsor

* CBT and training programs offered by independent vendors
* Online classes and training communities
* Courses at authorized training centers
* Self-paced workbooks and study guides
* Product documentation
* College courses
* Videotapes.

Each has attributes that may make it attractive to you, and each has drawbacks. To select training that will serve your purposes, it helps to distinguish between two types of learning you will need to undertake:

1. Adding to your body of knowledge
2. Learning new practical skills.

Think of the first item as the *what* and *why* of your subject area. Returning to the internetworking example, extending your knowledge would include understanding the functions and differences of switches and routers, and knowing which one you would need under what circumstances. This kind of learning revolves around concepts, theory, and case studies. You can reasonably expect to master the material through absorption methods: reading, listening, and watching presentations of the material. And yes, repetition and regurgitation of what you have just learned to help lock it into your memory.

Learning new practical skills is equivalent to the *how* of your subject area. It involves applying the knowledge you have gained; you perform instead of observe. You will install and configure a bridge and a router; you will deploy a firewall. The ideal way to accomplish this is to have the applicable hardware and software at hand, along with someone who can answer any questions and help if you get stuck. But that is not the only way. You may be astonished by what can be accomplished via simulation these days.

Both types of learning are valuable and important. How much you need of each kind will depend on the gap between your current knowledge and experience, and what you will require for the certification you have decided to pursue. Self study will carry you a long way. For some people and for some certifications, it is all that is needed. Other certified professionals swear that formal training classes are the way to go. A combination of the two may best meet your personal training needs. Let's explore the education options that you are likely to encounter.

Workbooks and Study Guides

Text materials, including study guides, workbooks, instructional texts, and product manuals, are very attractive to certification candidates (Figure 8.1 shows a page from fatbrain.com's collection of Cisco study guides). A big factor working in their favor is cost. You can frequently obtain workable study guides and exam preparation outlines directly from the certification sponsor via mail, or as downloads from the certification Web site. Texts that must be purchased are relatively inexpensive when compared to other routes for learning similar material. They are available through major bookstores and computer specialty book outlets.

FIGURE 8.1

Fatbrain.com Offers Loads of Books Packed with Cisco Expertise

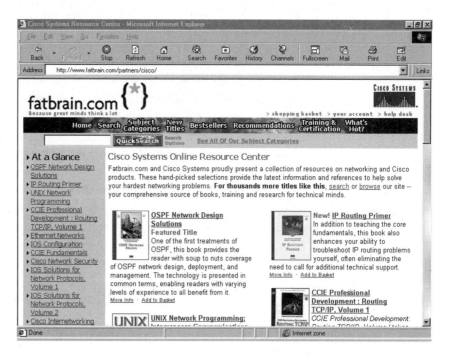

If you are not strongly motivated, learning by reading about a topic may not be the best alternative for you. But then, if motivation is really a problem, perhaps you should rethink your career goals with that in mind.

People may also bypass basic reading as a route to learning because they find it a slow and tedious way to learn. Whipping through the latest Dick Francis mystery may be pure pleasure, but page after page of dry technical exposition can seem like torture in comparison. Fortunately, you can drastically increase your reading speed and comprehension level by investing $6 and a bit of effort (see Speed Learning sidebar).

Speed Learning

If you have made it this far in this book, you can obviously read at a decent level. But what exactly does that mean? The average reader proceeds at a rate of about 250 words per minute. Especially "fast" readers race along at 400–600 words per minute. But the limits of human reading speed are vastly higher: 1200–3000 words per minute can be achieved through training. That same training will improve your comprehension and recall. You will not only read faster, you will understand and be able to recall more of what you read.

What kind of practical difference would this make in your certification training? If you have a 200-page manual to plow through (about 100,000 words), and your reading speed is above average at 300 words a minute, you will need nearly six hours of reading to get through the manual. Up your speed to 900 words a minute, and you will be able to read that same manual in under two hours.

How can you accomplish such a vast increase in your learning rate? By purchasing a slim paperback book for $5.99 and following the advice within. The book is titled *The Evelyn Wood 7-Day Speed Reading & Learning Program,* by Stanley D. Frank. (Avon Books 1992). Even if you just read and follow the steps in the first two chapters (about 40 pages), you will dramatically increase your reading speed. But going through a lot of pages in a little time is only one aspect of leveraging your reading abilities. Along with step-by-step instruction on how to accelerate your reading, you will find study tips and advice on how to increase your comprehension and recall and on how to prepare for exams.

When it comes to squeezing learning into a crowded schedule, this is one method that can really pay off. You can pick up this book (or a similar one) at most major book stores, or call Avon Books at 1-800-238-0658. You can also order this book online from Amazon Books (**www.amazon.com**) or any major online bookseller.

For some purposes, reading is no substitute for doing, but it has been a solid way to gain new knowledge or to expand upon what you already know. Table 8.1 lists learning characteristics of books. A book is the ultimate portable classroom. You can use it beneath the florescent lights of the company cafeteria, inside a clattering subway car, or deep in the shade of an ancient oak in your favorite park; and the battery never runs out.

TABLE 8.1
Learning Characteristics of Workbooks and Study Guides

Advantages	Disadvantages
Very portable	Not interactive, therefore less engaging
Can serve as a reference	May not be completely current
Relatively low cost	No external motivation, easy to get off track
Proceed at your own pace	Predetermined linear format

Product Documentation

One of the most overlooked preparation materials is product documentation. A vast storehouse of information about Cisco products and technologies is available through the Cisco Web site. The entry point to all of these goodies is at **www.cisco.com/public/Product_root.shtml**. You will find product-specific information as well as white papers covering diverse networking technologies. All are absolutely free for your viewing pleasure. Figure 8.2 shows one of the many documents available.

Computer-Based Training (CBT)

The term computer-based training refers to educational software developed and delivered via computer technology. This is also referred to by many other names, including computer-aided instruction (CAI), computer-based instruction (CBI), and courseware.

Good CBT programs are interactive. By requiring you to answer questions, step through tasks, and perform other actions, CBT *involves* you. By responding to the program, you become an active learner. Most people find that participation in this way increases their enjoyment of the process.

FIGURE 8.2
Free Networking
Study Materials—
Online
Documentation

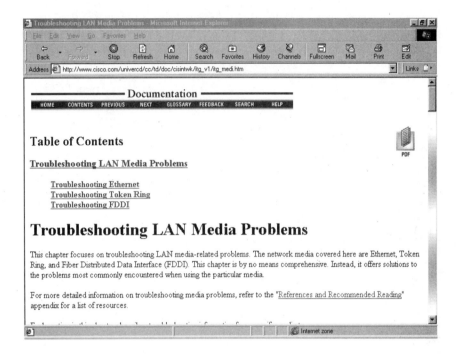

Another way CBT eases learning is by adding a "wow" factor. CBT software increasingly is a blend of multimedia wizardry, with voice tracks, video clips, animation sequences, and a big bag of tricks for transforming mundane information into, well, fun.

CBT software also provides freedom from the predefined, linear style of many other educational formats. You can elect to work with the topics in the order you prefer, and at the pace you choose. If you already have a particular area down cold, you can skip over it. If a lesson misses the mark, you can return to it as many times as you like.

On the down side, the software is limited in what its instructions include. There is no trainer to answer free-form questions or to urge you onward, and you have to be sitting at a computer (usually equipped with a CD-ROM and loads of memory) to use it.

Current CBT software seems to be developed in one of two styles:

1. Task oriented
2. Knowledge focused.

Task-oriented programs lead you step-by-step through the procedures native to the software, hardware, or environment you are studying. If the topic of the CBT is an Intro to Routers, a single lesson might cover how to add entries to a routing table. In a textbook you would read about it. In a traditional classroom, you would hear about it and possibly observe a demonstration by the instructor. With CBT, the applicable software is simulated on your computer screen. You will be instructed, often by text, but sometimes via voice clips, on the proper sequence of steps to perform. And you will follow the instructions as if you were actually adding a new user, clicking on the appropriate menu items, filling in variables, and coding switches. You can concentrate fully on what you are doing with no worry that you will inadvertently bring the entire LAN crashing down. There is no LAN, only an accurately reproduced interface with nothing on the other side.

Don't get too used to all that hand-holding because it will diminish as you advance through the course. Procedures that were spelled out in detail the first time won't be later on. You will have to "setup and configure the new router." Step nine might be to add items to the routing table. Since you already learned that procedure, you won't be walked through it this time around. This building-block, hands-on, simulation type of learning can prove very successful when your goal is to acquire a specific, concrete set of skills.

Knowledge-focused CBT takes a completely different approach. Instead of facing the simulation of a particular program's GUI (graphical user interface) and being given the goal of completing a specific task, you will find yourself in more of an open-ended, exploratory environment.

Learning Tree International (**www.learningtree.com**) is one company that makes impressive use of this style for some of its CBT courses. When you fire up the "Client/Server Computing" course, you are greeted by Ken, leader of the AcmeTech development team you have just joined. You are introduced to other team members, each with a particular perspective and area of expertise. You will probably call on them later. Or they may have questions for you. Your job? To help develop and implement a client/server environment at a prestigious university. Get to work. (Table 8.2 pinpoints learning characteristics of CBT).

Not all CBT software is created equal. Some programs place block after block of text on the screen, which will quickly fatigue your eyes. Others fail to utilize multimedia capabilities in an interesting and beneficial way. These and other shortcomings can limit the value of CBT software. Investigate your CBT options, preferably by test-driving a demo, before purchasing a CBT program. Most CBT vendors have demo versions available to download from their Web sites and/or available via mail. New programs are constantly appearing, so don't rely only on what other certification candidates report they have used. Don't limit yourself to software that includes the words "Cisco certification" in the title. There are plenty of concepts that are not Cisco specific that you will need to learn.

TABLE 8.2
Learning Characteristics of Computer-based Training

Advantages	Disadvantages
Somewhat portable	Less practical as a reference
Interactive	Requires fairly powerful personal computer to use
Moderate cost	No external motivation, easy to get off track
Proceed at your own pace	Often available in PC-compatible only, not Macintosh
Multimedia format is engaging	
Can review as desired	

Online Classes

One of the more recent developments in technical training is the use of the Internet as a delivery medium. Although online classes might appear to fall under the umbrella of CBT, they are distinct enough to deserve a category of their own.

Because online courses typically cost substantially less than their traditional classroom counterparts, training online is a cost effective option. Perhaps more important are the savings in time and aggravation. Distance learning makes it possible and practical to study at your own pace, on your own schedule, from anywhere you can link to the net. Courses often come with 24-hour access to subject experts, and if you want to, you can even earn CEUs while you explore the intricacies of TCP/IP or catch up on the features of the latest firewall schemes. Learning does not get much more convenient than this.

Distance education, while not an utter newcomer to the Web, is still a young industry. Technology barriers, such as the ever-present bandwidth bottleneck, place significant constraints of the format and delivery of course material. At the same time, distance learning offers an opportunity to develop entirely new learning models that take advantage of the delivery medium. The result is a menu of three flavors of course delivery to choose from: online multimedia courseware, the virtual classroom, and hybrids that combine features of each.

Courses that are delivered using online multimedia software are much like those that come on CD-ROM: they may incorporate snippets of video, audio clips, text-based instruction, software simulations, and self tests to measure your progress. Typically, a student signs onto the service, connects to the next module in the series she's currently following, and either works through the module online or downloads the module and completes it offline. Once a lesson is completed, the student takes an electronic self test and then moves on to the next lesson in the series. The self tests usually consist of multiple-choice questions, with a score calculated and provided immediately on completion of the quiz. The test program reports on missed questions, identifying the correct answer and/or identifying areas for additional student review.

Virtual classrooms, on the other hand, attempt to create an electronic parallel to a school setting. They do so by adding interaction with human instructors and other students as well as academic record-keeping and access to additional resources. The interaction is largely accomplished through a conglomeration of e-mail, newsgroups, dedicated forums, and scheduled chats. Study groups, remote access labs, exercises, and even telephone conferencing may also be incorporated.

To attend a virtual class, a student logs into the classroom to retrieve a lesson and related exercises. While online, she may participate in a discussion of the material by reading and posting on a class-specific message board. Instructor interaction is often accomplished via e-mail or message board. Unlike the multimedia courses, virtual classes often have specified start and end dates and lessons are presented on a fixed schedule, often weekly. Students can log in at any time during the week to complete the lesson, participate in discussions, and ask the instructor questions. A few virtual classrooms have specific meeting times and require all students to log on simultaneously and interact with the instructor in real-time.

Hybrid courses mix self-paced, multimedia courseware with access to class-specific message boards, chat links, and other resources. Students proceed at their own pace and are not obligated to comply with specific start and end dates, although there may be overall time limits. This means that one student may start the first module of a course at the same time as another student is finishing the fifth.

Most vendors permit you to sample a class before signing up. Use the opportunity to wander the virtual hallways and get a feel for the learning environment, because they vary widely. At Cyber-State University, for example, you'll encounter Professor Wire and his smorgasbord of jokes and puns. You may enjoy his witty interjections, or find them incredibly irritating.

Online courses may be offered by commercial education centers, colleges, consulting groups, and private individuals. The format and content details of a particular online course vary considerably from vendor to vendor. Prices run all over the spectrum, as does degree of instructor support, class quality, qualification for continuing education credits, and just about every other aspect you can imagine.

Ziff-Davis University

Ziff-Davis Corporation, publisher of numerous industry magazines, has jumped into the online training market with both feet, creating a virtual university named ZD Net University (ZDU). You will find it at **www.zdu.com**.

ZDU structures itself this way: Individuals pay a fee (currently $7.95/month or $69.95/year) to become members. While you are a member, you can register for and attend as many classes as you like. For each class, you log on at least once a week (at a time of your choosing) to read the instructor-posted assignment and submit questions that are posted on the class message board. According to ZDU, the message board is managed by "the instructor, teaching assistants, moderators and other students." Classes generally last four to eight weeks, and additional materials, including books or downloadable files, may be required. Instructors stage live chat "office hours." Many self-paced tutorials are available to subscribers as well.

For a processing fee (currently $15), ZDU will submit your information along with the course name and *recommended* number of continuing education units (CEUs), to the National Registry of Training Programs (NRTP) of the American Council on Education (ACE). *If* the CEUs are granted, you'll receive a notice from ACE via mail.

As this book was being written, ZDU had yet to offer any Cisco-related training courses in their catalogs, but it is a good bet Cisco training will be added in the near future.

CyberState University

CyberState U follows the virtual classroom model. Curriculum choices include Cisco A+, Computer telephony, Microsoft, and Novell certification preparation. Tuition is charged for each course and is often several thousand dollars. Courses are led by "Professor Wired." You will find it on the Web at **www.cyberstateu.com** (Figure 8.3) or call 888-Get-Educ for information. As this book was being written, CyberState's catalog included an two online CCNA courses: one for $1,795 and the second for $2,195.

Scholars.com

Scholars.com is another online training vendor offering a Cisco curriculum. It sells both an Introduction to Cisco Routers (ICRC) course and an Advanced Cisco Router Configuration (ACRC) course. As of February 1999, the package price for both courses together was $2595. The course-delivery format is a combination of self-paced courseware, access to "learning advisors," participation in forums, and practice questions and scenarios via e-mail. Figure 8.4 shows Scholar.com's Cisco certification page.

FIGURE 8.3
CyberState
University
on the Web

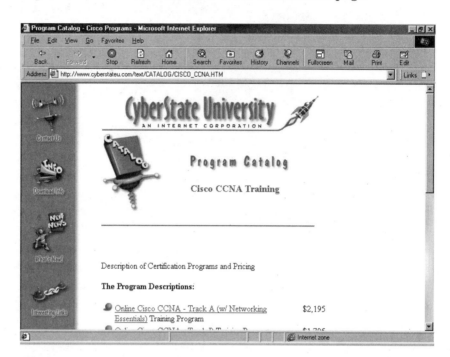

There are many more online instruction vendors besides those described above. Their course rosters may be limited to just a few classes or fill an extensive catalog. Their nature will vary considerably, too. Because this is an evolving business arena with exciting possibilities, you are likely to encounter an extensive variety of vendors, including colleges, individual entrepreneurs, technology businesses, and education companies. Table 8.3 outlines learning characteristics of online classes.

TABLE 8.3
Learning
Characteristics of
Online Classes

Advantages	Disadvantages
Self-paced (within time limits)	No future value as a reference
Access to expert instructor	Requires computer and Internet connection
Interaction with other students	Price, format, and quality vary widely

FIGURE 8.4
Training with
Scholars.com

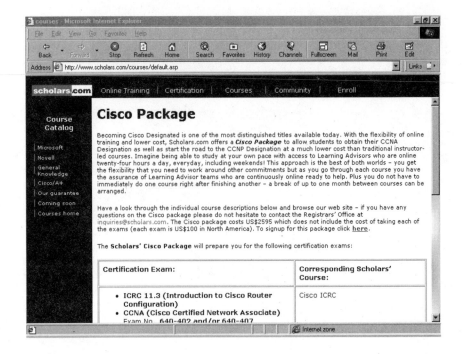

Training Web Sites

In addition to online training sources that include Cisco among their offerings, several sites exist solely to assist Cisco candidates. One of these is **CCPrep.com**, a subscription based site. Certification candidates pay a monthly fee to receive practice questions and lab scenarios with detailed explanations, as well as to pose questions to CCIEs on staff. As this book was being written, subscriptions cost $19.95 a month or $169 for a year. Figure 8.5 shows the CCPrep home page.

www.networkstudyguides.com is another subscription-based Web site catering to Cisco certification candidates. See Figure 8.6.

FIGURE 8.5

CCPrep.com

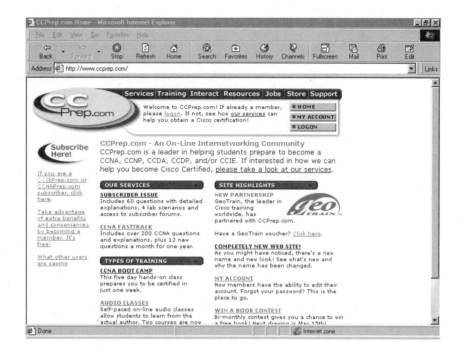

FIGURE 8.6

Studying with
Networkstudy
guides.com

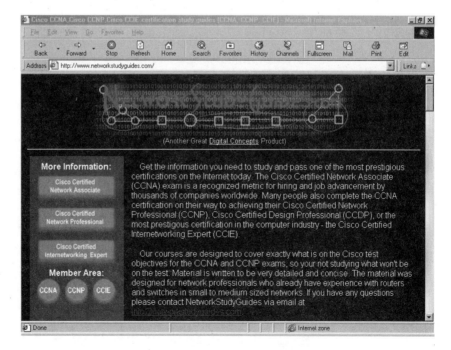

Authorized Training Centers

Cisco has quite a few (68 at last count) authorized training partners spread around the globe. As officially authorized partners, they adhere to the curriculum for each certification and class as defined by Cisco. These courses are required to be led by Certified Cisco System Instructors (CCSIs) and use Cisco's most current materials. They are also continuously monitored for quality. Some veterans of certification report that when it comes to in-depth, hands-on training, this kind of training is irreplaceable.

Because they work in partnership with Cisco, training partner center staff have the inside scoop on what it takes to pass particular tests, and what sort of practice is likely to pay off. You can get this same information elsewhere, but here it is likely to delivered to you practically on a silver platter. Your instructors will be professional technical trainers, extremely well versed in the issues at hand. Cisco requires its instructors to be individually certified for each course they will teach. If you run into a stumbling block, you won't be stuck for long.

Another big plus these centers offer is an appropriate computing environment. You will get your hands on the real thing. It will be free from the restrictions or potential for disaster that your employer's live network is likely to have.

The big downsides are cost and inconvenience. Intense authorized training can run up quite a tab. A single class can cost several thousand dollars. Of course, if your employer is willing to pay for it, cost will not be as big an issue.

Unlike other training you can pursue at your own pace, you will have to learn at a rate set by the rest of the class and the instructor. That rate may be slower or faster than you would like. You will have to adjust your work and leisure time to meet the training center's schedule, and if you miss a session, it may be difficult to catch up to the rest of the class.

To find a Cisco Training Partner (CTP) near you, you can either use the class locator page on Cisco's Web site (**www.cisco.com/pcgi-bin/ front.x/wwtraining/locator.pl**) or call Cisco training at 1-800-829-NETS (01-408-525-NETS if dialing from another country). In Europe the number to use is +32 2 778 42 02. In Japan, call 81 3 5219-6000.

Figure 8.7 shows Cisco's online class locator. Cisco also maintains a master list of training partners on its Web site at **www.cisco.com/ pcgi-bin/front.x/wwtraining/listAllTP.pl**. The reference section of this book also includes a list of Cisco training partners.

Shop around and compare price, course format, instructor experience, lab equipment, and convenience factors. You may find considerable variation among training centers. Table 8.4 details learning characteristics of training center courses.

FIGURE 8.7
Cisco's Online
Class Locator

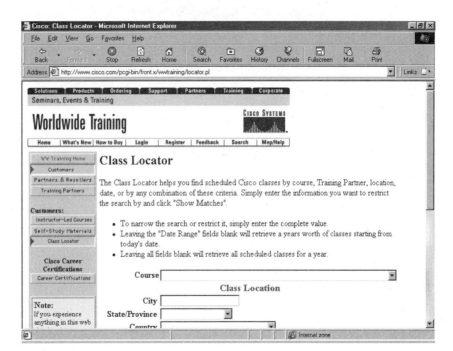

TABLE 8.4
Learning
Characteristics of
Training Center
Courses

Advantages	Disadvantages
Interactive	No future value as a reference
Access to expert instructor	Most costly
Access to expensive technology	Often requires time in large blocks
Interaction with other students	Not self paced
Easy to locate through sponsor	Compressed nature may reduce skill retention
Lots of training in a short time	May not be in convenient location

Cisco Academies

In 1993, the same year that Cisco launched its first certification, the company also began a program to promote Cisco training through high schools, colleges, universities, and technical schools. Cisco provides the curriculum and initial training that enables these "Cisco Networking Academies" to offer four semesters of hands-on Cisco training. The schools themselves must purchase the necessary equipment to set up a lab.

Students at these institutions participate in a four-semester program that includes multimedia training and hands-on networking activities. The current curriculum is specified by Cisco, and leads to the CCNA or CCNP exam. The curricula run about 280 hours each.

Attending one of these academies will enable you to overcome one of the biggest barriers to successful exam preparation—lack of equipment. (See Table 8.5 for learning characteristics.) They are operating at over 1,000 sites. To find out if there is one near you, visit the Cisco Academy Locator (**cisco.netacad.net/cnacs/ pub-doc/locator.shtml**).

TABLE 8.5
Learning Characteristics of College Courses

Advantages	Disadvantages
Interactive	No future value as a reference
Access to experienced instructor	Trainer may be less qualified than at a training center
Interaction with other students	Not self paced
Less costly than training center	Takes longer to complete course
Gentler learning pace	
Access to necessary equipment	
Often eligible for college credits	

Online Resources

An excellent way to augment any of these learning methods is to seek out additional information on the Internet. You can search for certification-specific resources or sites that contain the details of a particular technology that you are studying.

To locate sites with information of either type, connect to one of the search engines such as Yahoo! (**www.yahoo.com**), Infoseek (**www.infoseek.com**), or Excite (**www.excite.com**). Make your search as specific as possible. For example, to find Web pages relevant to the OSI model, something you'll need to know inside and out for these certifications, enter "OSI Model." Placing both words inside a set of quotes makes the search engine treat them as a phrase rather than separate keywords. This will return a list of links to pages that contain the exact phrase. To find documents relating to a particular certification test, you could use the keywords CCNA AND certification AND exam. You will get a list of pages containing all three of the keys, but they are allowed to be separated by other words not on your list. The more specific you make your search words and phrases, the less trash you will have to wade through to find the bits of treasure.

If you find that you are having little success, try a different search engine. Each search engine collects, indexes, and retrieves information in its own way. By executing an identical search on three different search engines, you will come up with three different (although overlapping) sets of results.

What types of resources can you expect to uncover with these searches? Both commercial and noncommercial sites will turn up. Some will be hosted by businesses who want to sell you their related services, others by individuals with special interest in your search topic. The bounty you will uncover is likely to include some of the following resources:

* Certification resource centers created by interested individuals (Figure 8.7 shows one of these)
* Resource sites about a particular technology
* Exam-specific learning aids, such as quiz programs, books, and testing tips
* Unofficial (that is, not officially authorized) training programs and books
* Sponsor-authorized training venues
* Related discussion forums
* Home pages of individuals who hold a particular certification

* Cisco Web pages
* Articles and papers about the technology or certification
* Online versions of software and hardware manuals
* Related newsgroups and mailing lists you can join
* Study groups organized around your certification.

FIGURE 8.8
GroupStudy.com
was Created by a
Cisco Certification
Candidate

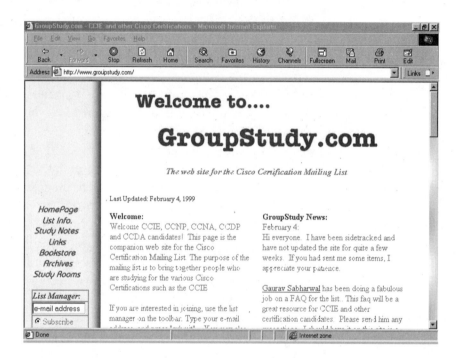

You will probably need to spend some time sorting the wheat from the chaff before you find the online resources that will prove most valuable to you. One of the great things about online resources is that when you find one good page, it will often contain direct links to other sites of similar quality and content. Table 8.6 provides learning characteristics of online resources.

Remember to take what you find on the Internet with a grain of salt. Excellent, accurate, and in-depth resources are out there, along with slapped-together, error-ridden pages. Most Web pages contain a link you can click on to contact the page's author. Don't hesitate to use it if only to get a feel for the person behind the information. You may well run across a kindred soul who is willing and able to serve as a fountain of knowledge about your certification program.

	Advantages	Disadvantages
TABLE 8.6 Learning Characteristics of Online Resources	Free	No guarantee of expertise
	Usually contain many useful links	Information may be out of date, inaccurate, or incomplete
	Tips and advice from certification veterans	May have to dig for the gold
	Place to connect with other candidates	

Unofficial Training Programs

It is a consumer truism that generic goods are generally less expensive than the name-brand version of the same item. That holds true for certification training, too. Entrepreneurs and others, who for one reason or another have not obtained official sponsor approval, have established themselves in the training business. The lack of a certification sponsor's seal of approval does not automatically indicate poor quality or anything shady about the operation. It may simply be a business choice not to go the authorized route, and plenty of trainers have, for one reason or another, made that decision.

These "unauthorized" vendors offer seminars, workshops, CBT software, software-based study aids, video tapes, textbooks, and study guides, virtually the same mix of resources you can obtain through official channels. As independent operators, they are free to develop their own curriculum and course format.

The good news is that unofficial vendors usually charge lower prices than their sponsor-authorized counterparts. Many are operated by skilled, knowledgeable professionals who know just what they are doing and how best to help you achieve certification. The bad news is that you cannot count on the presence of either attribute. Table 8.7 enumerates learning characteristics of unofficial training vendors.

Before purchasing goods or services, check out any unfamiliar vendor as thoroughly as you can. Find out how long the vendor has been in business, and if certification training is the product, inquire about the exam success rate of their graduates. Request the names and contact information of past customers, then contact those people to find out the details of their experience with the vendor. Spend time nosing around forums and Web sites for any bad press about the particular vendor. When people feel ripped off, they generally are not shy about sharing the details via an online site.

If a substantial amount of money is involved, it's worth it to call or write the Better Business Bureau in the vendor's home state and ask if there are any complaints on record against the company, and, if so, whether or not they have been satisfactorily resolved. Chances are that the vendor you are considering is running a quality operation, but it pays to be sure.

TABLE 8.7
Learning Characteristics of Unofficial Training Vendors

Advantages	Disadvantages
Usually less expensive than authorized	No guarantee of expertise
Not restricted to preapproved curriculum	Greater risk of inferior services and products
May get more candid view of product	

Training Videos

If you prefer learning from an instructor but classroom instruction does not suit you for one reason or another, videos are an alternative that you may find appealing. While you will not be able to interact with the instructor, you *will* be able to observe demonstrations of particular procedures. Voice, music, and visual stimulation will involve you, and, in many cases, animation, closeup shots, and virtual field trips will help to clarify concepts. Some videos apply a lead/follow approach. The video instructor demonstrates how to operate a particular piece of software, then you recreate the process using your own equipment. Many are passive affairs where you just sit and watch. Table 8.8 highlights learning characteristics of videotapes.

TABLE 8.8
Learning
Characteristics
of Videotapes

Advantages	Disadvantages
Relatively low cost	Not interactive
Self-paced	May contain excessive "talking heads" sections
Can review as needed	Require access to VCR equipment
Opportunity to see techniques in action	

Training videos often come with a support package that includes printed materials, review questions, and self quizzes. They are significantly less expensive than other forms of instructor-led training. In some cases, you may even be able to rent instead of purchase them, but if you do, you will not have them on hand for future reference.

It is important to remember that although a particular training option may seem ideal to you, it may not be available for your certification program, in your area, or in your price range, or it may not be available for some other reason. If you cannot obtain your first choice in training, there are probably several other options that will serve you nearly as well. There is also a lot of variation within categories, so be sure to shop around to get a clear understanding of what various training outlets have to offer.

QUOTE

Learning the Right Stuff

Hands-on time and access to equipment are critical to passing the lab. You can read all day long, but until you have sat down and done route redistribution or VLSM, you won't know it well enough to pass the exam. For the written portion, I usually tell the candidate to fork over the $200 and take the test cold. It will give them an idea of what the test is like and enable them to focus their studies. This industry is full of information, and a candidate can study for hours and hours and not be in the right ballpark. To invest 100 hours studying and then find out you were going in the wrong direction can be discouraging.

—Scott Urban, CCIE #3977

Keep in mind that different certification requirements may be best met by different training alternatives. To learn how physically to connect and configure a series of routers, for example, you might prefer a hands-on workshop with tools, equipment, and an experienced technician on hand. But to understand the layers of the OSI model and how they interact, a videotape, audio cassette, or book may do the job as well or better.

In the next chapter, as part of developing your personal certification road map, you will find out how to analyze your learning style and how to take that into consideration when choosing a training alternative. You will also determine just how much training you will need and how to evaluate individual training outlets.

CHAPTER 9

Your Personal Training and Certification Road Map

Once you have decided which Cisco certification to pursue, you are ready to lay out your plan for obtaining it. Is a detailed plan really necessary? Only if you want to save time, money, and frustration.

A certification plan is often referred to as a road map, and with good reason. The process of obtaining certification is very similar to the process of traveling from your home to a distant location. In both cases, there are many possible routes between your starting point and intended destination. Which route is best depends upon individual preferences. Is speed of the essence or do you prefer to see more along the way? Will you be camping out to save money or lodging at five-star hotels? Do you have the endurance and tenacity to undertake marathon drives or are shorter hops more to your liking?

The same issues apply to certification. Do you want to finish ASAP or delve more deeply into the elements? Are you aiming for minimal financial outlay or maximum comfort? Do you have the time and energy to immerse yourself for intense and extended training events or are shorter study and training sessions more to your liking?

Although it might be tempting to hop on the certification road as soon as possible and figure out each turn as it approaches, such impatience has a price. You are likely to spend more time and money than you have to and risk taking wrong turns along the way. By taking the time to understand your learning style and plot out which exams and courses you will take, in what order, and when, you'll be assured of meeting all the requirements and deadlines for your certification. You will also be able to move smoothly from one requirement to the next without constantly needing to interrupt your progress to stop and figure out what to do next.

Your completed certification road map will list the requirements you need to meet, in the order you will need to accomplish them. It will also identify the methods you intend to use to prepare for each exam and include a timeline to keep you on target.

Galton Technologies hosts a certification tracking system for Cisco's career certifications. Remember that the term career certifications encompasses all the Cisco certification except the CCIE designations. At this site (shown in Figure 9.1) certification candidates can track their exam completion progress and update their personal information. This is primarily a place to verify that Cisco's records gibe with your own.

FIGURE 9.1
Tracking Progress Toward a Cisco Certification

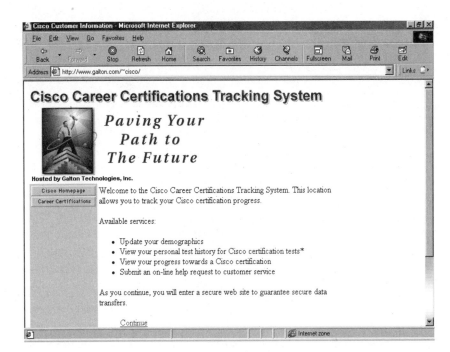

What this system does not do is set your deadlines for you or help you identify a plan of attack. That is why you will benefit from tailoring your own plan. Creating your personal certification road map involves the following steps:

1. Select a track
2. Record the requirements on your personal certification plan
3. Eliminate any requirements you can
4. Decide how you will meet the remaining requirements
5. Set deadlines.

Your plan will be an evolving document. Expect to adjust and fine-tune it as you progress toward certification.

A Word on Tracks

Many certifications allow some amount of customization so you can closely match them with your needs. This is like the electives component of college degree programs where you get to choose what to minor in. Correspondingly, you can act as some college freshmen do and choose the courses that are easiest to pass, or you can take advantage of this flexibility to follow a certification path tailored to your career goals.

These alternate paths are called tracks. They typically are organized in one of two ways:

* Around specific platforms and operating environments
* By job function.

Cisco uses both types of classifications to organize its certifications. For job function, it divides certification into support and design. Operating environments—i.e. routing and switching versus WAN switching—are used to further differentiate the certifications.

The best way to choose your track is to read over the descriptions created by Cisco. Select the option that most closely matches the goals you intend to achieve through certification. For example, if you are planning to leverage your career at your current position, choose the track that most closely matches the operating environment you work in or that best describes the functions related to your job. If you are intending to use certification to move into a new area, look for the track that best bridges what you already know and what you would like to know. If your goal is to advance your skills, select the track that best represents the skills you want to add or augment.

It is a good idea to discuss your options with other people who are familiar with the certification process and/or your goals. They can help you decide if a particular track or elective is "hot" or going out of style. There are several Internet venues for doing this. One of the best is the mailing list maintained at **www.groupstudy.com**.

Once you have settled on a certification track, begin filling in the personal certification plan in Figure 9.2 by listing the requirements you will need to meet, in the order that you intend to complete them. Be as detailed as possible. At this point, you should be able to list specific exams, experience requirements, applications to submit, fees to be paid, and anything else that will be needed to obtain your certification. Write only in the requirements column for now. This is the "what" of your certification plan. The other columns, which will address "how" and "when," will follow shortly.

FIGURE 9.2

Personal Certification Plan

Certification:_____

Target Completion Date:_____

X	Requirement	Target Date	Training/Study Method(s)	Notes

This is the point at which you will need to choose a testing path. Several of the Cisco certifications offer the option of taking the Foundation R/S exam in place of the ACRC, CLSC, and CMTD exams. The Foundation R/S exam lasts 2.75 hours while the total time for the other three exams is 4 hours. You can also save $100 by taking the Foundation R/S exam. The drawback is that you will have to prepare for the whole round of subjects at once, and weakness in one area may keep you from passing the entire exam. For these reasons, many certification candidates prefer to take the three separate exams rather than the combined exam.

Deciding How to Prepare

Now that you have spelled out and pared down your requirements, it is time to determine how you will approach each of them. Depending upon your background and skills, some requirements will entail more preparation than others. The next step of developing your personal certification plan is to therefore review each requirement and choose the study/training methods you will apply to achieve it.

Certification candidates have a rich array of learning alternatives to choose from—Chapter 9 explored them in detail. Deciding which method to apply toward a particular requirement is a highly individual process, and to make effective choices you first need to understand your personal learning style.

How Do You Learn?

People differ in how they perceive, understand, retain, and recall information. We all know individuals who can find their way anywhere providing they have a map to refer to, and others who are virtually guaranteed to get lost unless they are given oral directions. Give the map reader oral directions or the directions person a map and both will eventually reach their destinations, but their journeys will probably be longer and more stressful. Just like these travelers, learners have preferred methods of receiving and using information.

QUICK TIP

For an excellent (if extensive) discussion of many aspects of adult learning styles, read the Wave Technologies International white paper, *Learning: The Critical Technology*, which you can find at **www.wavetech.com/whtpaper/abttmwp.html**.

The people who study the science behind learning have identified and mapped these preferences in a number of different ways. By identifying and understanding your personal learning styles, you will be able to select the training methods and tools that will work best for you. To help you do that, an exploration of two of the more widely accepted models follows. As you work to understand your learning preferences, keep two important things in mind:

* There is no "best" learning style
* Sometimes options that cater to your learning preferences are unavailable or impractical. Although other learning styles may not be as ideal, they will still work.

One of the more common (and understandable) learning frameworks is organized around how we take in information. This theory identifies three basic learning styles based on human senses: visual (by sight), auditory (by sound), and tactile/kinesthetic (by touch and motion). Although most people can learn using any of these senses, most favor one over the others.

Visual learners take in information most easily by seeing it. If you prefer to look at pictures and images rather than listen to explanations, you may be a visual learner. The map reader mentioned above is a visual learner.

Readers are not necessarily visual learners. Many people "hear" the words in their head as they read them. For that reason, readers are considered auditory learners. Auditory learners understand ideas more quickly when they hear them spoken. If you learn more from a lecturer than from watching demonstrations on the same subject, then you may be an auditory learner. A tendency to "think out loud," is another indication that you learn through listening. In the earlier example of following directions, the person who prefers oral directions over a map is an auditory learner.

Tactile/kinesthetic learners prefer to touch and manipulate things. If you are one of those people who abhors reading directions and are happier diving right into whatever it is and figuring it out as you go along, you are likely to be a tactile/kinesthetic learner. A tactile/kinesthetic traveler typically has a good sense of direction and location and is less likely than the map reader or auditory traveler to get seriously lost.

The most effective instruction incorporates more than one learning style. The better teachers have been aware of this for some time and deliberately appeal to different learning styles.

Kindergarten teachers, for example, often apply all of these perception styles when teaching the alphabet. When introducing a new letter, they show what the letter looks like (visual), say the letter out loud and have the students repeat it (auditory), and direct children to trace the shape of the letter with a finger or crayon (tactile/kinesthetic).

QUICK TIP

To help determine whether you are more of a visual, auditory, or tactile/kinesthetic learner, take the online learning styles inventory at **www.howtolearn.com/personal.html** (shown in Figure 9.3).

FIGURE 9.3
Discover Your
Learning
Style Online

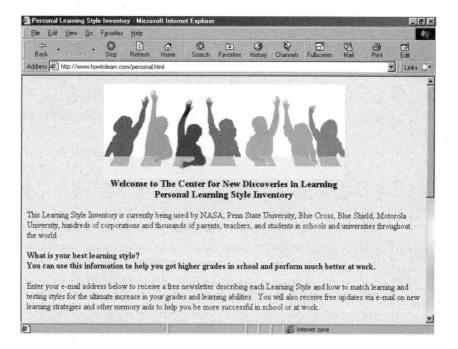

Peter Honey and Alan Mumford, building on the work of David Kolb, developed a second, widely referenced model. This framework is organized around how we think about things rather than around perceptive preferences. It identifies four types of learners: the activist, the pragmatist, the reflector, and the theorist. Once again, these categories are not mutually exclusive. It is likely that you have traits linked to more than one of these learning styles, but you will find one that describes you more accurately and completely than the others.

Individuals who fall under the first category—activists—are eager to dive right in and try out novel things. Do you enjoy new projects and frequently find yourself looking for the next project to tackle? Do you approach new ideas in an open-minded and enthusiastic fashion? Are you are always primed and ready for the next new experience? If so, then your learning style is probably activist.

Pragmatists are most interested in the application of what they learn. Do you return from a seminar filled with fresh ideas that you want to try out? Do you think of yourself as a practical person and like solving problems? Are you impatient with meetings that don't seem to be accomplishing a specific purpose? These are all signs of a pragmatic learner.

Reflectors are happiest when they can collect all the relevant information and study it carefully before reaching a conclusion. Do you prefer to make decisions at the last minute so that you can have as long as possible to consider potential ramifications? Do you enjoy collecting and analyzing data? Would you (or others close to you) describe yourself as a cautious person? If so, then you are probably a reflector.

Theorists like to understand how things fit together and what they mean. Do you prefer to analyze problems in an objective, step-by-step fashion? Do you look for the logic behind the ideas? Are uncertainty and ambiguity difficult for you to endure? These are all characteristics of a theorist learning style.

Once you have a good sense of your learning strengths, it is time to fill in some of the blanks in your personal certification plan. For each requirement you have listed, fill in the training/study method(s) you want to use. Keep in mind which learning alternatives are best matched to the learning styles you have identified as your favorites. If you have determined that you are a tactile/kinesthetic person, for example, you'll find hands-on options more effective. Consider interactive computer-based training (CBT) or instructor-led training (ILT) that includes lab work as your first choice. Ways to get hands-on experience with Cisco routers will be discussed later. An auditory learner should turn to books and audio and videotapes, while a visual learner should seek out alternatives that include videotapes, print materials that include extensive illustrations, and instructor-led training.

A reflector may be happiest poring over the details found in product documentation, while a theorist will prefer a study guide that pays more attention to the why of things. An activist may be best served by getting his or her hands on the technology in question before worrying about the details of how it works. A pragmatist should look for methods that begin by explaining what something is good for. Printed materials and instructor-led training are likely options for a pragmatist.

You can expect to find a lot of variety among products within a single category. Though some CBT programs involve much of interaction, others depend more heavily on reading from the screen. Some "talk to you" quite a bit. Others just settle for a beep and chirp now and again. Study guides can contain block after block of dense text or include diagrams, photos, and self tests.

How Certification Candidates Study

As part of a 1998 Gartner Group study sponsored by Sylvan Prometric, Hewlett-Packard, Microsoft, Novell, and Sybase, more than 6,000 certification candidates were asked about their training methods. The results show which study methods candidates used most and which proved most useful.

Self study was the primary method used by the majority (43 percent) of those surveyed. Twenty-seven percent of respondents reported using instructor-led training (ILT) as their predominant preparation tool. Less than 1% of those used Internet-based ILT as their primary study method. Figure 9.4 shows the breakdown of primary study methods reported.

Interestingly, the choice of a primary study method does not always correlate with the method that candidates identified as most useful. This is most apparent in on-the-job-training, which only 11.3 percent of candidates identified as their primary learning method, but 22.6 percent pegged as one of the most useful. Self-study methods were overwhelmingly designated useful (31.5 percent), and instructor-led training got the nod from just (18.7 percent). Figure 9.5 shows the study methods certification candidates found most useful.

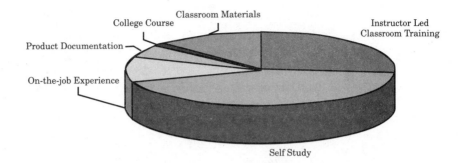

FIGURE 9.4
Primary
Certification
Study Method
Source: Gartner
Group, 1998

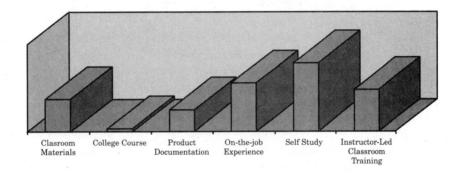

FIGURE 9.5
Most Useful
Study Method
Source: Gartner
Group, 1998

Finding Preparation Tools

Although there are many preparation tools available, you will need to conduct a bit of a search to uncover a good selection. Places to check include:

* Ask Cisco. Their Web site contains a class locator (**www.cisco.com/pcgi-bin/front.x/wwtraining/locator.pl**).
* Find out if there is a Cisco Networking Academy near you, also by checking the Cisco Web site (**www.cisco.com/warp/public/779/edu/academy/**).
* Contact vendors listed in the resource section of this book.
* Use Internet search engines, such as Yahoo! and Infoseek, to uncover sites that include the name of your certification along with the word "preparation."
* Visit Web sites and forums that you uncovered while researching your certification or find in the resource section of this book, and post a message asking for suggestions.

* Consider using generic (non-certification specific) self-quiz programs that let you create your own practice tests. You can find them in shareware catalogs and on the Internet.
* Call your local community colleges and inquire about computer technology offerings. These may not be officially authorized training, but may do the job.
* Visit a nearby bookstore or one of the bookstores on the Web, such as Amazon Books (**www.amazon.com**), and search for titles related to your certification and/or study topic. Figure 9.6 shows the results of an Amazon Books search for CCNA materials.
* Look in the business pages of your local phone book under computers—training.
* Browse the **comp.dcom.sys.cisco** Usnet newsgroup for suggestions.

FIGURE 9.6
CCNA Search
Results from
Amazon Books

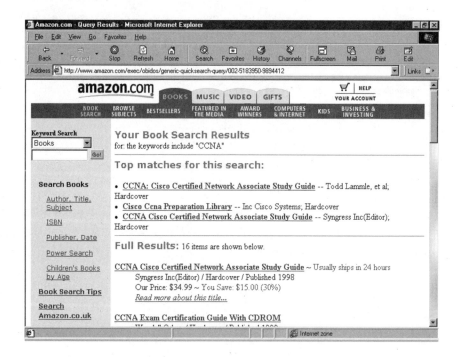

There are also a number of education clearinghouses on the Web. These have information on training companies and products and are searchable by geographic area and topic. Sites to visit include:

* Yahoo's computer training index (**yahoo.com/Business_ and_Economy/Companies/Computers/Services/ Training/**) contains hundreds of links to trainers and training companies.
* Nerd World Media's computer training list (**www.nerdworld. com/nw190.html**) is quite extensive.

Once you have added preparation methods for the requirements listed on your personal certification plan, pull out your calendar and fill in a deadline for each requirement. Setting these target dates will help you keep on track and give you a picture of the time frame. When setting deadlines, remember to allow for vacations, holidays, business trips, and the like. Give yourself a little more time than the bare minimum you think is necessary. Then if something unexpected comes up and you fall a day or two behind, your schedule won't be thrown completely out of kilter. Finally, as mentioned before, remember that your plan is not written in stone. You can change and adapt it to meet your needs along the way. But try to stick to the deadlines if you possibly can. Doing so will assure you make continued progress toward your goal of certification.

How to Evaluate a Training Center

There are two categories of training centers you will encounter: authorized and "other." Authorized training centers have an agreement with Cisco that specifies the details of their operations. The Cisco Training Partner agreement covers curriculum, course materials, facilities, equipment, and instructor qualifications. The theory behind authorized training centers is that you can obtain the same quality and level of training no matter which one you attend. However, the real world does not always conform neatly to a plan. Instructors are individuals with varying classroom presence and skills. Equipment upkeep may be more meticulous at one center than another.

The "other" category encompasses all training firms and programs that lack the official seal of approval. This may be because they do not (or cannot) meet sponsor requirements or because they want freedom from the complications of oversight and sponsor regulations.

Whichever type of facility interests you, it is important to evaluate how good a job the center is likely to do in providing the services you want. The two most important aspects to investigate are the instructor and the classroom.

To assess the skill of the instructor, ask the training facility for the name of the instructor who will be teaching your class. Request a copy of the trainer's resume and copies of past course evaluations from classes that trainer led. Find out if the training facility is willing to direct you to students who have taken classes from the trainer in the past. Opinions from such people are an excellent resource.

You may find the training center unwilling to provide such information. That may simply mean that they do not know who will be teaching the class; contract instructors are often brought in to teach courses. If that is the case, find out if the facility uses the same contractors again and again. If so, you can ask for information on each of the trainers who may teach your class. If the training company uses different trainers each time, they are taking a gamble with an unknown, and so are you. You may want to look elsewhere. Using new trainers each time may also mean that trainers have declined to come back for a return engagement, another potential warning sign.

The best way to assess a training facility's physical setup is to visit the classroom your course will be held in. If it is too far away, you will have to do your best to find out the relevant information via telephone. Ask what kind of computers will be used in class. Is the hardware up to date? How much RAM does each computer have? What speed are the CPUs? Is there a router for each student, or will you be expected to share? Are the relevant hookups, such as network and Internet connections, present?

Don't overlook the layout of the classroom itself. Is there room to spread out your materials and move around or are desks crammed tightly together? What presentation devices, such as overhead projectors or whiteboards, will be used to display information to the entire class? Are they clearly visible from all seats? Are the chairs comfortable enough to spend hours in, or are they ergonomic nightmares?

Inquire about lunch arrangements, satisfaction guarantees, and whether you can come in before or after class to practice on your own. The ability to use the equipment after hours is a valuable option to have. Think about your past training experiences and what you liked and disliked about them. If specifics come to mind, find out if they will occur at the facility you are now considering.

If you feel uncomfortable poking and prodding like this, remember that you are considering spending a significant amount of time and money at the facility, and you have every right to know just what you will be getting in return. Politely make your inquiries and jot down notes about what you discover. If the training facility has been in business for any time at all, they will be used to such inquiries. The time you spend checking on the center will be paid back tenfold if it saves you from enrolling somewhere that does not measure up. If you find a good center, you will be able to return to it again and again.

How to Set Up a Home Practice Lab

Although it may be possible to obtain CCNA certification without hands-on practice, that doesn't mean it is a good idea. There is nothing like interaction with the actual products to increase your understanding of the technology at hand. It is extremely unlikely you will be able to pass any of the other Cisco certifications without working with Cisco routers and switches. Although some lucky seekers of Cisco certification have a working environment where they can get hands-on practice with the equipment, many do not. For that reason it is common practice to set up a home lab.

With a home lab you can create scenarios that require you to use different components of the Cisco IOS (Internetworking Operating System) to accomplish tasks you are likely to encounter both in the real world on the job, and on the Cisco certification tests. Deciding what to put in a home lab and where to get the equipment has always been a challenge for Cisco certification candidates. Tom Thomas II, a Cisco employee, a CCNA, and a CCIE in progress, was asked about home lab configuration so many times, the he created the following list of suggested equipment:

CCNA Practice Lab Equipment List

(You should be able to pick this package up used for $2000 or less.)

2   Cisco 2501 routers or equivalent
2   software feature sets (IP & IPX) Cisco IOS 11.3 and if possible these should be the enterprise version
1   cable male DTE V.35
1   cable female DCE V.35
2   ethernet transceivers
2   console cables and adapters (shipped with Cisco routers by default)
PC with NIC card

Optional:
Token ring capability
FDDI capability

This equipment will allow you to connect the routers via the v.35 cables to simulate a frame relay cloud. By having these routers you will also be able to execute TFTP saves of your configurations, determine the operation of routing protocols, and become familiar with all the basic IOS commands needed to meet the objectives.

CCNP Practice Lab Equipment List

All of the recommended CCNA equipment plus:

A switch of some sort, this can be anything from a 1900 to 5000
ISDN (real or simulated)
Dial up connection
Capability to capture and decode packets

Optional:
All of the optional CCNA equipment
ATM/LANE

This equipment will allow you configure VLANs, VTP, and bridging for the CLSC section. It will also allow you to configure the various configurations and special features surrounding the dial up section as described in the CMTD section. It will also allow you to use some of the more advanced features found in the enterprise version of the IOS as discussed in the ACRC section.

CCIE Practice Lab Equipment List

All of the recommended and optional equipment for the CCNA and CCNP plus:

A 2502 or a 2503 and a 4000 with a 2 port serial and ethernet module with 6 cables and a transceiver.

1 Cisco 2509 router. This will be helpful to set up reverse telnet.
1 Cisco 3620 with a NM-1FE-TX fast Ethernet module, NM-1E1R2W i.e. 1 ethernet, 1 token ring and 2 WAN slots. WIC-IB-U i.e. 1 ISDN with NT-1
1 2521. This is a Token Ring, four port serial ISDN router
1 ISDN emulator
1 Catalyst 2924XL or 5000 switch
1 CAB-OCTAL-ASYNC. This is an 8 lead octal cable (68 pin to 8 male RJ-45s)

All routers should have 16 Megs of memory to hold the 11.3 enterprise version

The best lab to prepare for the CCIE is a real live enterprise network. You take what you learn there and then bring home your experience and test other possible solutions on your home lab. Then when you think you are ready, tear apart your home lab, pack it away for two weeks and rebuild it from scratch into a fully operational network all within 7 hours.

Where to Get the Gear

Cisco routers and switches can be quite expensive, and in order to keep the cost manageable, many certification candidates choose one of three options: borrowing equipment, purchasing used equipment, or renting time on someone else's equipment.

Borrowing Equipment

If you work at an installation that uses Cisco equipment, you may be able to borrow a router or two that is currently not in service. Don't try to practice on routers that are currently part of the company's internetwork, because it does not take much to cause major technical problems without intending to. There have also been reports that CCIE candidates in particular have been able to borrow equipment from a local Cisco field office.

Used Equipment

Used equipment is the best if not virtually the only way to proceed in setting up a home lab. It is dramatically cheaper than buying brand-new, still-the-box products. When you finish earning your certification, you can probably sell this equipment to other certification candidates and recoup much of your investment. Where can you get used Cisco routers and switches? The numerous sources include:

* Other Cisco certification candidates
* Dealers in used networking equipment (see resource section for list)
* Internet auction sites such as eBay (**www.ebay.com**) or Yahoo! auctions (**auctions.yahoo.com**)
* By posting equipment wanted ads in places such as the gocertify.com swapshop (**gocertify.com/swapshop.html**) and on Cisco user-group bulletin boards.

Renting Time on Equipment

To answer the need Cisco certification candidates have for temporary use of complex networking equipment, several companies have begun to offer access to banks of Cisco equipment via the Internet. These are subscription services—fees are typically charged by the hour or by the month. Vendors include:

* Virtual Rack (**www.virtualrack.com**)
* Mentor Labs (**www.mentorlabs.com**)
* Net Educate (**www.neteducate.com**)

Figure 9.7 shows the Net Educate Web site.

FIGURE 9.7
Net Educate
Web Site

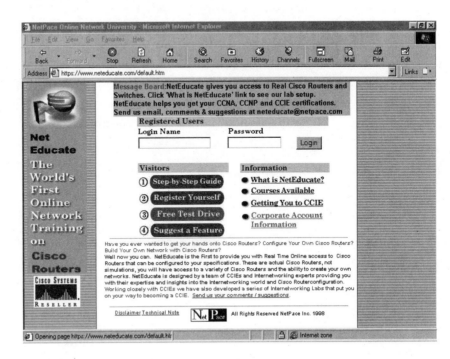

Following Your Plan

As you step through the requirements in your personal certification plan, it helps to take a methodical approach. Your process should go something like this:

1. Read objectives for the exam
2. Read Cisco's how-to-prepare guide for that exam
3. Complete any study/training classes and materials
4. Get hands-on experience
5. Review/practice
6. Register for the exam
7. Take the exam.

Don't hesitate to modify these steps to suit your personality and needs. Some people prefer to schedule their exam first and use the exam date as motivation to keep on track. You will also find that, for some requirements, your existing knowledge and experience will make it possible for you to skip steps and still perform just fine on the exam.

Once you have completed the preparation of your plan, store it somewhere close at hand so that you can refer to it at will. Whenever you complete a requirement, mark an X in the column provided for that purpose. Those Xs will accumulate into a tower of accomplishment, and before you know it, you will reach your goal and become a Cisco certified computer professional.

CHAPTER 10

Study Secrets

Is it possible to graduate from high school, college, or even graduate school without mastering effective study skills? In a word, yes. Learning how to learn rarely receives the attention it should in our system of education. It seems to be assumed that it is something everyone knows instinctively, like putting your hands out to catch yourself when you stumble.

In fact, extending your arms to cushion a fall is not instinctual, it just feels that way because you have been doing it for so long that it has become second nature. If you observe young children who have just begun to walk, you will notice that they stumble a lot, and when they stumble, they fall, usually face first. It is only after repeatedly banging their foreheads or noses that they begin to catch themselves with their hands.

At first glance, studying might also seem like an inherent skill that you either do or do not have. Like putting your hands out when you trip, it is a learned behavior. Similarly, once you have mastered effective techniques, you will be able to apply them again and again throughout your life. At first it will require deliberate effort, but with time and practice, it, too, can become second nature.

You already know how to study, you say? If you are really fortunate, then you do. More likely, you know just enough to get by. When study skills are lacking, an increase in effort can sometimes compensate for lack of ability. Studying does not have to be a mind-numbing feat of endurance, and exams do not have to tie your stomach in knots. Nor should you feel embarrassed if your study skills are weak; it is not that difficult to fix them. Once you do, you will find the act of learning can become downright pleasurable.

As an adult learner, your educational circumstances are significantly different from what they were when you were in high school or college. It is likely that you have more demands competing for your time, including a full-time job and possibly a family. You have an advantage over your counterparts in a very important way—motivation. You are studying because you have identified a goal you want to obtain (Cisco certification). You have a concrete vision of how achieving your goal will benefit you. You are placing at least some of your own money on the line. Getting down to business will be easier this time around.

Learning to study effectively means gaining control and understanding in three main areas: environment, methods, and motivation. The skills you already have in these areas can be strengthened and augmented with new techniques. First, let's look at a few myths about studying.

You Might Have Heard That...

Smart people don't have to study.

This is one of the most widely held misconceptions about studying. Everyone knows an individual who appears to glide through academics with little effort and get excellent scores on exams yet never seems to crack a book. How can this be?

Some people do need less study time than others, but that often can be linked to efficient and effective techniques rather than to a high I.Q. score. Consider reading speed. One student may read at a rate of 250 words a minute and will take about six hours to read a 90,000-word book. A faster reader, cruising along at 500 words per minute, will finish that same book in only three hours. Is the slower reader not as smart? Not necessarily. He is just not as skilled a reader.

The other contributing factor to the myth that smart people need not study has to do with where they study. Rather than trying to concentrate in the midst of a crowded cafeteria, for example, they hit the books in a private (and quieter) environment. Only those who live with them see them studying. If word starts to circulate that they are so smart that they don't have to study, why deny it?

Cramming is a good way to remember things.

Cramming is the way to forget things! Think back to a time when you applied this technique yourself, probably out of desperation over an exam looming the next day. You may have achieved a decent score on that test, but what do you remember of the material now? Or even just a week after the test? If you are like most people, the facts quickly evaporated from your mind.

The human brain strengthens the connections between bits of information through repetition. Although cramming may stuff enough facts into short-term memory to pass an exam, short-term memory is just that, here today and gone tomorrow. Storing information in long-term memory requires repetition and sustained effort. Certainly, last-minute studying does have its place: as a review tool. Its true effectiveness is as a supplement to a more sustained kind of learning that will place information at your service today, next week, and next year.

The more you study, the more you learn.

Longer study periods covering greater quantities of material may, in fact, be detrimental to your ability to recall the information. Your attention span is not unlimited. Everyone reaches a saturation point where information seems to flow into one brain cell and then proceed directly out of another. It is as if your brain is saying "give me a break!" In fact, that may be just what is happening. Recent research suggests that the human brain requires time for new information or skills to become "hard wired," and that introducing a second skill or batch of information on the heels of the first interferes with that process. Essentially, the brain needs time to process what it has just received.

Think about learning two phone numbers. If you work on both simultaneously, you will probably exchange digits between them and take more time to be able to correctly recall either one. However, if you take them one at a time, and get the first down cold before taking on the next, such confusion is unlikely to occur. More studying is not automatically better.

Background noise can help you concentrate.

Studying with the television running may feel like less work, but it is also working less. When part of your mind is occupied filtering and interpreting background noise, it is not available to focus on the information you're studying. Background music also interferes with your ability to concentrate, although music without lyrics is significantly less distracting than music with them. For best results, focus your full attention on your task. You will finish sooner and can then fully enjoy your music or television show.

Studying requires substantial, uninterrupted blocks of time.

Ideally, you should have at least some uninterrupted periods. But not having them does not preclude study opportunities. Squeezing "study snacks" into the margins of your daily life can be very beneficial. Consider the times you find yourself waiting: for the bus, for an elevator, for the next available bank teller, or for a take-out lunch. If you carry notes, in some form, in your pocket, you can whip them out at these times and grab a few minutes of power studying. Over the course of a week, these "study snacks" can add up to a significant meal of information.

When to Study

You need not be a time management expert to recognize that most people cram an incredible array of activities into the course of a week. If you are one of them, you may be wondering how to squeeze study time into an already crowded schedule. Although small amounts of study time can prove quite valuable, longer, uninterrupted blocks are necessary. Finding them can be a challenge. Fortunately, it is one you can conquer.

Every week contains 168 hours. That's more than 10,000 minutes. A basic eight to five job, with no overtime and a half-hour commute each way, cuts 50 hours off the top. Allocate another 45 minutes to shower, dress, and eat breakfast before leaving the house, and that's another 3¾ hours gone. What about sleep? At eight hours a night you are snoozing away 56 hours each week. Take another half hour a day to microwave and eat dinner and the total reaches 113 hours. That's 6,795 of your precious allotment of minutes expended on basic living, without even getting to sleep in on Saturday morning.

That's the bad news. The good news is that the above barebones regimen still leaves another 55 hours or so (specifically, 3,285 minutes) in your time bank. It's up to you to spend it wisely.

Granted, much, if not all, of that time is already spoken for. Some of it is devoted to activities you won't want to give up. If you examine your use of time closely, chances are you will be able to massage your schedule and slide study time into your life fairly painlessly.

If the time slots open to studying are not obvious, a time usage chart will reveal them. To make one, mark 15-minute time increments along the left side of a piece of paper. Create seven columns across the top, one for each day of the week. During the next week, record what you do throughout the day by listing the activity and blocking off the amount of time used. Figure 10.1 shows a partially completed time usage chart.

FIGURE 10.1

Sample Time
Usage Chart

	Monday	Tuesday	Wednesday	Thursday	Friday	Saturday	Sunday
7:00	Rise &						
7:15	Bkfst						
7:30	Commute						
7:45	to-work						
8:00	Work						
8:15							
8:30							
8:45							
9:00							
9:15							
9:30							
9:45							
10:00	Break						
10:15	Work						
10:30							
10:45							
11:00							
11:15							
11:30							
11:45							
12:00	Find-Keys						
12:15	Lunch						

At the end of the week, add the total amount of time you spent on each activity. Analyze your chart to determine:

* Which activities do you spend the most time on? Is the amount of time you devote to them reasonable? If not, think about how you can cut back.
* Which are the biggest time wasters? Does your time chart show hours of television watching, excessive phone calls, or frequent nights out? Looking for misplaced items is a frequent time waster that probably will not even make it onto your chart.
* What can you cut back or eliminate to make room for studying? The time wasters are prime candidates for the ax. You can let the answering machine take phone calls, become more organized so you don't spend as much time finding things, and/or turn off your television. You also might identify com-

mitments, such as volunteer work or league sports, that you can reduce while you are working toward certification.

This is not to say that you should completely cut out your social life and leisure activities. In fact, those are things you should be careful to include in your schedule. To succeed as a learner, you also need time away from the books so you can relax and maintain your health.

When choosing study times, keep the following principles in mind:

* Schedule study time during those times of day that you feel best. If you are a morning person, consider getting up early so you can get in a half hour before work. Are you a night person? Then skip the evening news and work on your certification program instead. You will absorb material quickly and more easily when you are fully alert.

* Learn to say no. During this time, try to avoid taking on extra work. Some people find it hard to refuse any request, especially those that come from coworkers or charities. But a simple reply like: "I'd love to be able to do that for you, but right now my schedule is booked solid. Maybe another time?" will protect your study time without hurting feelings. If you are someone who finds it difficult to say no, practice in front a mirror until the words just flow from your lips.

* Build a cushion into your time estimates. Avoid the temptation to schedule things to the minute. Inevitably, something unexpected will occur. If you have not allowed time for it, you will end up chasing your schedule for days afterward.

* Study the worst first. If you are dreading a particular study unit or practice material, take it on first. Chances are you will discover it isn't nearly as onerous as you expected, and with the hardest part out of the way the remaining materials will be a cake walk.

Where to Study

Where you choose to study affects how successful you will be at learning and remembering the information you cover. While it is possible to study on the subway, a park bench, or at the kitchen table, your best study space is likely to be elsewhere. What makes a study area ideal? The perfect study environment is one where you can work in distraction-free comfort. It is physically and psychologically conducive to the work at hand, without being so comfortable it puts you to sleep.

Selecting a regular study place has another advantage: mental conditioning. Think of Pavlov's famous dogs. Each time the animals were to be fed, Pavlov rang a bell. Soon, the dogs began to salivate at the sound of the bell alone. They developed a physical response to the expectation of food. They were conditioned to respond to the bell.

Similarly, you can condition yourself to study. If you use the same study spot again and again, you will begin to associate it with studying. Over time, your mind and body will become conditioned to learn whenever you enter your study area. Sitting down and getting to work will become more automatic.

Your chosen space should have adequate lighting; bright, but not glaring. It should provide a chair and desk or table. The chair should be a standard desk chair, or one you might find in a conference room or classroom. Don't study in a cushy arm chair. You will end up slouching and holding your study materials at an awkward angle, both of which can interfere with your ability to concentrate and cause muscle soreness. If you are lying back in a soft chair, especially in a warm room, you may doze off.

The work surface can be a desk or table. Whichever it is, there should be plenty of space to spread out your study materials. It should be at a comfortable height so you can study for extended periods without strain. The surrounding environment should be quiet and free from distractions and interruptions. That means the television and radio should be off, and, if you are at home, let the answering machine answer the phone. Don't park yourself in front of a picture window either; a blank wall will be less distracting. Instruct family members and coworkers not to interrupt you. Have all your study materials—calculator, notebook, extra pens, and so on—at hand so you won't have to get up to fetch something.

Schedule regular study times. It will help you get into the habit of studying and will aid the conditioning process mentioned above. Choose a time of day when you usually feel alert. Consider eating a high-protein snack beforehand so you don't get hungry.

Study sessions do not have to be marathon events. If you need a break, take one. Get up, stretch, and wander down the hall for a few minutes. Try to limit breaks to ten minutes or less. Four one-hour study sessions will prove more beneficial than one four-hour session.

Common study locations include a library, an empty conference room, or a kitchen table. Lack of the perfect study area should not keep you from the task at hand. Though a comfortable, well-lit, and distraction-free environment is best, reality may dictate other circumstances. Do your best to schedule study periods following these ideal conditions, but when it comes down to it, if life interferes, study where and when you can.

How to Study

Once you have nailed down the when and where of your study plan, it is time to focus on study techniques. By making effective use of your study time, you can cut down the amount of time needed while simultaneously increasing your comprehension, recall, test scores, and self-confidence.

Study skills are best organized by task. Thanks to the perennial fountain of students and teachers, methods have been developed for getting the most out of a textbook, taking effective notes, tricks to improve your memory, test preparation, and more. Although there are also tips and tricks for writing papers, you are not likely to need to do that in the course of certification training, so they are not covered in this book.

The key to all of these methods is your involvement. To be an effective learner, you need to be an active learner. The information that comes your way via self study and classroom activities will not stick with you just because it passes by your eyes or ears. But if you operate with the intention of making it stick by using methods that have been proven to work, you will learn and remember.

How to Read a Textbook

One of the most effective and most widely taught textbook study methods has been around since the 1940s, when it was first developed by Dr. Francis Robinson. It is called SQ3R. The acronym is derived from the five steps of the system: Survey, Question, Read, Recite, and Review. Following them will greatly increase your comprehension and recall of textbook material. They can be applied to an entire book, to a single chapter, or to any reading assignment. Let's go over the steps in order.

Survey

The first step is to survey the reading material. Just as a construction surveyor determines the lay of the land, your goal is to determine the overall shape of the book. Read the title, preface, introduction, and table of contents. Then flip through the rest of the book (or chapter), reading only the boldface headings and subheadings. Scan any illustrations to see what they are about. Surveying an entire book should take less than a half hour. When you're finished, you will have a good feel for what the book is about and how it's organized.

Question

The next step, signified by the Q in SQ3R, is to question. This very important step transforms you from a passive reader to an active one. Instead of expecting the book to feed you information, you will be able to work to extract it by focusing on learning the answers to questions you develop in advance. To develop your questions, scan back through the reading material, again focusing on the headings and subheadings. This time, rephrase them as questions. Table 10.1 shows headings from a book chapter about Visual Basic, along with questions that could be derived from them.

Read

The third step (the first R) is to read each section keeping the questions you formulated in the previous step in mind. Pay especially close attention to the first and last sentences of each paragraph. The first sentence, called the *topic sentence*, will reveal the main idea of the paragraph. The last sentence typically brings discussion of that particular idea to a conclusion.

QUICK TIP

The first time through new material, leave your highlighter pens on the desk. Otherwise you will tend to underline too much and the wrong things. Save highlighting for a later read-through, when you will be better able to identify key points.

TABLE 10.1
Headings and Questions from a Visual Basic Text

Section Heading	Question
Specifying Visual Basic Data Types	What data types are available in Visual Basic?
Creating Variables and Constants	How are variables and constants created?
Creating User-Defined Types	What is a user-defined type, and how do I create one?
Determining Scope	What determines the scope of a variable or constant?

Recite

The second of the three Rs in SQ3R stands for recite. After you read each section, *without consulting your notes or the text*, do your best to recite the questions you developed and their answers. You can do this silently or out loud. Out loud is better because it applies an additional sense, your hearing, to enhance your learning. If you cannot answer the questions from memory, look back through the text and try again. When you can answer the questions from memory, go on to the next section.

Review

The final R stands for review. This is where you begin seriously building your memory of the information. Go back over all the questions you created for all the sections you read. Try to answer them again. To add kinesthetic (touch/movement) learning, write out the questions and their answers. If you jot them down on index cards, you can them review the information anywhere, anytime you have a few spare minutes. Repetition will help solidify the information in your mind.

That is all there is to it. Next time you open a textbook remember the acronym SQ3R. Then do it. After you (S)urvey, (Q)uestion, (R)ead, (R)ecite, and (R)eview, you will know a lot more than if you had simply read the book.

How to Get the Most from a Class

Just as you can get more from a textbook by becoming an active reader, you can boost your classroom comprehension by becoming an active listener. To become an active listener in a classroom setting, you will need to prepare, pay attention, participate, and take notes.

Before Class

What you do before class dramatically affects how much you learn during class. If you prepare properly, the actual class time will be almost a review, reinforcing information you have already learned. You won't be struggling to keep up because you will have developed a good idea of what is coming and familiarized yourself with the concepts and language that are likely to arise.

* Preview the material to be covered. Before the first meeting of a new course, obtain a course outline from the professor, along with a set of objectives. Read over it to find out what will be covered. Determine exactly what you will be expected to know when the class is complete. If a textbook accompanies the course, scan through it ahead of time, using the survey method described above.

* Prior to each class session, check over the course outline to see what material is due to be covered. If you have a textbook with corresponding chapters, read it using the SQ3R method *before* class.

* Arrive early. The first few minutes of class time are often very important. During this time the instructor is likely to introduce the topic at hand and sketch the shape of the material to come. If you are busy opening your notebook and greeting

your neighbor, you will not be paying attention and you will miss out on this important information, and you will be a step behind for the remainder of the class session. It is much wiser to arrive ten or fifteen minutes beforehand to get yourself organized and mentally in gear.

During Class

* Pay attention. You cannot remember what you have not learned in the first place.
* Take notes. Research has shown that students who take notes during class remember more than those who don't, *even if they never look at those notes again.* The process of taking notes forces you to pay attention and to organize your thoughts.
* Participate in discussions. Again, this forces you to be an active listener. Besides that, you will also have the opportunity to clarify any points you find confusing. By speaking, you will also reinforce your learning by verbalizing some of what you have read and heard.

After Class

* Stay at least a few minutes late. It can be tough to pay attention when others around you are packing up their books, but those last few minutes of class are as important (if not more) than the first few. Your instructor may use them to summarize what was covered, or, if time has run short, may cram fifteen minutes of material into the last five. The end of class is also when you are likely to find out what will be covered next session and what you should do to prepare.
* Review your notes immediately after class and fill in any gaps. This will take just five or ten minutes and could save you hours later on. While you will remember most of the lecture/material for a short time, by the next day, unless you have reinforced it mentally, much of what you heard will slip away.
* In conjunction with reviewing your notes (or in lieu of, if time does not permit you to sit down with them immediately after

class), conduct a mental review of the class session. You can do this in the car on your way home or in the cafeteria. Recall what the main points of the session were and why they are important.

Note Taking 101

Taking good notes is not a hit-or-miss proposition, but a learned skill. Effective note taking will help you focus on what is being said, understand it, and recall the material later on. You can gain all of this without requiring a minute more than you will spend sitting in class anyway.

Although taking notes is not as simple as pulling out a piece of paper and recording what the instructor says, it is not much more difficult either. To begin, start each class with a fresh piece of paper and record the date and lecture title (if there is one) at the top. Then draw a vertical line about two inches from the left edge of the page, dividing it into two columns. Most of your notes will go into the second, wider column. The first column is for comments, words, and other marks that will enable you quickly to identify key sections of your notes. Little or nothing will go there until you review your notes later.

When class begins, start writing your notes. Don't try to record every word the instructor utters. Instead, aim to capture key points and subtopics, using a structure similar to outlining. Distinguish between major and minor points by indenting or underlining. Write in your own words, not the instructor's. By rephrasing what is said, you will deepen your understanding of it. The exception to this guideline is if the material is a definition, formula, or rule. In those cases, it is best to record exactly what the instructor says, to ensure accuracy.

For expediency in note recording and review, use descriptive words and phrases instead of whole sentences. You can save additional time by developing your own shorthand. To do so, substitute symbols and abbreviations for words or parts of words that appear frequently (see sidebar for shorthand suggestions). Add new shortcuts gradually, so you don't find yourself with a page of jumbled shortcuts that you cannot decode easily. Remember, your personal shorthand is intended to save you time, not add confusion. Let it develop over time.

Shorthand Substitutions

Replace *ing* with *g*: *configurg* instead of *configuring*

w/ for with: *w/ program loaded* instead of *with program loaded*

w/o for without: *w/o reformat* instead of *without reformat*

R for are, *U* for you: *U R here* instead of *you are here*

+ for and: *compile + bind first* instead of *compile and bind first*

Use digits instead for numbers: *4 principles* instead of *four principles*

< for less than or lower: *< cost* instead of *lower cost*

> for greater than or more: *> flexibility* instead of *greater flexibility*

= for is the same as: *time = money* instead of *time is money*

leave out vowels that aren't critical: *prgrm* for *program*

Deciding what to include or exclude can be challenging at first, but once you develop your skills and grow familiar with your instructor's style, it will become second nature. Try to capture the main ideas and their subtopics. Listen for key phrases that indicate important information will follow, such as:

* "The four principles are"
* "Most importantly"
* "The most frequent mistake is"
* "Always remember"
* "In conclusion"
* And of course, "will be on the test".

Through voice and body language, the instructor may give cues that key points are imminent. Watch for increased animation or a change in the pitch of the speaker's voice, which should alert you that important points are forthcoming. Pay close attention to anything that is emphasized through use of the chalkboard. If you miss something, leave a blank space in your notes so that you can fill it in later.

Review your notes as soon as possible after class. This is the time to use that left-hand column. Use it to highlight especially key points and to serve as a quick index to your notes. For example, you might mark **!** next to an important point and **?** next to something you need to clarify. Identify sections of your notes with key words describing the topic, so that you can locate them easily. Figure 10.2 shows a sample page of notes from a class about the OSI reference model.

Make sure you record your name and phone number on the inside of the front cover of your notebook. Then, if you accidentally leave it somewhere, you may get it back; otherwise a moment of inattention may cost you all your notes.

FIGURE 10.2
Sample
Lecture Notes

5/20/99
OSI·ref·mod

	7·lyrs:·Phys,·dta·lnk,·ntwrk,·trans,·sess,·present,·app
*	Pls·Do·Not·Throw·Sausage·Pizza·Away·(PDNTSPA)
	phys=bits
1	
	data·lnk·=·LLC·+·MAC
2	MAC·=·phys·addrssng
	Data·in2·frames
	Ntwrk·lyr·=·logical·addrsng
	-·IP·here
3	-·routers·opr8·here

How to Remember

Do you have a good memory or a bad memory? While the ability to recall information does vary between individuals, it is another study skill (and life skill) that you can significantly improve.

In *Learn To Be A Master Student* authors Robert Rooney and Anthony Lipuma identify three basic functions of memory: labeling information as you learn it, storing it in your brain, and recalling it. You can improve two of these functions. The third, storing, does not need enhancement. Your brain already has more storage capacity than you can possibly use in your lifetime, no matter how much information you stuff in there. Don't you wish your computer's hard drive were like that?

The labeling part of the memory process involves deliberately identifying information as you learn it. This can be accomplished through linking new information with other things you already know or by organizing it in a way that makes it easier to remember. There are several tricks you can use to improve your labeling skills, including mnemonics and memory mapping. Both will be described shortly.

Your ability to recall information improves with practice. Every time you remember a particular piece of data, your brain becomes better at retrieving it. The brain path to where it is stored becomes more clearly delineated and more deeply entrenched. The process can be compared to finding your way to a new place of employment for the first time versus finding your way there for the 21st time. That initial trip requires considerable attention and maybe a wrong turn or two. By the time you've worked there three weeks, you can practically drive there in your sleep (and some mornings it probably feels like you do).

You can also create more than one pathway to a particular piece of information. Doing so enables you to do what you would have to if you encountered a road closure on the way to work—take an alternate route. The more routes you have to work (and the more pathways you create to the information stored in your brain), the less likely it becomes that you will get stranded without reaching your destination.

GRASP

The word grasp means to lay hold of with the mind. Here's how to GRASP what you want to learn.

* (**G**)et it the first time. If you are not paying attention, you won't learn, and you cannot remember what you haven't learned.
* (**R**)emember to remember. Learn with the intention of remembering information for a long time (not just until the next exam).

✳ (**A**)ssociate new information with something you already know, or arrange it in a pattern that is easy to remember.

✳ (**S**)tudy the same information different ways to create more than one path to retrieving it.

✳ (**P**)ractice remembering. The more you recall a piece of information, the easier it will become.

Mnemonics

Remember SQ3R? That's right, it stands for Study, Question, Read, Recite, Review. Because you have linked the acronym to the process of reading a textbook, you can more easily remember the individual steps. SQ3R and GRASP are examples of mnemonic devices—memory cues that help you label and recall information. Other mnemonics you have probably encountered include: Every Good Boy Does Fine, which helps you remember the notes (EGBDF) associated with the lines of the treble clef; and ROY G. BIV for the colors of the rainbow (red, orange, yellow, green, blue, indigo, violet). Remember the verse "Thirty days hath September?" That is a mnemonic, too.

Mnemonics are powerful tools that make memorization easier, more interesting, and even fun. They also enable you to remember longer. How many years has it been since you first met good, old ROY G. BIV?

You can create your own mnemonics. Acronyms are a form of mnemonics that the computer world is awash in already. Consider WAN (Wide Area Network), RAM (Random Access Memory), IOS (Internetworking Operating System), PROM (Programmable Read Only Memory), and ISDN (Integrated Services Digital Network), just to name a few.

To create your own acronyms, consider the items you need to memorize. Can you rearrange them so that the first letters form an acronym you can remember? What if you needed to memorize the stages of the systems development process, in order? They are:

1. Requirements Stage
2. Evaluation Stage
3. Design Stage
4. Implementation Stage.

How handy that the first letters form the acronym REDI! Just remember that to develop a new internetwork, you have to get REDI first. In this example, the items needed to be recalled in order. But if they do not, feel free to play with them, rearranging them to see what you can come up with.

Another powerful type of mnemonic is rhyme. Putting information into rhyme format or to the tune of a familiar song creates a fun association that makes it easier to recall.

Another helpful memory trick is to count. For example, if you know that there are seven layers in the OSI network model, you will know to keep trying if only six come to mind at first.

The Power of Pictures

Consider using pictures to help you remember, especially if you are a visual learner (Chapter 9 explained how to determine your learning style). Visualize or actually draw a picture that illustrates a concept you want to remember. You can put yourself in the picture or not. If you can conjure up a humorous scenario, so much the better.

For example, if you study communication, you will discover that communication requires: a sender, a receiver, a message, a channel to convey the message, and feedback that informs the sender if or how the message was received. The sender transmits the message over the channel to the receiver. Anything that disrupts the smooth operation of any of the elements is called noise.

How might you turn this information into a memorable image? Here's just one of the infinite possibilities: Picture your boss and her boss talking via two tin cans connected by a string. At various points between the sender (your boss) and the receiver (her boss) the string (the channel) bulges with words (the message). Now picture yourself standing midway between the two, hoisting a chainsaw over the delicate string. Can you guess which element you represent? The noise, of course. The feedback, in this case, might be your boss's boss hurling his tin can in frustration.

Another way you can capitalize on the power of pictures is through a technique called *memory mapping*. This does not require a class in cartography or any artistic ability. If you can draw basic shapes and lines, you can create a memory map.

Memory maps are similar to other tools you may be familiar with—data flow diagrams and structure charts. All of these tools provide a way to organize information in a logical fashion by arranging it as parts of a diagram. The act of creating them helps you organize your thoughts and forces you to identify how the pieces of whatever you are mapping fit together.

To create a memory map, begin by drawing a shape of your choice, such as a circle, square, diamond, or star, in the center of a blank page. Inside the shape, write a word describing what you are mapping. For each main idea associated with the topic, draw a line extending outward from the shape. Add additional lines branching off of the main ones for associated ideas and topics. Figure 10.3 shows a memory map for the GRASP system.

FIGURE 10.3
GRASP
Memory Map

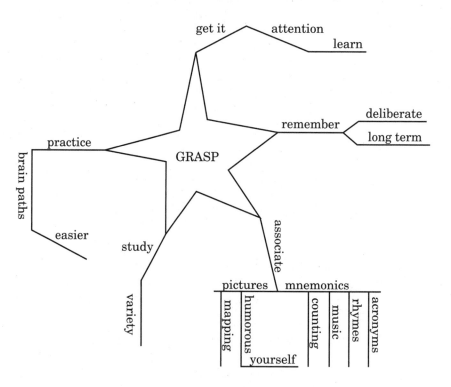

No two memory maps will look alike. Each is unique to the topic and to the person who created it. Illustrating and organizing information this way utilizes both motion and sight (visualization) to help you remember it later on.

Study Groups

Contrary to popular assumption, a study group is not a place to learn new information; it is a place to practice and reinforce what you have already learned. Depending on other group members to provide you with an introduction to something you have not studied yet is risky—it may be presented inaccurately, and once you learn something the wrong way, learning it correctly is more difficult. It is wiser to get the facts down first, then use a study group setting to reinforce them.

Study groups are good for increasing your understanding of a topic. Since no two people see things exactly the same way, another participant may be crystal clear on a concept you are struggling with and can guide you through it. You can return the favor for a different concept. You can also compare interpretations. The process of discussing subject matter will clarify material and solidify it in your mind.

Study group members can also drill each other with flash cards or exchange essay questions. This sort of interaction is very valuable when preparing for tests.

You may be able to join an existing study group, but more likely, you will have to form your own. Look for two or three individuals working on the same material (or certification) as yourself. You may find them online or through a class you are participating in.

Set regular meeting times—once a week is a common interval—and choose a site conducive to your purpose. A library may not be a good option unless there is a room you can use so your discussions won't disrupt others. An empty classroom or someone's dining room table are also possibilities. Limit meetings to about an hour per session; any longer and the extra time is likely to be spent on socializing rather than studying.

If you are preparing for certification through self study, your best bet for forming a study group is likely to be via the Internet. Prowl forums and newsgroups devoted to the topic(s) you are interested in, and consider posting a message seeking individuals interested in forming a virtual study group. You can also use the Web search engines to seek out such groups. Use the name of your certification and the phrase "study group" as search keys. One popular place to find Cisco study partners is at the **groupstudy.com** Web site, where study groups have been known to form spontaneously, and the webmaster is quite willing to set up virtual study rooms as needed. Figure 10.4 shows the study area of the site.

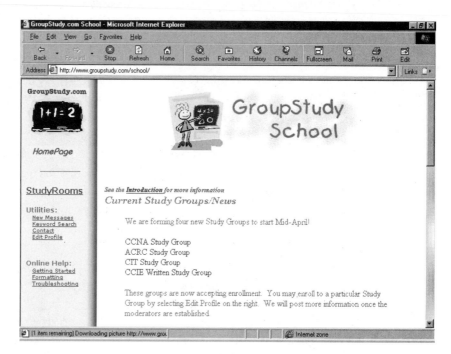

Self Quizzing

One of the simplest ways to practice recalling information is via the self quiz. Talk about versatility and convenience—you can self quiz almost anywhere. You can do it with spiffy software, audio tape, or cheap 3 × 5 index cards. You can time yourself, or not. How often do you get the chance to make up your own questions for a test?

Depending upon your choice of certification and how deep your pockets are, you can purchase quizzes that other people have made specifically for your certification.

Figure 10.5 shows a screen from BeachFront Quizzer's preparation package for Cisco certification.

Many of these prepackaged quizzes are available in software format. Others come in workbooks. This book's resource section includes contact information for the most widely known vendors of Cisco certification preparation software. Their product lines are always evolving, so visit their Web sites or telephone their offices for information on current offerings.

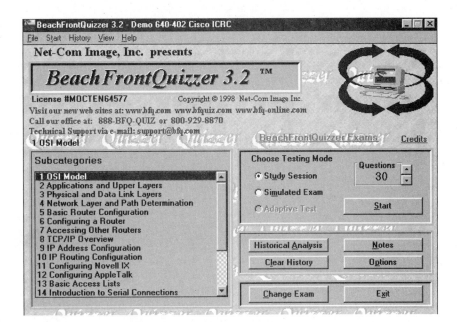

FIGURE 10.5
BeachFront
Quizzer's
Preparation
Program for ICRC

Besides Cisco-specific software, there are a number of shareware programs that allow you to create quizzes on any topic of your choice. These can be especially useful if commercial programs are too expensive or unavailable for the material you wish to practice. Figure 10.6 shows WinFlash, by Open Window (**www.openwindow.com**). A free trial version is available on the company's Web site.

If you prefer to go low tech, you can create a set of flash cards using 3 × 5 index cards. Write the question on the front of the card and the correct answer on the back. If you keep a deck of these cards on hand, you can sneak in practice whenever it is convenient to do so. When you think you have one set of cards down cold, put them aside and start another. Come back to the first set later, and see how much you remember.

Books on tape are becoming popular with people on the go. You can create a quiz on tape to listen to during your daily commute or during exercise workouts. To do so, prepare a list of questions and answers. Then insert a fresh tape into your tape recorder and press record. Read a question aloud, let the tape roll for a few seconds (however long you want to allow yourself to answer the question you just read), then read the answer aloud. Repeat the procedure for each question on your list. When you play back the quiz later, try to answer the questions before the recorded answer plays. Before you record an entire quiz, run a test batch of a few questions to verify that the tape recorder is set up and operating properly.

FIGURE 10.6
WinFlash
Self-quizzing
Software

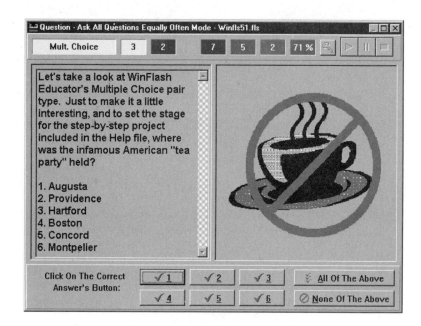

Taking Tests

If you asked learners to choose the aspect of the educational process that causes them the most anxiety, the overwhelming majority would cite tests. Why? Because a test presents an opportunity for failure, and nobody likes to fail. In fact, fear of failure sometimes leads people who know the material cold to blank out on test day, and just what they feared most would happen, does.

Consider what will happen to you if you do fail a test. Will your coworkers burst into laughter when you return to the office? Will your spouse or lover leave you? Will you lose your job and, as a result, be unable to pay your mortgage, which will then cause you to lose your house and end up lying penniless, in a gutter and alone some cold night? Of course not.

So, putting first things first, don't blow this test thing out of proportion. If you do not pass the test, you will probably have to take it again; big deal. It might not be your idea of a good time, but it is hardly life-shattering. The fact is, if you prepare effectively, you are infinitely more likely to succeed than fail.

Before the Test

What constitutes effective preparation? Most important, it does not begin the night before the exam. As discussed earlier in this chapter, cramming is an ineffective learning tool and only marginally successful as a last-minute act of desperation. Pull an all-nighter and your mind may be stuffed with facts, but they will be shrouded in a fatigue-induced fog. When the fog dissipates, the facts are likely to go with it.

If, on the other hand, you have been studying throughout a course, you are already halfway prepared for the final exam because you've GRASPed the majority of the information and only have to review and practice recalling it the way the test will ask you to.

The first step is to find out as much as possible about the format and content of the exam. Questions to answer include:

*   What will you be expected to know?
*   Which question format will be utilized—multiple choice, essay questions, or true-false? Currently most computer certification tests are multiple choice.
*   How long will you have to complete the test?
*   Will you be able to return to questions later if you skip over them?
*   Will points be subtracted for wrong answers?

You should be able to obtain the answers to these questions from your certification sponsor, instructor, and/or testing center. Many of these questions are also answered in Chapter 11 of this book. Once you have identified the characteristics of the particular test, you can tailor your review methods accordingly.

Review the material you have identified as likely to be on the test. Try to guess what questions will appear on the test, then practice answering them. You can practice by reciting aloud, creating written or recorded self tests, or using commercially available self-testing software and certification preparation guides. If you belong to a study group, quiz each other and discuss your answers.

QUICK TIP

Pay special attention to vocabulary and terminology words. Make certain you know exactly what they mean. If you do not understand a question, you won't be able to answer it.

Develop an overall test strategy, depending on the type of exam. The following advice focuses on multiple-choice exams, the most common format of current Cisco certification test questions. These exams count an unanswered question the same way as an incorrect answer. If you will not be penalized for wrong answers (as opposed to skipping the question entirely) then it pays to guess when you don't know the correct answer.

On most exams you will be able to mark questions to return to later. When this is the case, be sure to MARK the questions or you will NOT be able to return to them. Answer the questions you are certain of first, marking the more challenging ones, and then return to the marked questions when you have finished the easy ones. This strategy enables you to answer a larger percentage of the questions and to answer the easiest ones right away.

The night before, do a brief review and remind yourself that you have prepared and are as ready as you are going to be. Don't stress yourself out poring over your notes again and again. Instead, spend the evening in some pleasant, relaxing way, then get a good night's sleep so you will be rested and ready to excel.

The Day of the Test

On the day of the test, allow yourself plenty of time to arrive at the test site. Would you rather arrive at the last minute, adrenaline pumping from the stress of too many red lights, or ten or fifteen minutes early, time you can easily fill with a final review of your note cards or trip to the restroom?

Make certain to bring several forms of identification, including a photo ID, and, of course, if you have not already provided it, payment.

If you feel tense or anxious, apply a few relaxation techniques. One of the most basic is breathing. Take a deep breath, filling not just your chest, but every nook and cranny of your insides all the way down to your abdomen. Inhale from your navel, like a baby does. Exhale slowly, and feel your muscles relaxing as your breath carries the tension out of your body. Repeat the breathing several times.

When the test begins, follow your preplanned strategy.

* If the test format is suitable, remember to go through and answer the easy questions first.
* Pay close attention to instructions. Are you supposed to select just one answer or all answers that apply?
* Read each question carefully, and twice. It is easy to misread a question and end up with the wrong answer as a result. It is also a waste and something you can avoid.
* Be alert for modifiers like *always*, *never*, *not*, and *except* that can radically affect the meaning of the question.
* Mentally answer the question *before* reading the answer choices. Then look for the choice that most accurately reflects your answer. This can spare you unnecessary confusion created by the test itself.
* If you don't know the answer, make an educated guess (see sidebar).
* If you finish before the time limit, and the software permits it (which is not always the case) go back over the test and verify your answers. But *don't* change an answer unless you have good reason to believe it is wrong. Research indicates that when we are in doubt, our first guess is usually our best.

If other people are taking the exam at the same time, don't pay any attention to when they finish. Just because others are done before you does not mean that they will end up with a better score. Correspondingly, if you finish first, it does not mean you must have missed something. Take your time, keeping an eye on the exam clock if there is a time limit, and concentrate on regurgitating what you have learned. If you have prepared using effective techniques, such as the ones detailed in this chapter, you have nothing to worry about.

Making an Educated Guess

If you find yourself facing a question you just don't know the answer to, consider guessing. If there are four possible choices, you automatically have a 25-percent chance of randomly selecting the correct answer. Apply some guessing techniques, and the odds shoot upward in your favor.

Successful guessing relies heavily on the process of elimination. For that reason, the first step is to eliminate any choices that are clearly wrong. If you have four answers to choose from, and you can discard two of them as incorrect, you've gone from a one in four chance of picking the right answer to a one in two chance.

Unless your exam format allows more than one answer choice for each question (which is unusual), "all of the above" is basically equivalent to "more than one of the above." If "all of the above" is an option, and you can see at least two correct answers, then choose it.

Sometimes you will find that, in the course of presenting the question and answers, one test item will provide hints that can help you answer another. Be alert for these and use them when you find them.

Many test-taking experts advise that if you have no idea which choice is correct, and "all of the above" is an option, you should choose "all of the above." By the same token, if you cannot decide between two similar answers, choose the one that gives the most complete information.

A Half Dozen Ways to Beat Procrastination—Today

Effective study techniques are powerful productivity boosters—if you use them. But if the procrastinator's mantra—"I'll do it tomorrow"—starts playing in your head, it can wreak havoc on your certification plans. Procrastination often masquerades as some other, ostensibly legitimate, demand for your time. Only on close examination is the disguise pierced. The following are examples of what you can do to the keep the procrastination beast on a leash.

Study 15 Minutes a Day

For some, unfathomable reason, when it's time to study, the laundry in the corner suddenly becomes more urgent than the new material. So does mowing the lawn. Anything that delays the dreaded moment of sitting down and beginning becomes more attractive than work.

Getting started doesn't have to be so difficult. Set yourself a daily deadline by which you must sit down and commence 15 minutes of studying. That's right, a mere 15 minutes.

When that deadline arrives, force yourself into your study space and work until the time is up. The method's magic is that once you get going, you won't want to stop! You are virtually guaranteed to continue long beyond 15 minutes and accomplish plenty.

Put Procrastination to Work for You

Make procrastination your slave instead of your master. When you are reluctant to begin a particular project, consider other study tasks you could be doing instead. Is your personal certification plan current? Have you reviewed your vocabulary list lately? Why not go back and draw a memory map for that concept you covered last week? Even if you don't get to the project you really ought to be doing today, other valuable tasks will be completed: there really is nothing like procrastination for getting things done. And once you begin, you just might find yourself picking up the work you are avoiding and completing that as well.

Quell Household Distractions

People who study at home know what it is like: the nearby refrigerator seems to call your name. Friends and family telephone to chat just as you settle in to study. You are wearing your last pair of underwear and really should run the laundry through.

While it is certainly the prerogative (and even pleasure) of someone who studies at home to tend to a chore during a break, don't let this can become a should. As in I should do this chore or I ought to do that one because I am right here and it needs to be done.

During study hours you are not at home—you are at work. If the refrigerator is a problem, weaken its pull by stocking it with lettuce and fruit instead of high-fat treats. When callers disrupt your concentration, let the answering machine pick up or simply offer to return calls later. If tasks, such as piled-up dishes, beg attention, imagine how you would respond if your study space were uptown at the library instead of upstairs. Would you drive home and suds up or leave them for later? Save your chores and errands for after study time. They won't go anywhere.

Respect What You're Doing

Frequently, adult learners give their educational efforts a back seat to everything else and consequently get little done. The logic goes something like this: It is not that important, after all, I do it out of choice, and I already have a job.

The person who lets this thought pattern continue is placing serious limits on his or her success. Your certification goals are meaningful and valuable. You are just fortunate (and clever) enough to be in charge of your own future. Education and professional advancement are something you have decided to go after. Don't let insecurity stop you!

It may help to review your accomplishments. Go over your personal certification plan and review what you have already achieved. Revisit your reasons for pursuing Cisco certification in the first place. Count your successes and see how you can build on them.

When you interact with others, don't be afraid to talk about your educational accomplishments and struggles or that troublesome exam. To become a confident and successful student, you must act and feel like one.

Get Regular

While a flexible schedule is overtly a plus, a regular routine will ensure productivity. Identify certain hours to study every week. You can pick how many and which ones, but decide on a core set of hours, with others you can add or omit as needed. Instruct members of your household not to interrupt you during those times unless there is blood or fire involved.

Have a designated study space and go there during your study time; your equipment and supplies will be at hand and you will become conditioned to work when you are in that space. If you have children, arrange child care during your scheduled hours or plan to study when they are in bed or at school. Alternatively, study at work, the library, or another site away from home.

Entering the Zone

Imagine an ideal performance state, a "zone of productivity" where your learning flows unimpeded as if from a greased mechanism. It is a lofty aspiration, but you can certainly make strides in that direction, starting today. After all, it will only take 15 minutes.

Putting It All Together

Keep in mind that there are many study methods available. The methods you have read about here are solid, specific approaches to common learning tasks. They are by no means the only solutions available. If you want to learn additional study methods, check out your local bookstore and library for books about studying.

Thanks to the many colleges and universities connected to the Internet, you can also access study tips via the Web. Educational institutions around the world have put study advice online for your free, 24-hour perusal. Virginia Polytechnic Institute (**www.ucc.vt.edu/stdysk/stdyhlp.html**); University of California, Berkeley (**128.32.89.153/CalRENHP.html**); the University of Texas (**www.utexas.edu/student/lsc/handouts/stutips.html**); and Dartmouth (**www.dartmouth.edu/admin/acskills/index.html#study**) are good places to start. Figure 10.7 shows Virginia Polytechnic's Web-based study skills resource center.

At first it may feel like the effort needed to be an active learner requires more time and energy than it is worth. Once you get into the swing of it, you will find that the time you put into learning how to learn will be paid back ten times over; you will be able to remember more and maybe even study less.

FIGURE 10.7
Virginia Polytechnic
Offers Study
Advice Via the
Web

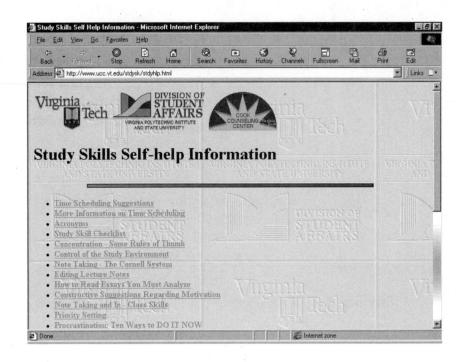

FIGURE 10.7 Virginia Polytechnic Offers Study Advice Via the Web

CHAPTER 11

All About Cisco Tests

With the exception of CCIE lab exams, Cisco certification tests are administered through Sylvan Prometric testing centers. Over 1200 of these centers serve more than 80 countries worldwide. Sylvan Prometric provides testing services for many of the best known certification programs. If you have taken a certification test before, you probably took it at a Sylvan testing center.

Registering for an Exam

When you are ready to register for exam, there are two ways you can reserve your spot. The first is to call Sylvan Prometric's Cisco testing phone number, which is (800) 204-3926. This number works in United States and Canada. Phone numbers from outside United States are listed in the sidebar, but you can also find them through Sylvan Prometric's Web site at **www.2test.com**. If you prefer, you can choose instead to register online through **www.2test.com** (shown in Figure 11.1). In addition to allowing online registration, this Web site incorporates a test center locator that lets you find the test site most convenient to you.

FIGURE 11.1
Sylvan Prometric's
Registration
Web Site

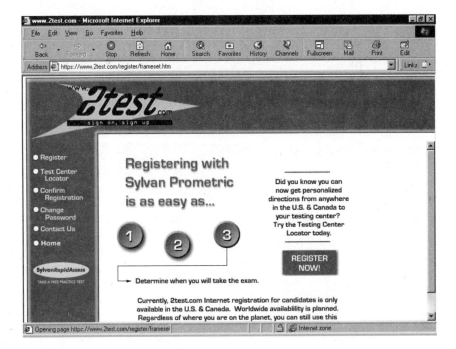

Whichever way you register, you will be asked for an ID number. This number will be used each time you register for an exam and allows Cisco to track your progress. In the United States, the testing candidate's Social Security number is usually used. However, Sylvan can assign you a different ID number if you request one. Take care to use that same ID number every time you register for an exam. Use care when providing your address information as well, as that is what Cisco will use to contact you, send you welcome kits, and so on. If you register via telephone, have the clerk read your information back to you to guarantee that it is correct.

Cisco Certification Test Registration Phone Numbers

North America

United States and Canada (800) 204-3926

South America

South America and Central America (612) 820-5200

Europe

Austria 0660 85 82

Belgium 0800 1 7414

England +44 1 81 607 9090

France +33 1 42 89 31 22

Germany +49 2159 923 30 / 0130 83 97 08

Italy 1678 7 8441

Netherlands 06 022 75 84

Switzerland 155 69 66

Australia and Pacific Rim

Australia +61 2 9414 3666

Japan +81 3 3269 9620 / 0120-387-737

There is no required waiting period between registering for a Cisco exam and taking it. However, testing center seats do fill up, so it is a good idea to reserve your spot several weeks in advance. It is also a good idea to verify the accuracy of the reservation several days after you make it. Confirm that you are registered for the test you intend to take, and at the time you specified.

If you fail an exam you can retake it the same day if there is space available in a testing center. There is no limit on how many times you may retake an exam.

The test center will download your exam the night before your scheduled appointment. On exam day, you can call the test center as soon as they open to verify that your exam has been downloaded and is ready for you. Although download failures are rare, this can save you traveling to the center only to find no test awaiting once you arrive.

Bring two forms of identification, one of which must be a photo ID, to the testing center with you. You will be provided with a small wipeoff board, like a whiteboard, along with a marker to use for notes and calculations during the exam. You can ask for paper and pencil instead, which many people find more comfortable to work with. Whichever you use, you will be required to return it before leaving the testing center.

QUICK TIP

Cisco certification exams are closed book. No notes or other resources, including a calculator, can be taken into the exam room with you. You will also need to leave any last-minute study materials with the receptionist. To avoid forgetting them when you leave, consider leaving your car keys/bus pass as well. This will make it impossible to depart without your other belongings.

You will take the test in a room dedicated to that purpose. There may be other people taking different tests in the same room. Exam rooms are typically monitored via video camera to deter cheating. When you sit down in front of computer containing your exam, the test administrator will log you in using your unique Sylvan testing ID.

Before taking the certification exam, you will have the option of completing a practice test to familiarize yourself with the testing software. This is really necessary only if you have not used practice tests as part of your preparation, or if you feel uncomfortable with computer-based testing.

When you finish the exam, your score will appear on the screen. Do not continue past that point until you have your official score sheet in hand. Although it is extremely unlikely that your score will be lost, better safe than sorry.

After your exam, Sylvan Prometric transmits your results to Cisco where they are entered into your candidate record. Your records may be updated within a few hours or it may take up to several days.

Beta Exams

When Cisco is getting ready to introduce a new exam, it often does so by making a preliminary version available. These are called *beta exams*. They are available through the standard Sylvan Prometric outlets and typically are free, or on occasion half-price. Candidates who do not want to wait for the final version, or who want to cut their certification costs, often find beta exams attractive.

Although beta exams may differ from the final version of the exam, passing one still counts toward certification. If you take a beta exam, you will not receive a score printout immediately following the exam—you will have to wait six–eight weeks for one to be mailed to you from Cisco. Beta exams are available for a limited time, typically a month or less. Career certification beta exams are announced on Cisco's beta exam page at **www.cisco.com/warp/public/10/wwtraining/ certprog/testing/beta_exams.htm**. CCIE beta exams are announced on the CCIE news page at **www.cisco.com/warp/public/625/ccie/whatsnew.html**.

Exam and Question Formats

All Cisco certifications exams (other than lab exams) are administered via computer. Each test has a specific number of questions, time limit, and passing score (see Tables). These change from time to time as Cisco updates its exams, so don't count on information you receive from previous candidates as 100% accurate. You will be reminded of the parameters for your particular exam at the beginning of your session. Table 11.1 shows the exam details as this book went to press.

Exam ID	Name	$	# Questions	Length (Minutes)
CCNA Exams				
640-407	Cisco Certified Network Associate (CCNA)	100	70	90
640-410	Cisco Certified Network Associate (CCNA) WAN Sw	100	63	60
CCNP R/S Exams				
640-403	Advanced Cisco Router Configuration (ACRC)	100	72	90
640-404	Cisco LAN Switch Configuration (CLSC)	100	70	60
640–405	Configuring, Monitoring, & Troubleshooting Dialup Services (CMTD)	100	64	90
640-406	Cisco Internetwork Troubleshooting (CIT) 3.0	100	69	60
640-409	Foundation Routing & Switching (FRS)	200	132	165
CCNP WAN Sw Exams				
640-419	Multiband Switch & Service Configuration (MSSC)	100	100	120
640-425	BPX Switch & Service Configuration (BSSC)	100	101	120
640-411	MGX ATM Concentrator Configuration (MACC)	100		
640-422	Cisco StrataView Plus (CSVP)	100	70	60
640-451	StrataView Installation and Operation (SVIO)			

continued

Exam ID	Name	$	# Questions	Length (Minutes)
CCNP Specializations (optional and still being rolled out)				
640-442	Managing Cisco Network Security (MCNS)	100		
640-443	Managing Cisco Routed Internetworks (MCRC)	100	89	90
640-444	Managing Cisco Switched Internetworks (MCSI)	100		
640-445	SNA Configuration for Multiprotocol Administrators (SNAM)	100		
640-446	Campus ATM Solutions (CATM)	100		
640-447	Cisco Voice over Frame Relay ATM (CVOICE)	100	69	105
640-450	Cisco Data Link Switching Plus (DLSWP)			
CCDA Exam				
640-441	Designing Cisco Networks (DCN)			
CCDP R/S Exams				
640-403	Advanced Cisco Router Configuration (ACRC)	100	72	90
640-404	Cisco LAN Switch Configuration (CLSC)	100	70	60
640-405	Conifiguring, Monitoring, & Troubleshooting Dialup Services (CMTD)	100	64	90
640-025	Cisco Internetwork Design (CID)	100	100	120
640-409	Foundation Routing & Switching (FRS)	200	132	165

continued

Exam ID	Name	$	# Questions	Length (Minutes)
CCDP WAN Sw Exam				
640-413	Designing Switched WAN Voice Solutions (DSWVS)	100	60	60
CCIE Qualification Exams				
350-001	CCIE Routing & Switching Qualification Exam	200	100	120
350-004	CCIE ISP Dial Qualification Exam	200	100	120
350-007	CCIE WAN Switching Qualification Exam	200	123	120

QUICK TIP

Just prior to taking an exam, brush up on exam strategies by reviewing the "Taking Tests" section in Chapter 10.

There are several types of questions you will encounter:

✳ Multiple choice with a single answer
✳ Multiple choice with multiple answers
✳ Freeform response
✳ Scenario based.

Single-answer multiple choice questions are very straightforward—read the question and choose the best answer from the list of possible answers. If you don't know the answer to a question of this type, eliminate the choices you know are wrong, and choose from what is left.

Multiple-answer multiple choice questions are a bit trickier since you will not have the benefit of knowing how many of the answers should be picked. Instead, you will be directed to "mark all correct answers."

Again, use the process of elimination. For example, if you see that all of the above is a choice, and one of the other options is definitely wrong, you can eliminate two of the possible choices right away. To keep track your progress use your marker board/note paper to write down a shorthand version of each answer. As you consider each answer option, cross it out if it's wrong, or put a check mark next to it if it's correct. This makes it possible to jump around in the list of answers without missing any or losing track of choices you have already made. Read these questions carefully! Sometimes you will be given the number of answers you should select as part of the question, such as "which three functions are performed by the OSI transport layer?"

Freeform response questions are usually used to test your knowledge of command syntax. You might be asked to type in the command to accomplish a particular task.

When answering this type of question, be very careful to avoid typos and to spell the command and its parameters correctly. Misspelling the command will cause the question to be scored as wrong.

QUOTE

Learning vs Cramming

The most common mistake I see people making is thinking they can learn enough through study questions, quizzes and "brain dumps" to pass these exams. Cisco exams demand understanding of subtle distinctions and fine points. Many of the study questions out there are written by people who don't have the understanding to write good questions in the first place. Caveat emptor!

—Pamela Forsyth, CCIE, CNX, Master CNE, MCSE, and other certifications

Scenario questions attempt to add a level of real-world complexity to exam questions. A typical scenario question will present you with a paragraph or two about a specific networking situation, followed by a series of questions related to that scenario. Often the scenario will be accompanied by an exhibit—a diagram of a network configuration, for example. The questions that are based on a particular scenario may be in any of the previously described formats.

Sample Exam Questions

Question 1. NBT would be recommended in which one of the following scenarios?

a   When IPX is being used in a WAN environment
b   Anytime a window application is being used
c   When IP is being used in a WAN environment
d   Only for small diameter networks
e   When configuring each computer with an IP address is not practical.

Answer:

c   When IP is being used in a WAN environment, NetBIOS over TCP/IP (NBT), NetBIOS is not routable.

Question 2. In which of one of the following scenarios might LAPB be appropriate?

a   digital links
b   any WAN link
c   Frame Relay
d   dedicated leased lines
e   unreliable analog lines

Answer:

e   unreliable analog lines

Question 3. If an organization required a highly reliable internetworking environment in several US locations to carry high volume traffic, and money was not an issue, which of the following would you recommend?

a   X.25
b   Frame Relay
c   ISDN
d   ATM
e   T1

Answer:

d   ATM

Question 4. Type the command to display the list of networks Router_A has a path to.

Answer:

Router_A#

Sample questions © Copyright CCprep.com

CCIE Lab Exams

The CCIE Lab exam is a challenging hands-on assessment your internetworking skills. It costs $1,000 US and stretches over two days. Before you can sign up for the lab exam you must pass the CCIE qualification exam. Unlike the computer-administered exams, CCIE lab exams are only offered through Cisco locations. CCIE Routing & Switching candidates have their choice of numerous locations. Availability of the CCIE ISP Dial and CCIE WAN Switching lab exams is much more limited (see sidebar). The exams are standardized among sites and selecting the location is a matter of geographical preference.

CCIE Lab Locations

Routing & Switching Labs

San Jose, California USA
(800) 553 NETS or (408) 526-8063
ccie_ucsa@cisco.com

Research Triangle Park, North Carolina USA
(800) 553 NETS or (408) 527-7177
ccie_ucsa@cisco.com

Halifax, Nova Scotia, Canada
(800) 553-NETS or (902) 492-8811
ccie_ucsa@cisco.com

North Sydney, New South Wales, Australia
+61 2 9935 4128
ccie_apt@cisco.com

Brussels, Belgium
+32 2 778 46 70
ccie_emea@cisco.com

Beijing, China
+86 1 0648 92398
ccie_apt@cisco.com

Tokyo, Japan
+81 3 5219 6409
ccie@cisco.co.jp

Capetown, South Africa
+32 2 778 46 70
ccie_emea@cisco.com

ISP Dial Labs
Halifax, Nova Scotia, Canada
(800) 553-NETS or (902) 492-8811
ccie_ucsa@cisco.com

San Jose, California USA
(800) 553 NETS or (408) 526-8063
ccie_ucsa@cisco.com

WAN Switching Labs
San Jose, California USA
(800) 553 NETS or (408) 526-8063
ccie_ucsa@cisco.com

Stockley Park, United Kingdom
+32 2 778 46 70
ccie_emea@cisco.com

According to Jeff Buddemeier, Cisco's technical lead for the CCIE program, the lab setup incorporates five routers and a catalyst switch. Each candidate has his own rack and patch panel. You will also receive a set of Cisco documentation to use throughout the exam. You cannot bring any other notes or documentation into the exam with you.

Your first task will be to create a network to specification. This will take up all of the first day and half of the second. Halfway through the second day, while you are out of the room, the exam proctor will insert faults into your network, and you will have to find and fix them, as well as be able to document the problems and their resolutions.

There are a total of 100 possible points on the exam. To pass, you must achieve a score of 80 or better. You must achieve a passing score on each section of the exam to be allowed to progress to the next. For example, a perfect score on the first day would be 45 points. You have to earn at least 30 of them to be allowed to return for the first part of day two.

Table 11.2 shows the scoring breakdown.

Day	Task	Points	Total so far	Min score to continue
1	build	45	45	30
2 (part 1)	build	30	75	55
2 (part II)	troubleshooting	25	100	80 or better to pass

The lab starting time varies depending upon location, but will be somewhere between 8:00 a.m. and 9:00 a.m. each day and run for 7½ hours. There is a half hour break for lunch. A proctor will be in the room to clarify questions and handle any emergencies that may arise, but basically you are on your own.

The failure rate for this exam is high. According to Buddemeier, only about 20% of candidates pass it on the first attempt. On average, CCIE candidates require two to three lab exams before they earn a passing score. Think of your first time through as a learning experience, and if you manage to pass, that is a bonus. There is no limit on the number of times you can retake the exam.

As with all certification exams, lab exam content and structure are subject to change, so when you are ready to consider taking the lab exam, it's best to get the latest information from Cisco. Cisco's Web site contains specific instructions about how to prepare for each of the CCIE lab and qualification exams:

* CCIE R/S: **www.cisco.com/warp/public/625/ccie/routing. html**
* CCIE WAN Switching: **www.cisco.com/warp/public/625/ ccie/cciwa_ds.htm**
* CCIE ISP Dial: **www.cisco.com/warp/public/625/ccie/ isp_dial.html**.

It cannot be stressed enough that you must get lots of hands-on practice if you hope to pass this exam. If you do not have equipment to practice on at work, you will have to set up a home lab (see Chapter 9) or find another way to gain access to the equipment.

When taking any of these exams, keep the big picture in perspective. Your goal is to obtain a particular Cisco certification. Part of that may well require taking one or more exams more than once. If you fail an exam, instead of berating yourself, turn it into a learning experience that will help you pass next time. Immediately upon leaving the testing room, sit down with pen and paper and write down everything you remember about the exam, particularly the areas you were weak in. As soon as possible, review these areas using your study materials. If the materials you have do not adequately cover the topics, get additional materials that do. Then reschedule the exam and take it again. Keep your goal of certification in mind and persist until you have accomplished it. And if you are determined and stick with it, you will achieve your goal of becoming Cisco certified.

PART 3

Utilize Your Certification to the Max

CHAPTER 12

Advertising Your New Status

You have planned, studied, passed the tests, filed your application, signed whatever you needed to sign, and been granted the Cisco certification you chose. Give yourself a well-deserved pat on the back, but don't rest on your laurels. Choosing the right certification and obtaining it is 80 percent of the job. The other 20 percent is making the effort to capitalize on what you have already accomplished. Many professionals before you have discovered ways to put their certifications to work. By following what others have done, and perhaps adding a few inventive flourishes of your own, you can maximize the positive effect certification can have on your career.

Looking Good in Print

Since the day Cisco first launched the CCIE certification, individuals who earned the designation have been granted the right to use the CCIE logo. Logos for all the other Cisco certifications were in the works as this book went to press. These logos are professionally designed and are protected and marketed by Cisco Systems, which promotes understanding of the logo's significance to your potential customers, to employers, and to others throughout the computer industry. This creates brand recognition, something marketing organizations across industries work to achieve. By utilizing these logos to promote yourself, you can benefit from the effort and financing that have gone into the sponsor's logo program. Doing so is one of the easiest ways to advertise your status as a Cisco certified professional, and can help inspire the confidence of potential clients and employers.

Certification logos can be used on your business cards, resume, marketing materials, Web site, e-mail signature, and almost anywhere else you can think of. To prevent misuse and abuse of these logos, you will receive guidelines for proper usage. Although such control over your use of the logos may feel annoying, it is really for your benefit as much as for Cisco's. By assuring that these logos are used in a professional and consistent manner, Cisco is protecting and building their value.

Logos generally are provided in several formats. This makes it easier for you to use them for various purposes, and you end up with a more professional result. It is possible to convert files between graphical file formats using special utility file conversion programs, but some resolution may be lost, which is one reason certification sponsors generally offer logos in various formats. Electronic formats, such as GIF, JPG, EPS, and TIF, can be imported into word processing, desktop publishing, graphics (such as Web design), and other computer programs. Typically the menu command to use will be some variation of **Insert|Picture** or **Import|Image**.

Camera-ready logos, another format for logo distribution, are, as the name implies, suitable for photographing, with good results. They are provided in a high-resolution, sharply printed format and can be physically pasted directly onto originals before reproduction. These are most often used on promotional materials, such as brochures, that are run off in quantity by a printer.

Commercial printers sometimes prefer to receive graphics in a particular format—the one that works best with their system. If you are having the logo included on your business card or on other commercially printed materials, ask the printing company which format will produce the best results. They may prefer camera-ready or a particular file type.

Besides incorporating a certification logo on your personal materials, consider the marketing potential it offers your employer. If you are the first person at your company to obtain Cisco certification, by doing so you have added value to the company's service offerings. Cisco resellers need multiple certified individuals on staff to qualify for various reseller levels, and thus will benefit substantially from your certification. Your company may well want to advertise your new status for its own benefit.

Consider a company specializing in expanding existing networks that can claim "Cisco Certified Internetwork Expert (CCIE) on staff," or "Cisco Certified Design Professional (CCDP) on staff." Such announcements would, of course, be accompanied by reproductions of the relevant logo. This type of employer marketing of your certification is a win-win situation. The employer wins through gaining increased credibility, which may well lead to added revenue, and you gain by boosting your value to your employer and earning a reputation for yourself as an expert.

Marketing Magic Via the Internet

More than a few publications rave about the potential of the Internet and World Wide Web as marketing tools, and most of the claims are true. The Web is a versatile medium. It is affordable, accessible, and for most computer professionals, a do-it-yourself opportunity, especially for computer-related services and products, such as your services as a computer professional. It provides access to an incredible number of interested potential customers/employers, and recruiters and employers use it as a tool to uncover talent and fill positions. You can use it to market yourself as a computer professional, to establish a professional reputation, and to display your talent to those who might be interested in compensating you handsomely for it.

The potential of the Web as a marketing medium to advertise your certified status is limited only by the extent of your creativity. To begin with, you can use it to:

* Communicate with your clients via electronic mailings
* Draw interested clients and employers to you by creating a Web site
* Make professional networking a pleasure
* Establish name recognition and expert status for yourself.

Information on posting your resume online is included in Chapter 14, which covers how to use certification to land a new job.

You can do all this with minimum financial outlay and a bit of your time. Best of all, the Web is an enjoyable medium to work with, and even though you will be using it for professional purposes, the process can be as much (or more) fun as it is work.

A Quick Guide to Getting Connected

You don't need an ISDN connection, high-powered server, or any other high-end equipment to turn the Internet into your personal marketing tool. As a computer professional, you may already be

Internet savvy and able to find your way onto the information superhighway with your eyes closed. If that is the case, skip ahead. For those who are not already logged in, here is a quick overview on getting connected from home.

The computer you use to access the Internet does not need to be especially powerful or cutting edge. Your current personal computer will probably do the job nicely. If you don't have a computer at home, it may well be time to buy one. A PC with a 486 or higher processor, 16MB of RAM at the bare minimum (more is better), and loads (preferably a gigabyte or more) of disk storage will do the job, but seriously consider a Pentium II or higher so your investment won't be totally obsolete before you finish unpacking it. Apple fans might prefer the iMac, which comes adequately prepared to connect to the net. Whichever system you choose, don't skimp on disk space. Between the needs of your Web browser software and the bounty of interesting files you will want to download, you will need plenty of storage at your disposal. The modem should be capable of 28.8Kbps (Kilobits per second) or higher. Although it is possible to travel the Web using a modem as slow as 2400 baud, doing so may test the limits of your sanity. Imagine watching a full-length feature movie at less than a tenth of its normal playing speed, and you will have a good understanding of why modem speed is so important.

The modem can be internal or external to your computer. Which one you choose is largely a matter of personal preference. Internal modems don't take any extra desk space and are slightly lower in price. However, you will have to open your computer system unit to install it, and some people experience hardware conflicts that can be difficult to track down and resolve. External modems give you the benefit of pretty flashing lights to reassure you that your connection has not crashed, which can be comforting during a long download. They are also easier to install. You just connect them to the serial port in the back of your computer; there is no need to open the system unit.

The telephone line can be the same one you use for everyday household conversations. You will connect your modem to the wall jack in the same way you would a telephone, using the same type of phone cord. People who spend a lot of time connected to the Net (which is not hard to do with all that interesting stuff out there!) often add a separate phone line so their home phone number is not tied up for hours on end.

If you have call waiting, set up your modem to dial *70 each time it dials. This will disable the call waiting for the duration of the call, and prevent an incoming call from causing your modem to disconnect abruptly.

The final thing you will need to get connected is access to the Internet. You get this by purchasing a subscription from a company that provides this service. When you dial the company, your call is answered by one of their computers, and linked to the Internet via a high-speed connection. The going rate runs about $20 a month, although you will find rates that run slightly higher or lower. The fee usually includes e-mail and space on the company's computer for your personal Web page.

Companies that connect you to the Internet come in two varieties: online services and Internet service providers (ISPs). Online services are company-run "virtual communities" that only subscribers can fully access. They provide topical discussion forums; software repositories; news, weather, and business feeds; and a host of other electronic services, including Internet access. The Internet access is sometimes called an Internet gateway. The online services with the most subscribers are America Online (AOL), CompuServe, and Microsoft Network (MSN). ISPs, on the other hand, provide Internet access only. MCI, AT&T, and Sprint are three popular providers.

Each of the two subscriptions has its pros and cons. Online services provide an oasis of relative calm within the chaos of the Internet. Within the service, information is organized by topic, and some degree of control over content is exercised, which means that rude, nasty individuals are usually booted off the service. They also have extensive technical support available for people who need it, which can be very important when you are first starting out.

ISPs, on the other hand, do one thing and one thing only—provide Internet access. You will usually find an Internet connection via an ISP to be significantly faster than one through an online service's gateway. And once you are connected, you are usually pretty much on your own. For many people, especially IT professionals, that is exactly as they prefer it.

As with most other products and services, quality varies between vendors. Some vendors don't have an adequate setup, which can lead to lost connections, busy signals, and other impediments. AOL has long been lambasted for this. Logjams at peak times of Internet usage (evenings) are also common. Having an Internet connection you cannot connect to can be very frustrating! You may decide to switch vendors if your connection is consistently unsatisfactory, so don't lock yourself into a year's service in exchange for a price break until you are positive that you will receive good service in return. It is always a good idea to ask friends and colleagues which Internet access vendors they recommend and which they don't. Many of the online services offer a one month free trial so you can test them out at no charge. If you live in a large metropolitan area, you will have many companies to choose from, but in some other locations, the options will be more limited. It should not take long to get your computer, modem, telephone line, and Internet access lined up, and once you do, you will have access to the marketing wonder of the Information Age.

Internet Connection Resources

This list includes some of the Internet access providers available to you. Online services will often send you free software and a free trial period. ISPs rarely provide the free trial and sometimes charge a one-time set up fee.

Popular Online Services

America Online (AOL); 800-827-6364; **www.aol.com**
CompuServe (CSi); 800-848-8990; **www.compuserve.com**
Microsoft Network (MSN); 800-228-7007; **www.msn.com**

Internet Service Providers (ISPs)

Finding an ISP with a local phone number can be a challenge. It is a good idea to inquire at a local computer store or ask friends which provider they use. There are many ISPs that serve a limited geographical area—usually right around their office. These often offer more personalized service and support than do their nationwide counterparts. ISPs that serve every state in the USA include:

aaaa.net; 888-732-1266; **www.aaaa.net**

Big Planet; 801-345-7000; **www.bigplanet.com**
City Online; 888-4-CITYOL; **www.citycom.com**
CompUnet; 217-362-5907; **www.gocompunet.com**
EarthLink Network; 800-395-8425; **www.earthlink.com**
Epoch Internet; 888-77-EPOCH; **www.eni.net**
FNet; 805-373-8688; **www.ftel.net**
GTE; 800-927-3000; **www.gte.net**
IBM; 800-455-5056; **www.ibm.net**
NetLimited; 888-NET-LTD1; **www.netlimited.net.**

If you can access the Internet, search for a new provider by area code, using The List, at **thelist.internet.com**. It contains information on over 6,800 ISPs, including service and pricing information. It is worth a trip to the local public library to view this list—libraries often provide free Internet access for patrons.

Direct E-mail

Whichever Internet access you have, chances are it comes with unlimited e-mail access. This means that you have free access to one of the more effective forms of advertising: direct mail marketing. The trick with e-mail, even more so than the earthbound variety, is to target your recipients carefully. In cyberspace, junk mail is very poorly received. If you are perceived as a junk emailer (also called a *spammer*), you will do your image more harm than good. Word travels fast on the Internet, whether or not the message is positive.

How can you make appropriate use of e-mail to advertise your status as a Cisco certified professional? One method is to send an FYI update to your past and present clients (and/or your employer's), reminding them of your skills, availability, and, of course, certified status. Keep such messages short and to the point. For example:

> ABC company is pleased to announce the we now have a Cisco Certified Internetwork Expert (CCIE) on staff. This certification, granted only by Cisco Systems, signifies the attainment of the highest standards in design, installation, and management of complex network environments.

This would be followed by another paragraph or two about the services ABC company currently offers and a call to action, such as: "To boost your network performance, call ABC," along with contact information.

If any companies or recruiters have your resume on file, you would then send them a variation of the above message, along with an updated version of your resume.

Your Cyber Billboard

Whether you obtain Internet access through an online service or ISP, your account will usually include space on the provider's server for your personal Web pages. You are paying for this as part of your basic subscription fee, so don't let it go to waste. ISPs, in particular, may charge extra for Web page storage, but usually the fee for a basic personal site will be nominal. Some Web sites will even host your home page free, without your having to be a subscriber to a particular service. Yahoo! maintains an index of such sites at **www.yahoo.com/Business_and_Economy/Companies/ Internet_Services/Web_Services/Hosting/Free_Web_Pages/**.

Creating a Web site that will showcase your talents does not require a degree in graphic design. The site can be a straightforward, one-page affair, or a multi-part masterpiece, depending on your goals, aspirations, and how much time you are willing to devote to the project. Thanks to the plentiful supply of Web design software packages available today, you don't even have to learn HTML (hypertext markup language), which is used to hard code Web pages. Instead, you can point, click, and highlight, inserting pictures, text, and links where you would like them. As you paint the screen with images and text, the design program translates the results into HTML for you. Figure 12.1 shows one such program.

You can find these Web design tools (sometimes called HTML editors) at your local software outlet or download them from Web sites on the Internet. The AOLPress program, for example, can be found at **www.aolpress.com**. You can jump to reviews of various HTML software programs and find out how to obtain them from Yahoo!'s index of HTML editors at **www.yahoo.com/**

Computers_and_Internet/Software/Internet/World_Wide_Web/HTML_Editors.

FIGURE 12.1
Using Microsoft's
FrontPage 98 to
Design a Web Site

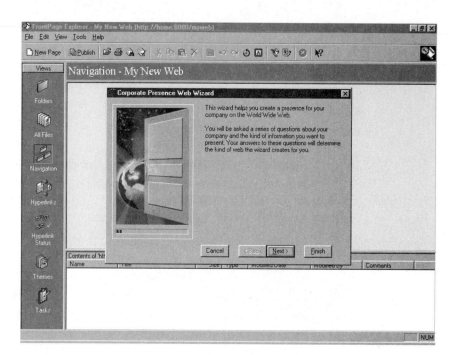

An endless supply of available HTML tutorials will provide you with step-by-step advice on the creation of your Web site. You can find Web design books in the computer section of your local bookstore or order them from one of the online bookstores, such as Amazon Books (**www.amazon.com**) and **fatbrain.com**. You can also find plenty of free advice, much of it pretty good, on various Web sites. For starters, check out:

✳ The NCSA (National Center for Supercomputing Applications) Beginner's Guide to HTML (**www.ncsa.uiuc.edu/General/Internet/WWW/HTMLPrimer.html**) is an excellent place to get the basics on what HTML is, its various components, and how to put it to work for you. You can also download this file to print out or read using Adobe Acrobat Reader, which can be obtained free at **www.adobe.com**.

✳ If you already have HTML basics down cold, you might want to learn the ins and outs of more advanced techniques, including floating frames, marquees, meta tags, and more. You can read about all of these at **www.htmlgoodies.com**, Joe Burns' extensive HTML site (shown in Figure 12.2).

FIGURE 12.2
The HTML
Goodies Web Site

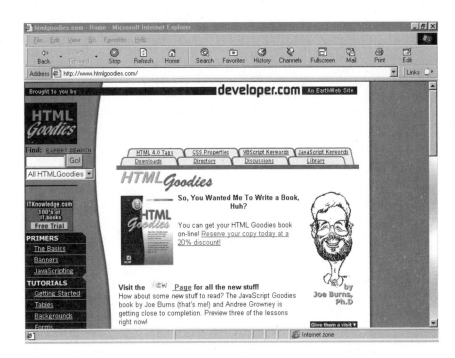

What to Put On Your Pages

Give some thought to what you want to include on your Web pages. It is good to develop an overall plan before beginning, so your site will have a cohesive feel. You don't have to create the whole thing all at once. Start with a main page (this will be your home page), and add to it over time. Strive to make your site interesting by providing a variety of content.

QUICK TIP

Check out what other computer professionals are doing with their Web pages to see what works and what doesn't. You can jump to many of them from Yahoo!'s high-tech resumes index at **www.yahoo.com/Computers_and_Internet/ Employment/Resumes/Individual_Resumes/**.

Think of your main page as a table of contents for your site. Your contact information should be there, along with a brief introduction so visitors know what they are looking at and who created the site. You'll also need links to other pages in your site, accompanied by descriptions so visitors can choose whether or not to view them.

Web Site Design Tips

Go easy on the graphics. Pictures take longer to download than text, and visitors may jump to another site rather than wait for a page full of graphics, no matter how amazing, to download.

Make navigation between pages simple. Visitors should be able to return to the main page with a single mouse click.

Don't get too fancy. Web pages with purple lettering on black backgrounds, or other jarring combinations, prove nearly impossible to read. When in doubt, it is best to be conservative with the use of color. For similar reasons, stick to one or two fonts in various sizes.

Don't incorporate large blocks of text that span the width of a monitor. Narrow columns with wide margins will be easier on the eyes.

If you use a background texture or image, make sure it doesn't obscure the clarity of the text that overlies it.

If you include links to other sites, check them periodically to ensure they still work. There are many free programs to automate this task. FrontPage does it as well.

Include an e-mail link to your electronic mailbox, and display the address too. Sometimes people may not have the mail portion of their Web browser working properly, and they will want to know your e-mail address to respond using another mail program.

Do not put personal information you don't want the whole world to know on your Web site. This may include pictures of your children or your home phone number.

Verify that your page appears properly to individuals viewing it with different Web browsers.

Possible pages include: your resume; links and/or reviews of Web resources that are linked to your area of professional expertise; reviews of products you work with; links to the Web sites of clients who maintain an online presence; examples of your work; testimonials from satisfied customers (get their permission first); or a tutorial on something you are qualified to teach about. Make it a goal to create a page that will prove useful to people who stop by.

Ideally, you should make your Web site a resource that visitors come back to again and again. To accomplish this, it is important to add new material periodically. It is a good idea to build this task into your schedule, otherwise it will fall by the wayside and before you know it your Web site will be full of outdated material and broken links—transforming it from a positive career tool to a potentially negative one.

QUICK TIP

Few interesting Web sites begin with the author's resume, so create a separate page for yours, and link to it from the main page.

You will also want to build what are called "keywords" into your site, especially on the main page. Keywords are words and phrases individuals searching through the Net are likely to use. The trick is to figure out which words the users you want to draw to your site are likely to be using. Think about words that are common to your field of expertise and to your goals. Include both the acronyms and the spelled out words. For example, you might work in the words internetwork, networking, and independent consultant.

QUICK TIP

It is possible to embed hidden keywords within a Web page by rendering the keyword in the same color as the background, thus making it invisible to the human eye, but readily available to computer search engines. Unscrupulous individuals have been known to incorporate the word sex in this way, to draw unsuspecting visitors to their Web site. The visitor arrives, of course finds no sexual content, and has no clue why your page turned up. This kind of trickery is not likely to enhance the professional image you would like to present and is best avoided.

When you are ready to present your Web site to the world, you will need to upload it to your access provider's computer. Typically, this is accomplished using a special file transfer program, and your provider should supply you with instructions on how to do so.

If You Build It, Will They Come?

Creating a Web site and launching it into cyberspace does not automatically generate a readership. A few people will stumble across it, but your goal is to achieve much more than that. One measure of a Web site's success is the number of accesses (called *traffic or hits*) it receives. To build up traffic to your Web site, you will need to spend a little time promoting it, but doing so won't take long.

To advertise your Web site, add the URL to your print materials, including your business card and marketing brochures. It should become a standard part of your contact information and be included in your e-mail messages as well.

A second, arguably more powerful, way to promote it is via the Internet. You need to get your site included by the search engines (Yahoo!, Infoseek, AltaVista, and so on). To do this, you can visit the site of each search engine and follow the individual instructions. Or you can use one of the free tools, such as freeSubmit (**www.webpedia.com/tools/freesubmit**), that lets you submit your URL(s) to multiple search engines without having to visit each one independently. The freeSubmit site is shown in Figure 12.3.

FIGURE 12.3
The Submit It!
Web site

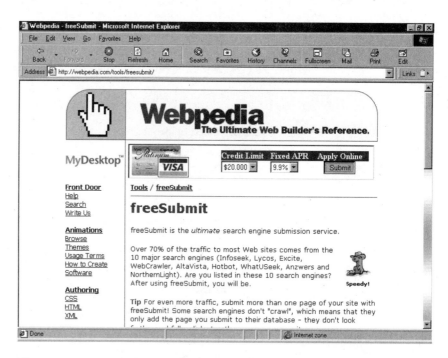

If your time is in short supply, consider signing up with a submission service. For a fee, these services will submit your Web site information to a specified number of search engines. To locate one, visit Yahoo!'s index of Web site announcement and promotion services (shown in Figure 12.4), at **yahoo.com/Computers_and_ Internet/Internet/World_Wide_Web/Information_and_ Documentation/Site_Announcement_and_Promotion/.**

FIGURE 12.4
Plenty of Site
Promotion
Help Available

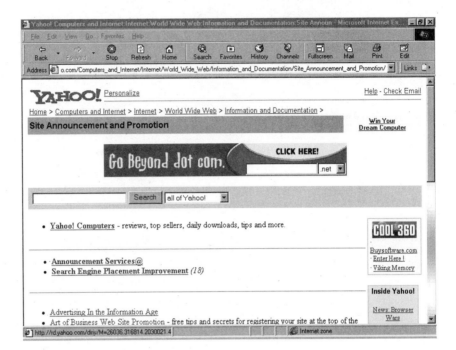

For the interested Web site promoter, many additional methods for increasing traffic to your site exist. Read about them in some of the excellent articles on the subject. You'll find plenty of them at the following sites:

✳ The Website Promoters Resource Center (**www.wprc.com**) is an excellent and robust site that contains tools and advice related to Web site promotion via targeted e-mail, banner advertising, URL submissions, and press releases. If you want a consultant to assist you with your promotion efforts, you can find one here.

✳ ClickZ (**www.clickz.com**) contains loads of tips, resources, and articles related to online marketing. You can also elect to receive a free electronic subscription to the ClickZ newsletter.

✳ Promotion World (**www.promotionworld.com**) explains how to promote your Web site and build up traffic, all free.

You can also subscribe to *The Promotion World Informer*, a weekly electronic newsletter packed full of tips and tricks for promoting your Web site.

Clearly the Internet is not only a natural ally for the computer professional, it is also an easy-to-learn, low-cost marketing tool. Your potential employers and clients are out there trolling for experts like yourself. Why not make it easy for them to find you?

Networking and Lurking

In the career sense, networking means getting the word out about who you are and what you do. It means getting to know the people who may prove beneficial to your career at some point in the future. Perhaps they will introduce you to the hiring manager of a company you want to work for, or maybe end up needing your professional services themselves. How do you know which people those are? You don't. It is impossible to predict who will remember your name and pass it on when a need arises. Fortunately, the Internet provides an efficient networking medium, and you won't even have to endure any boring speeches or attend distant professional dinners to connect with clients and peers. You can do it all from your personal computer.

One of the strengths of the Internet is its power to bring people together. Individuals whose paths would never cross in a different environment can meet online and exchange mutually beneficial information. Part of the nature of the Internet community is that people are interested in helping each other out. Perhaps this is related to the age-old urge to offer advice, or maybe it is just a special, cyber brand of goodwill. Either way, professionals online typically expect to receive help and advice and to offer it. By jumping into this community give and take, you can tap into the power of networking without leaving your desk. You can use this environment to promote your professional abilities.

The primary places for such networking are forums and newsgroups. The two have much in common, and the terms are sometimes used interchangeably, but they are actually quite different. Both are repositories of discussion and information related to a particular topic. However, a forum is part of the World Wide Web, and as such, can be accessed using a Web browser. It will bear a name such as "The Client/Server Forum." Newsgroups, on the other hand, are a part of the Internet called Usenet. They are accessed using a program called a *newsreader*. Often the terms forum and newsgroup are used interchangeably. Newsgroup names follow a standard format that indicates the subject matter at hand. Abbreviations or word fractions, separated by dots, are strung together to identify the topic. A newsgroup titled **comp.jobs.offered**, for example, is clearly identified as a place for messages about computer job openings. Table 12.1 lists common newsgroup abbreviations and their meanings.

TABLE 12.1
Newsgroup
Abbreviations

Abbreviation	Meaning	Example
alt	Alternative	alt.books.technical
biz	Business	biz.marketplace.services.computers
comp	Computer	comp.jobs
misc	Miscellaneous	misc.jobs.wanted
rec	Recreational	rec.games.computer.quake.playing
sci	Science	sci.physics.research
soc	Society	soc.activism
sys	Systems	comp.dcom.sys.cisco
os	Operating System	comp.os.linux.network
lang	Language	comp.lang.c

A forum is associated with a particular Web site or online service. Forums generally serve a smaller readership than newsgroups. They may be sponsored by a company with related products and services or by an interested individual. When you post a message to a forum, you often have the option to hide it from everyone but the person you are replying to. Although this is sometimes a good option to use, many times a reply will be of potential interest to others who follow the messages, so you won't want to conceal it. A forum is more likely (although not guaranteed) to be moderated, which means less off-topic ranting and raving.

Messages posted to a newsgroup are visible to all and anybody who wishes to read and respond to them can do so. They are more likely to include a high number of junk postings—off-topic, often off-the-wall rantings. They also boast a greater number of readers and messages. In both forums and newsgroups, you can read messages, respond to them, and post questions of your own. However, neither is a place to post advertisements for yourself or your services; doing so will get you an e-mail box full of angry complaints (a.k.a. flames).

Using newsgroups and forums to network and promote yourself is simple: all you have to do is share your expertise. The self-promotion is incidental to the advice you are offering and, thus, is acceptable according to the rules of Internet good conduct (sometimes called *netiquette*). It is also a powerful way to put your name and affiliations in front of many people, as well as demonstrate your expertise. To make this work, you will need to do two things: create a signature and identify appropriate newsgroups and forums.

Your Signature

A signature is the closing section that will end each e-mail and posting you create. Think of it as your electronic letterhead. Your signature should include your name; business title; e-mail address; phone number; phrases conveying additional information about you; and, sometimes, a personal slogan. Depending on the nature of your message and where you post it, you may choose to include your physical address, too, or exclude your phone number. Some e-mail software will allow you to include a graphic, such as a certification logo, in your e-mail, but if you do so, consider that not all recipients will be able to view it properly.

The promotional parts of the signature are your business title and slogan. The business title conveys what kind of professional you are. The slogan can be a quote you feel is representative of yourself or you think is funny and can be included or excluded as you prefer. Any slogan should always be succinct—preferably one line. Figure 12.6 shows a signature a Cisco certified professional might use. It is a good idea to create several variations of your signature to choose from so that you can select the signature most appropriate for the environment you are posting to.

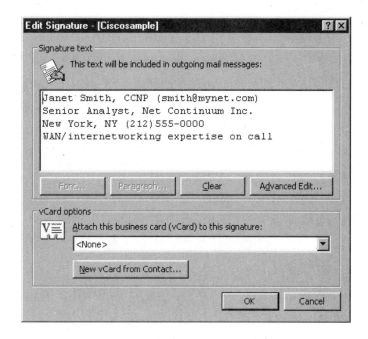

FIGURE 12.5

Example of a
Personal Signature

Prowling the Net

Once you have created your signature, it is time to identify target
newsgroups and forums among the thousands of them that exist.
Obviously, it is impossible to peruse them all. Although you can
probably find some automated program to post your message to
all of them, that would be a big mistake (remember netiquette?).
Besides, in this case quality is more important than quantity. So
pick a few newsgroups or forums you will want to visit regularly.
How many depends on how much time you are willing to devote.
Two is a manageable number to start with.

You will need to do a bit of exploring to uncover outlets that
match your professional interests. Don't limit yourself to com-
puter-specific sites; if you are interested in a particular industry
or technology, seek out forums and newsgroups related to it.
Businesses and individuals in those industries may have need of
your expertise as well. Here are a few possibilities to get you
started:

* **comp.dcom.sys.cisco** (Usenet)
* **de.comm.internet.routing**

* **discussions.earthweb.com** (IT discussion forums and
  Usenet gateway)
* **www.groupstudy.com** (CCIE mailing list).

The first thing to do when you discover a promising newsgroup or
forum is lurk. In Internet lingo, lurkers are individuals who are
present but don't participate. In your case, that means read and
pay attention, but don't post anything. This will enable you to get
a solid feel for what material is discussed in the forum and what
does not belong. It will also protect you from inadvertently posting something inappropriate that will generate ill will and start
you off on the wrong foot. After several visits as a lurker, you will
be able to decide if the outlet is one you would like to participate
in, and if so, what type of participation is most appropriate.

When you have found a forum or newsgroup that appeals to
you and you have lurked enough to be certain of the content and
format, you are ready to make your premiere appearance. Watch
for a question that you can answer with authority. When one
appears, create a thoughtful, grammatically correct, spell-checked
posting that addresses the issue at hand and concludes with the
signature you have developed. Every time you do this, you are
advertising your professional expertise, and, if you have done
your signature file right, your credentials. Over time you will
become known to the people in the forum as a thoughtful, experienced professional. When they need just such a person, or know
someone who does, your name will come to mind.

CHAPTER 13

Moving Up

Career advancement can follow many paths, and enhancing your professional credentials through earning a Cisco certification opens more of them to you. Now you are faced with the enviable (if somewhat daunting) task of deciding which route to pursue; you have come to an intersection on your career path, and you get to choose in which direction to proceed.

Straight ahead lies the path of least resistance—continuing as you are in the same job with the same responsibilities. You might choose to keep on straight ahead if you are content with your current position and/or have too much going on in other, non-work areas of your life, to devote mental energy to choosing one of the turns. Taking one of the turns, on the other hand, will require a bit of energy and effort, as they both involve upward movement. Turn one way to move up within your current organization, or the other to advance by moving on to a different employer (possibly even yourself). This career intersection is fast approaching, and you have earned yourself a green light through certification. It is time to step on the gas.

Up or Out?

Before you press the career accelerator too hard, you will need to decide which way you are going to turn at this intersection. Since you have already made the choice to undertake certification, you are probably not completely satisfied with the status quo. That eliminates proceeding straight ahead, and leaves you with deciding whether you would like to advance within your current company, or look elsewhere. If your current workplace is not meeting many or all of the needs you defined as important, and is not likely to, then moving on may be your best option. Chapter 14 includes advice and hints on choosing that direction. If, on the other hand, your current employment has a lot going for it, and has the potential to meet most or all of the needs you defined as important, then moving up within your current organization is your logical choice, and this chapter will help speed you on your way.

There are two basic moves you can make to advance your career at your current place of employment: up or over. Moving up means increasing your responsibilities and place within the hierarchy of the organization without straying far from your current areas of expertise and/or department. Moving up makes you a more senior member of the organization. It should always come with a raise. Moving up can also mean staying where you are but going after a raise to reflect your increased value now that you have become certified.

A lateral move, on the other hand, may bring no raise or even a reduction in pay, but will provide you with something else of value instead. That something else may be a bridge into a new part of the company that offers potential for greater advancement in the long run. Or it may be sliding into a new technical specialty that has attracted your interest.

Laying the Groundwork

Whether you are after a promotion or a raise, careful planning will maximize your likelihood of success. Before actually reaching the moment where you utter the words describing what you want, you need to do advance work to solidify your position. The goal of this work is to remind your employer just how great an asset to the organization you are, and how valuable. This is not something you can do in a single day, at least not without hampering your chances of success. What you want to do instead is parade your value in front of the decision maker(s) in subtle and not so subtle ways, over a period of time. What you don't want to do is come across as pushy. That is more likely to work against you than for you. Instead, your goal should be to strike a balance, going far enough to keep your accomplishments visible, without becoming annoying. You should be doing this the whole time you are working toward your certification—don't wait until you have passed your final Cisco exam—that is when you will make your move, capitalizing on the groundwork you have put in place along the way.

Understand Your Manager

When planning your advancement campaign it is important to distinguish between what you feel is important and what your boss thinks is important. You cannot give yourself a raise or promotion, the boss can. If you don't already know the boss' opinions of what makes an employee outstanding, do a little detective work. Is high value put on technical skills? Independent work? Fast work? Teamwork? Skillful interaction with customers? Does he notice whether you arrive at 7:50 or 8:01? Everyone has opinions and pet peeves; do your best to scope out those of your boss. If you have received employee evaluations in the past, go back over them for clues. Has anyone in your department been promoted lately? Try to determine the basis for that move. Once you have identified what matters to those in control of granting your raise or promotion, you can describe your accomplishments in ways appropriate.

Share the Good News

By now you have notified your manager that you have successfully obtained Cisco certification, but have you explained just what that means to the company? One way to do this is to pass on the results of research studies that have investigated the issue. Several studies have been conducted, some by certifying organizations and others by independent research organizations. The results quantify the value of certification to employers. You can obtain some of these studies free, via the Internet, and pass them on to your boss with a note that says something to the effect of "thought you might find this interesting." Because the data come from someone other than you, it will seem less like you are tooting your own horn. Unfortunately there are no such studies done specifically on Cisco certification, so you will have to extrapolate and encourage your employer to do the same. Resources you can view and download from the net include:

* **www.ibm.com/Education/certify/news/proidc.phtm**—
  This is an IDC study titled: *Benefits And Productivity Gains Realized Through Certification.* This study was sponsored by IBM, Lotus, Microsoft, Sybase, and Sylvan Prometric. It begins: "IT certification has a significant positive effect on IS productivity and network uptime," and continues with graphs

and data that back up and expand up on that claim (see Figure 13.1). This oft-quoted white paper is beginning to be a bit dated, but is still a decent resource for your purposes.

* **www.itaa.org**—Visit this site for details on how to obtain the Information Technology Association of America (ITAA) IT Workforce Study, which identifies a severe future shortage of IT workers in the US. It would not hurt for your boss to be aware of some of these statistics, like the one that states "Sixty-eight percent of IT companies cite a lack of skilled/trained workers as a barrier to their companies' future ability to grow."

FIGURE 13.1
Certification
White Paper

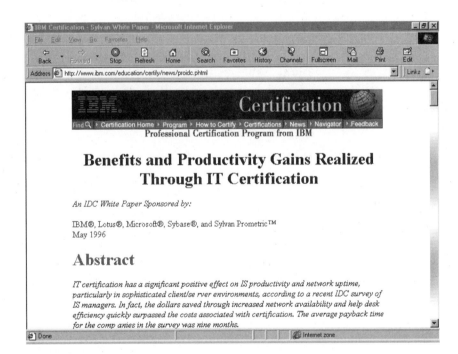

Magazine articles touting the value of Cisco certification and certification in general are also worth passing across your boss' desk. You can find quite a few online or in your local library's periodical room. The following references will get you started:

* "Certification and the Bottom Line" (*ComputerWorld*, 4/18/98)
* "Cisco Certified Experts: A Headhunters Paradise" (*Smart Reseller Online* 5/15/98)

✳ "Certification Pays Off" (*Information Week* 10/26/98)
✳ "Certification Sense" (*Smart Reseller News* 11/20/98)

Be a (Visible) Problem Solver

Whether you are after a raise or promotion, you can help your position considerably if you can create a reputation for yourself as a problem solver. This is a step that will require extra time, since you will need to do this without compromising your current responsibilities. However, companies love problem solvers, and if you can manage to become one, advancement within the organization will come more easily.

In order to solve problems, you first have to identify them. It is easiest to start with your personal area of authority. Examine quantifiable aspects of your daily activities, such as number of support incidents handled, system down time, turnaround time for various tasks, or the incidence of software bugs. For each topic you examine, ask yourself:

1. Is this number the best it can be?
2. If not, why not?
3. What can realistically be done to change this?
4. How much will it cost to change this?
5. What will changing this accomplish for my organization?
6. Considering the answers to 4 and 5, is this worthwhile change to implement?

You are looking for items that will improve the company's bottom line in a quantifiable way. Likely areas include heightening customer satisfaction (and thus retention), cutting costs, speeding production, or increasing quality. You may run across numbers that could be improved, but with methods that are not cost effective. Those are worth a second look—to seek a creative approach that would be cost effective.

QUICK TIP

Look for problems that are widely visible, so that your solutions will have a widely apparent impact.

If you are fortunate and talented enough already to have your own bailiwick operating like a well-greased machine, then expand your problem search outside it. What do your coworkers complain about? Your customers? Or, best of all, your boss? The next time you hear them complain, instead of just empathizing, probe a bit for details and make a mental note to brainstorm potential solutions.

You may think that you will have trouble identifying problems and coming up with ways to solve them, but any company has processes that can be improved. Most employees are quite busy coping with the day-to-day tasks that make up their job responsibilities, and expend little if any time and energy on analyzing and problem solving. You will find that once you develop a problem-solving mindset, potential areas for improvement will practically jump out at you, and the difficulty won't be in picking them out, but in deciding which ones you have the time, energy, and interest to pursue.

Becoming a company problem solver has additional benefits. Coworkers will appreciate you (though maybe with a tad of envy attached) because you make their jobs easier by solving their problems. In addition, witnessing the positive impact on your personal efforts on the day-to-day operations of the organization can be quite satisfying. Of course, it will also enhance your image with the company execs.

If you are not already keeping a log of your accomplishments, you should be. Remembering everything you have done over the course of a year without one is practically impossible. Your log does not have to be anything fancy—a simple notebook or computer file will do. When you get or finish an assignment, record the date and a brief summary (a sentence or two should do) describing the task and possibly its consequences. If your boss praises you for something, jot that down too. Your entries don't need to go into intricate detail, but serve instead to jog your memory. If you make to-do lists, you can hold on to those as well (or instead) as evidence of what you have accomplished.

Be Part of the Team (Better Yet, Be the Captain)

Shining through your own work is important, but add a reputation for teamwork and/or leadership and you will have an especially winning combination. The ability to work with others is valuable precisely because its not always easy to do. How can you demonstrate your people skills?

* Join a company-wide task force
* Play on the company softball team
* Organize the company picnic or holiday party
* Volunteer your time to a company-sponsored charity activity.

Each of these has the added bonus of increasing your visibility both inside and outside your current department. You look good AND your boss looks good because your activities will reflect on her as well. These activities also provide you with an opportunity to hone leadership skills in a lower-pressure environment.

Although organizing the company picnic might not be your idea of a good time, find a way to be enthusiastic. If your heart is not in the project/activity, don't sign on or your efforts may well backfire.

Asking for a Raise

If a coworker walked up to you in the lunch room and asked what your paycheck was last week, you would probably be speechless for a moment or two. Whether for better or worse, this is just not a question you go around asking — individual compensation details are very personal, and often cloaked in secrecy. Talking about them is practically taboo, and asking for a raise can feel quite intimidating.

This environment of secrecy benefits employers, because it provides them with an edge when it comes to negotiating compensation; they know what every other person in the office pulls down, you can usually only guess and estimate. But if negotiating a raise is rather a game of wits, employers don't hold all the cards. There are plenty of steps you can take to load the deck in your favor. Assuming you have already begun laying the groundwork as described above, here is a step-by-step guide to going after that raise:

1. Figure out what you're worth
2. Study the organizational pay structure

3. Bone up on the organization's performance data
4. Prepare your case detailing why you're worth more
5. Choose your moment
6. Ask for the raise.

What Are You Worth?

To receive a raise, you will need to prove that your value to the organization justifies one. You can do this by:

✳ Proving you are being paid at below market rate, or
✳ Proving that you are worth more than the market rate because of the contributions you make to the company's bottom line—often because of special skills or experience.

In either case you will need figures to support your position. Developing them is not difficult, although it does involve a bit of homework.

Salary Surveys

Salary surveys are a good place to find out the going rate for your type of position. Fortunately, surveys covering computer professions are plentiful and easy to obtain. Chapter 3 reported on the results of a recruiter survey of pay rates for Cisco-certified individuals. The fastest way to get additional IT salary information is available is via the Internet.

The JobStar salary survey site (**jobstar.org/tools/salary/sal-comp.htm**) is a great place to start. There you will find a collection of links to salary information specifically relevant to computer professionals. Figure 13.2 shows the JobStar computer and engineering salary information page.

To find additional salary resources, use one of the major search engines such as Infoseek (**www.infoseek.com**) or Yahoo! (**www.yahoo.com**) to ferret them out. Search using the phrases "salary survey" AND "computer." Pay attention to the dates and source of the information, to make sure that it is both current and credible.

You can also get salary surveys from professional organizations and societies. Trade publications such as *InformationWeek* and

Computerworld carry them periodically. Research and consulting companies in the computer field often publish salary surveys too. Source Services Corporation, for example, prints an annual survey available free to anyone who requests a copy.

FIGURE 13.2
JobStar
Salary Center

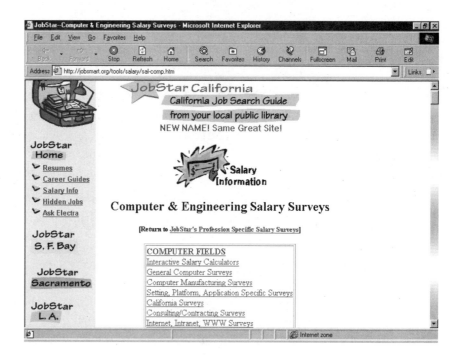

When using a salary survey to determine the going rate for your position, you need to match your job responsibilities and organization type as closely as possible. Don't go by the job title alone, as the same job can go by different names. Instead, focus on the description of duties. Some surveys break down pay rates by employer size, which will enable you to narrow your research even further.

Depending on the area of the country (or world) you are in, pay rates will vary. A programmer in New York City, for example, will typically receive a higher salary than one in Lima, Ohio. Of course, there will be higher living expenses too. Look for a salary survey that provides regional information so you can determine the relevant pay rates for your geographical area. You can also check with recruiting and employment agencies in your area.

They may have job listings similar to yours, and will have a good sense of going rates.

Salary calculators let you enter your skills, years of experience, and other qualifications and provide a custom estimation of your salary worth. Keep in mind that there are probably variables that these tools don't account for—such as special additional skills and so on—but they can still be a good place to start. Figure 13.3 shows a Web-based salary calculator.

FIGURE 13.3
Pencom's Interactive Salary Calculator

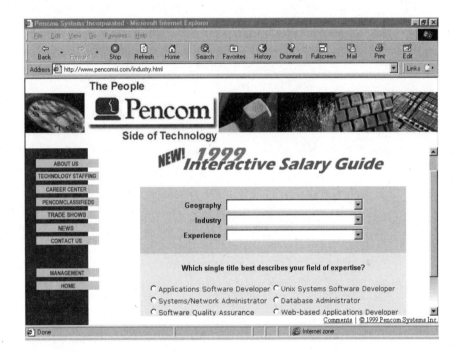

Internet Sources of Salary Surveys

www.dice.com/ratesurvey contains the results of the 1999 IT salary survey conducted by Contract Professional magazine and dice.com.

www.currents.net/resources/iwantanewjob/calculate/index.html contains an interactive salary survey calculator from Computer Currents and iwantanewjob.com.

www.experienceondemand.com/features/edpstats1998.html is Source Services' online national salary snapshot. From here or by calling 1-888-ONDEMAND you can also request a full survey (and career guide), which will contain figures specific to your geographic area, be mailed to you at no charge.

www.datamasters.com/survey.html contains current US regional salary information from DataMasters.

www.computerworld.com/home/features.nsf/all/980907mgt contains statistics and analysis from Computerworld's 1998 Salary Survey.

www.jdresources.com/salaryf.html is the Web site for J & D Resources' IT salary survey, and provides national rate ranges by job title. Historical salary information is included.

www.realrates.com/survey.htm is the Web page for The Real Rate Survey of rates received by computer contractors and consultants.

www.jobfactory.com/salary.htm contains a salary comparison calculator that you can use to translate salary information for one geographic location into equivalent information for a different location.

How Does Your Employer Pay?

The next thing to investigate is the compensation structure used by your employer. It is important to understand that you are much more likely to obtain a raise by working within the organization's pay structure than by ignoring or trying to circumvent it.

Many companies will provide job descriptions and pay ranges if you ask. You may also be able to find out the amount of the maximum raise given. It is also important to ask how your performance is evaluated, and how raises are determined. There may be a formula in place that you should know about. For example, if you are already at the top of the pay scale allowed for your current position, then your efforts would be better spent pursuing a promotion than a raise.

Find out if raises are given at a particular time (often following an annual performance review), but don't assume that such guidelines are carved in stone. If you can provide evidence that you deserve an increase even though it has not been a year since your last one, go ahead and go for it.

This information should be available through your human resources department, and possibly on the company intranet. If not, ask coworkers or your supervisor if they know where you can obtain copies of the current policies.

How Has Your Organization Been Performing Lately?

You may have a sense of how your organization has done the last few years, in terms of growth and profits. Taking the time to bone up on the details will enable you to bargain from a position of knowledge. If your boss says "we can't give you a raise—the company has been running in the red for the last two years," you won't be taken by surprise. On the other hand, if your employer's profits have been climbing, you can incorporate that fact into your case for a salary increase.

By the way, poor organizational earnings are not a bona fide, iron clad reason to turn down your request for a raise. They are a factor to take into consideration when making your request, and definitely something you should be aware of, but do not mean you should cancel your plans for advancement. Even if your company is operating in the red, if you are doing an excellent job, or have increased your value to the company through certification, you still have legitimate qualities to take to the salary bargaining table.

To find out your company's financial standing, read the annual reports for the past few years. You may also be able to look up the information online, through a business database resource such as Hoover's (**www.hoovers.com**). Look at historical information and future projections as well as a snapshot of the firm's current financial health. It would not hurt to do research for newspaper and magazine articles about your company and its products and services as well.

Preparing Your Case

When you have completed the first three steps, you are halfway there. Now you will use the information you have gathered to make your case for why you should be given a raise. First compare your current compensation to the figures you obtained through your salary research. If yours is at or off the low end of the scale, you are in a good position to argue that you are not being paid at market value for your work. Don't forget to point out that you are actually worth more than the market average, since you have continued your professional development and obtained certification. Use the certification-related research and statistics you uncovered earlier to bolster your position.

If you are going to use the market rate approach, be prepared to identify the functions you perform, and provide the survey data that will support your claims of below-average compensation. Multiple survey sources will be greeted with more credibility than a single source, and make your position very strong.

If you discover that your compensation ranks in the upper portion of the range for your area, skills, and responsibilities, then the going rate argument won't due you much good. The good news is that if you are at the top of the scale, you can feel reassured that the organization values you and your work; the bad news is, you may have to work harder to make your case for a raise, though it certainly can be done. On the other hand, you should conisder pursuing promotion to a higher-level job, with increased responsibilities and correspondingly higher pay by getting a promotion.

To justify a raise when your compensation is already at or above the ranges uncovered by your research, you will need to show why you are especially valuable to the company, and therefore worth compensating at a higher rate than average. The best way to do that is to translate your activities into dollars. If you have followed the earlier advice about becoming a problem solver, you can start there. How much money have you added to the company's bottom line through your efforts? Did you train coworkers in a technology? Find out what the going rates are for such training if it had been obtained from an outside source. Have you become more efficient at performing particular tasks? If you can complete a job that took you 50 hours last year in only 40 hours this year (perhaps due to your certification-related training), that's a 25 percent increase in productivity. If you do the math for other activities where your efficiency has increased, you will be able to translate those into quantifiable savings for the company too.

If you want to carry your calculations a step further, figure out your hourly pay rate (don't forget to include the dollar value of your benefits) and multiply it by the number of hours of work you have saved the organization. The result will be a dollar savings you have provided your employer. Using the above example, you have saved the organization 10 hours of your time (which you were able to devote to other tasks thanks to your new efficiency). If you determine that your hourly rate is $25 then you save your employer $250 each time you complete the task. If you do it once a quarter, that's $1000 per year in savings that you have personally generated. When you analyze your other improvements in a similar way, the dollar amounts may quickly add up.

Don't forget to consider whether your certification qualifies your employer to become a Cisco reseller, or to become a higher-level reseller. If you are the only Cisco certified individual on staff, or one of only a few, you may be especially valuable to your employer.

Once you have your approach figured out, practice your pitch in private or in front of someone you trust, like a spouse. You can also use a tape recorder or video camera to record your practice session, and review it until you are satisfied with your performance. Your presentation will come out much more smoothly if you have run through it a few times in advance. You will also be able to relax a bit more, once you know you can state your case effectively.

Timing

When your boss has just returned from receiving a chewing out at a meeting, it's the wrong time to ask for your raise. After an annual meeting that included announcements of the organization's staggering gain in market share, led by a product produced by your division is a great time. Chances are that your range of timing opportunities will fall somewhere between these two extremes. Pay attention to the atmosphere in your workplace, and choose a time that seems favorable.

Raise Day

When your homework is complete and the time seems ripe, broach the subject of your raise. Something simple like "I'd like to speak to you about a raise. Can we schedule a time to talk?" will do nicely. Although it is unlikely that you'll be offered a meeting on the spot, be prepared just in case. If you get put off for a week or more, do your best to be patient, and use the delay as an excuse to get in a few more practice sessions and to further prove your worthiness.

When your meeting time arrives, follow these dos and don'ts:

* Do dress and groom yourself to business perfection the day of the meeting. Not only will it improve the image you present, but it will relieve you of any worry about your physical appearance.
* Don't say that you *need* a raise. Need is not the issue. What the company *owes* you isn't exactly relevant either. What matters is that you can prove that your increased value justifies the raise.
* Do provide documentation that details your accomplishments. Your boss won't be able to remember everything and will be able to use your documentation to make a case to higher ups, if necessary.
* Do provide figures and be prepared to produce on-the-spot evidence that backs them up.
* Don't be confrontational. This is more like a sales meeting than a boxing match, and hostility won't sell anyone anything. Make eye contact, but don't engage in the staredown.

Above all, relax. You know you have prepared your case as best you can. You have practiced and know what you will say. You are as ready as a person can be. Whether you get the raise or not, stand up, shake hands, and thank your boss for taking the time to meet with you. Remember, post-certification is not the only time you can ask for a raise, it is just an especially good one.

Securing a Promotion

Shortly after you have earned certification can be a good time to make a play for a career move upwards through a promotion. This is especially true if you chose your certification with an eye toward a transition into a new specialty.

Begin by laying the groundwork for career advancement, as described above. Pay special attention to increasing your visibility within the organization. Once that is under way, follow these steps to go after your promotion:

1. Identify a target position
2. Research the position
3. Get an interview with the right person
4. Prepare for the interview
5. Interview for the position
6. Follow up.

Promotion to What?

To gain a promotion, you will first need to identify a target position. Tell your boss you are interested in getting a promotion. Ask what the next step up is and what the requirements are. If the position one up from yours is not likely to be open any time soon, or does not interest you, look around for other options. Many organizations have an in-house job posting system, either on a bulletin board somewhere or accessible via the company network. Some organizations collect such postings in a notebook in the human resources department, and you will have to go there and leaf through them.

When examining your alternatives, pay special attention to transition positions that will open the door to further advancement. For example, if many of the organization managers came from a particular department or a particular position, you should focus on jobs in those areas first. To find this out, you can ask your boss or other "higher ups" how they came to hold their current position within the company. Most will be flattered that you are interested, and happy to share with you the story of their advancement. If you are lucky, you might even land a career mentor this way.

It is not necessary, or even desirable, to limit yourself to positions that seem easily within reach. Don't be afraid to stretch a little and pursue jobs even if you only have some of the qualifications. You might just land one of them.

Honing In On Your Target

Once you have identified a target position, find out everything you can about it. Is it a newly created position or a recently vacated one? If the job is not new, why did the person who previously held it leave? If the person is still at the company, or somewhere nearby, consider inviting him to lunch and asking about the details of the job and reasons he left it. You might find out that his boss is difficult to work for, which could lead you to reconsider your choice. At the very least you will gain an understanding of what duties and responsibilities the position really entails. Be sure to ask what the person liked most and least about working in that position.

If the individual who previously held the position is inaccessible to you, you will have to dig up details in other ways. Study the functions of the department the job falls under. Take someone from that area to lunch and pump him (nicely, of course) for information. It is fine to explain why you are asking. In fact, you might even gain an edge if she happens to like you.

One way to learn more about a particular position is to volunteer to take on some of the tasks it includes. This will involve extra work, since you will still have to complete your own job functions, but is an approach that has several things going for it. First of all, you will gain first-hand experience by test driving part of the job. Second, you will be demonstrating your ability to perform the functions, and to do them well. Third, you will show your initiative and willingness to go the extra mile by extending yourself in this way.

Get On the Schedule

After you have chosen a position to pursue, find out who will be conducting interviews for the position, and who will be making the hiring decision. These may not be the same person. Approach the appropriate contact and state that you are interested in pursuing the position, and would like to schedule a meeting to discuss your candidacy. When choosing a date, allow yourself adequate time to prepare, but don't make an appointment so long into the future that your anxiety builds over the delay.

Preparing for the Interview

Unlike asking for a raise, for which you can create and present a case that proves your position, an interview for a promotion to a new position will be structured and directed by the person doing the interviewing. Learn everything you can about that person. How did he advance to the position he now holds? Does she have particular peeves and preferences you should be aware of? If you can turn up someone else who has been interviewed by the same person, ask what the interview was like, what questions were asked, and overall how the interview went.

Once you have researched the position and the interviewer, begin planning your approach. How will you demonstrate that you hold the skills and qualifications needed for the position? Create a list that records each requirement and how you fulfill it. Don't forget to mention your ongoing technical training, but don't limit yourself to technical qualifications. Pay attention to human relations, leadership skills, and personal work habits too, which can be very important as you advance within the organization. This process will help solidify your qualifications in your own mind, so that they will flow smoothly from your lips during your interview.

Prepare a few questions to ask the interviewer. They might be about some of the technical details of the position or cover other issues. If you can phrase the questions in a way that demonstrates the knowledge you have gained through researching the position, so much the better. For example, you could say, "I know the sales department runs a token ring LAN with 52 workstations; is the number of workstations expected to change significantly over the next year? The point is to show that you are interested, informed, and thoughtful. You may not get to use all of your questions, but prepare several to have in mind.

Consider reading a "how-to-interview" book to refresh your memory on successful answers and body language. *Ace the Technical Interview* by Michael Rothstein (McGraw-Hill 1998) is written specifically for IT job candidates. You will find it, and many additional titles, in the career center of your local library or bookstore.

The Interview

Knowing that you are fully prepared will enable you to complete the interview process in a confident, relaxed manner. You may well feel stress from the pressure of the interview, but stress can be good as well as bad—it keeps you on your toes. Keep the following tips in mind:

* As always, dress for success. Choose attire that corresponds to the dress code of the position you are applying for, not the one you already hold.
* Be on time and pay attention to your body language. The interviewer will be taking cues from how you act as well as what you say.
* Maintain friendly eye contact and speak with sincerity.
* Do your best to avoid fidgeting. If you are a fidgeter by nature, direct your restlessness to a covert site: you can always jiggle your toes inside your shoes and the interviewer will never know.
* If you find yourself in a stressful situation, or unexpectedly challenged by the interviewer, remember that there is a good chance that you are probably being tested for your reaction to the situation. Keep your cool, and maintain your position if challenged on something (although it is certainly good to acknowledge another's point of view).
* Avoid discussing salary. Let the interviewer bring it up, if it comes up at all during the session.
* Bring extra copies of your resume in case they are needed.

As the interview gets under way, work to be an active rather than passive part of the process. Listen carefully. Ask questions to clarify just what the interviewer would like to know. When answering, draw from your prepared material. Work in information that shows how you are suited to fill the position. Don't forget to ask some of the questions you prepared earlier. You may be interviewed by more than one person—either in sequence or all at once. Be prepared for this and take notes on interviewer names and titles.

At the conclusion of the interview, shake the interviewer's hand and thank him or her for making time for you. Restate that you want the position, and are looking forward to hearing about the decision.

Follow Up

Interview follow-up is an often neglected part of the process. By making sure you don't overlook this step, you will put yourself ahead of many of your competitors. If an agency arranged the interview for you, telephone your agency contact as soon as possible after the interview to report how the process went and whether or not you want the position.

Also as soon as possible after the interview, write a letter thanking the interviewer. Summarize the nature of your meeting, and reiterate your qualifications for the position. If you met with several individuals in the course of the interview, remember to thank them as well. Include a fresh copy of your resume.

If you don't hear within a few days, it is all right to call and ask when a decision will be made about the position. Just don't make a pest of yourself with numerous calls or messages.

If you don't get the job, don't take it too personally. There are often many candidates competing for a position, and you may have to repeat this process several times before you obtain a promotion. Ask the interviewer why you were not chosen. It might be easier for both of you if you phrase the question in a way that explores why the other candidate was better suited to the position instead of asking for a list of your shortcomings. Consider whether you can augment your qualifications to strengthen your candidacy next time around.

Increasing Consulting Rates

If you are an independent consultant, you cannot really seek a promotion, but you can boost your rates to reflect your increased value as a certified professional. At the same time, you need to be careful not to price yourself out of the market.

The best way to determine the rates you can reasonably charge is to find out what other consultants who provide the same services bill. There are several places you can turn to for this information. One is the placement firms who connect professionals like yourself with potential employers. A firm in your area should be able to give you an idea of the local rates.

Contracting opportunities posted on the Internet are another source of rate information. You can search computer job boards for contracts that require skills like your own, and look for postings that contain rate information. A good place to look is DICE at **www.dice.com**. Another excellent Internet source is Janet Ruhl's real rates survey (**www.realrates.com**), which collects rate information from consultants who visit the site and makes it available to anyone interested. The Real Rates site is shown in Figure 13.4.

Another possibility is to frequent forums and mailing lists where other Cisco-certified individuals are found, and connect with other consultants like yourself. E-mail them privately, and inquire if they are willing to share information on their billing rates or pay on previous contracts.

Use your rate research to determine a range for your services and skills. Remember to take into account your experience level and any special qualifications, such as level of Cisco certification. If previous clients question your new rates, explain that you have simply revised them to reflect current market rates for services like your own.

FIGURE 13.4
Janet Ruhl's Real
Rates Survey

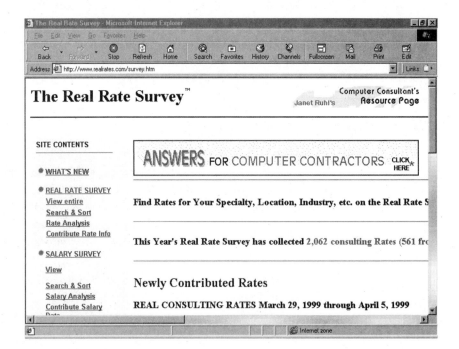

What to Do If Your Efforts Don't Work

Taking a planned, organized approach to career advancement will usually bring prompt results. This is especially true in the current IT industry environment, where demand for skilled technical people continues to outpace supply, and demand for Cisco-certified individuals is especially strong. However, your first or second attempts may still be unsuccessful. Persistence is an important factor in career advancement, in any profession. If your first efforts at moving up don't come to fruition, analyze the reasons why, take aim at a new goal, and try again. Whether or not your efforts result in immediate advancement, keep a professional attitude. Things to keep in mind include:

* *Have a graceful fallback plan.* If the boss says no to your raise or promotion, or your clients balk at your rate increase, what will you do? Have your response planned in advance so that it can roll off your tongue, despite your disappointment. Remember, you can always try again.

* *Don't burn bridges is a trite saying but wise advice.* You never know if the person you aggravate today will be your boss or coworker at some time in the future. Make every effort to be considerate and professional. Don't let anger or hostility cloud your judgment (and potentially your future advancement).

* *Don't make a pest of yourself.* Persistence is important, but not to the point of becoming an annoyance. Constantly reminding your boss that you want a raise or a promotion will make you an irritation and work against you. Work to demonstrate your value and monitor yourself to prevent this problem.

Finding Career Advancement Advice on the Web

Although most Internet career sites focus on finding a job rather than moving up within your current organization, there are several useful advancement resources you might want to visit.

careerplanning.miningco.com is the Mining Company's career advancement site. It features articles, links, and a forum where you can post your questions and advice with others. The site is shown in Figure 13.5.

www.hardatwork.com/Escalator/career1.html is the Web site of the Hard@Work Career Escalator. It contains an ongoing discussion of career

advancement topics, articles on promotions, raises, career breakpoints, and interview help.

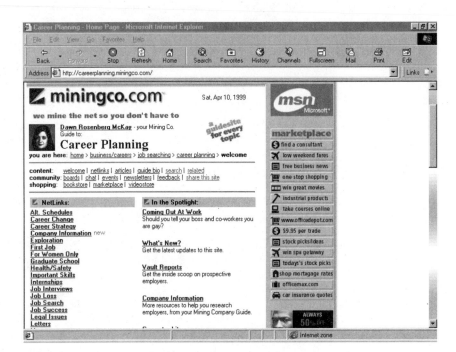

By preparing carefully, you will boost yourself to the front of
queue for raises and promotions. You will also be able to move
upward more swiftly than coworkers who wait for advancement
to come to them instead of going after it. Throughout your career,
you should work to keep your skills current with workplace
needs. That will require constant reassessment and planning for
where you want to go next. Although career advancement
requires strategizing and effort to succeed, the payoff will be well
worth it.

CHAPTER 14

Moving On

An earned Cisco certification gives your marketability a sudden boost and is often used as a springboard to a new position. In fact, many professionals pursue certification with the primary intention of using it to land a new job. A 1998 survey of certification candidates revealed that 17 percent of them expect certification to be a deciding factor in helping secure a new job. That's up two percent from 1997. More than half the respondents are pursuing certification as a means to advance in their profession.

Although Cisco certification can also help you move up through the ranks at your current place of employment, for one reason or another, many professionals prefer to move on to an entirely new job situation. If you are ready to move on, or simply want to explore the possibilities, you first need to develop a profile of the type of job you would like to obtain. Next, you will need to dust off your resume and update it to reflect your certified status. Then, dive into the job market and begin exploring your options. There are loads of jobs out there, and one of them is bound to be just right for you.

Before You Start Your Search

Before diving into a job search, take the time to define exactly what is you want to accomplish by finding a new position. As a starting point, examine your current job and identify its shortcomings and strengths. Rate it on items such as amount of responsibility, on-call duties, compensation, potential for advancement, access to technologies that you are interested in working with, and your general overall satisfaction with the work environment. By identifying where your current employer falls short, you can increase your chances that the new position you find will prove a step up. Sometimes an assessment like this has a surprise result: you find out your current job is actually providing you with most of which you want. If that is the case, consider an upward or lateral move at your current place of employment. Many individuals with newly earned Cisco career certifications use them to obtain a position that brings daily hands on work with networks using Cisco routers and switches. This provides them with experience and an environment that can be used as a springboard to the elite CCIE certifications.

QUOTE

Entering a New Specialty

I got my first certification because I'd identified it as a way to help me break into a line of work that interested me—computer networking. At the time, that meant becoming a CNE. I began preparing for the CNE tests by reading Novell's CompuServe support forums, known as NetWire, and I responded to a classified advertisement I saw online there for an entry-level CNE wannabe. I got the job. The first day they told me to install a server. I did it, and I liked it. It didn't take me long to get my CNE after that.

However, as I'd gotten more involved with computer networks, I'd also started hearing about "Paper CNEs," and I didn't want to be one. I decided that I was going to excel at computer networking, and I wanted a certification that would set me off from the crowd, so I proceeded to become an Enterprise CNE. My following certifications were really just a continuation of this theme—using tests to prove that I am good at some aspect of networking. The harder the test, the more I liked it.

—David Yarashus, CCIE, MCSE, CNX, ECNE, and several other certifications.

As you prepare to enter the job market, remember that it can be a stressful place. You are going to encounter rejection, especially if you go for positions at the upper range of your qualifications. Don't take it personally. Rejection is not an indication of your personal worth. Rather, it signifies that there was no match between yourself, the position, and the hiring manager. If you don't collect a few (or even many) of those "we regret to inform you" letters, then you are probably not aiming high enough.

Another stress factor to consider is the wait. It is unlikely your first resume will hit the optimum target. Patience is necessary, as is persistence. Don't expect immediate success or you will almost certainly be disappointed. You may have to dig into vacation time to attend interviews and devote some of your leisure hours to researching positions and companies and performing other marketing tasks.

On the up side, remember why you started the certification process in the first place—to advance your career. Whether you are after higher pay, a position with greater responsibilities, entrance into a new area of expertise, or any other positive career move, changing jobs is a powerful way to put your certification to work for you.

Pay-Off Time

I believe my certifications have earned me higher pay than I would have had otherwise, but it's difficult to quantify that precisely. I know that my pay increases have
averaged almost 20 percent each time I've changed jobs over the last three years
(five times). I think the certifications have played an important role. Of course, I've
sought out employers who have reason to value the certifications most highly.

—Pamela Forsyth, CCIE, ECNE, MCSE, and other certifications

A Resume Tune-Up

Once you have clarified the type of position you are after and
reminded yourself of the nature of job searches, it's time to sharp-
en your resume, which will of course include information on your
new Cisco certification(s). Later on you may create unique versions, tailored to a particular job opening, but first, you will need
a starting resume; one as strong as you can make it.

Resumes can be as individual as the person who creates them
and may be classified into a half dozen formats. For a comprehensive discussion of resume formats and wording, visit your local
bookstore or library for a resume writing guide. You can also try
one of these handy online resume aids:

* **content.monster.com/resume/**—Contains numerous sample resumes and cover letters, as well as articles to help you
  hone a perfect resume of your own.
* **www.his.com/~rockport/resumes.htm**—*How to Write An
  Exceptional Resume* is an excellent, in-depth presentation on
  resume writing goals and practices. Figure 14.1 shows this
  Web site.
* **www.bio.com/hr/search/ResumeRocket.html**—This article, "Resume Rocket Science" puts resume writing in perspective and will help you make yours the best it can be.

Meanwhile, here is a resume refresher, which may be all you
need. The two most widely used resume styles are chronological
and functional. Any format you choose should lead off with your
name, address, telephone number, and e-mail address. An
employment objective often follows, such as:

FIGURE 14.1
Exceptional
Resume Advice
Web Site

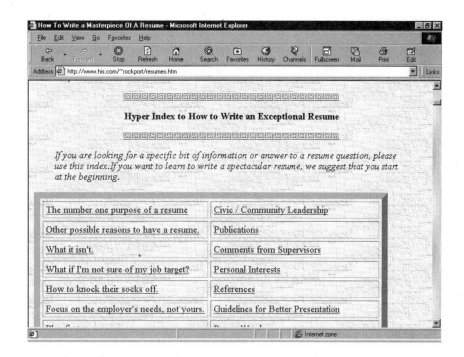

Professional Objective: A position managing a medium to large WAN in a corporate environment.

Because specific technical skills are of critical importance when hiring computer professionals, they are listed prominently. Depending on the diversity of your experience, you may decide to lump them under a single heading, such as technical skills, or break them out by category. This is one possible place to list your certifications.

Software/OS: C/C++, Cisco IOS, COBOL, Oracle, Pascal, RPGII, SQL, Visual Basic, MS-DOS, Windows/NT

Hardware: Cisco 2500 Series, HP/3000, IBM compatible microcomputers, NCR Tower

Certifications: CCNP, CCIE in progress

Work history or education follows next, depending on which you think is strongest. The work history section is where the chronological and functional styles diverge. Chronological resumes organize work history by employer, starting with the most recent (usually current) and working backwards. They work well to emphasize continuous growth in a single profession. Each entry includes dates, employer, location, and job title, followed by a succinct description of duties and accomplishments. For example:

1990–Present   Associate Systems Analyst, ABC Corporation, Hartford, CT

Responsible for software and hardware installation and maintenance of 200 node network with Internet link. Prepared and presented training seminars and materials at the data center and the customer site. Performed technical support activities for relational database products.

Resumes organized in the functional style highlight work experience by job function rather than by date and employer. This format is especially useful when changing professions or if you want to emphasize the scope of your experience over the continuity. For example:

Project Leadership: Directed development of in-house customer support workstation from design phase through implementation. Supervised and coordinated team of four programmer-analysts. Delivered projects on time and under budget.

In the Education section, achievements should be listed from most recent to least recent. That means your certifications should be first. If you have a college degree, don't bother to list your high school diploma.

Your resume should also list professional affiliations, honors and awards, publications, and any additional qualifications you hold. *Don't* include personal information such as family/marital status, age, race, religion, health information, or a physical description of yourself. Such information is irrelevant to your qualifications for employment.

No matter how perfect your resume is, it will not get you the job; you will have to do that in person through one or more interviews. What your resume will do is get you that interview in the first place. For that reason, it is important to make it as perfect as you can and to emphasize your strengths.

You may be able to create a powerful resume on your own, especially if you have an existing resume to work from, but take advantage of one or more of the how-to books available to guide you through the process. If you don't feel satisfied with the result, consider using a resume preparation service. You can also obtain resume help from the career resource office of a school you have attended.

Books To Help

Knock 'Em Dead 1999: The Ultimate Job Seeker's Handbook by Martin John Yate (Adams Media Corp.)

The $100,000 Resume by Craig Scott Rice (McGraw-Hill)

Jobsearch: The Complete Manual For Job Seekers by H. Lee Rush (Amacom)

How to Get Your Dream Job Using The Internet by Shannon Bounds and Arthur Karl (The Coriolis Group)

Resume Writing: A Comprehensive How-To-Do-It Guide by Burdette E. Bostwick (John Wiley & Sons)

But Is It Computer Friendly?

Resume layout has long been a challenge to those who are not desktop publishing wizards. It can take a dozen reprints to get the margins just right; settle on sharp, decent-sized fonts; and otherwise manipulate your resume so that it looks appealing. Today that is only half the job. You also need a resume that is appealing to computers.

If you submit your beautifully designed masterpiece electronically, as is often required these days, it may arrive at the other end looking scrambled. Unless you are Picasso, that will not work in your favor. To get around this problem, you need a version of your resume that is computer readable.

The safest bet when transmitting resumes electronically is to use ASCII format. ASCII (American Standard Code for Information Interchange) can be read by many different kinds of computers. Saving your resume in ASCII format will keep the text, tabs, and spacing but lose all other formatting, such as indents, special fonts, bold print, and underlining. Once you have created a reasonable ASCII resume, you will be able to transmit it electronically and have it arrive looking the same as when you sent it.

To create an ASCII version of your resume, use your word processor and select a font that is not proportionally spaced. Courier is a good choice. Don't apply any formatting as you input your resume information. You can still make it appear clean and appealing through the use of spaces and tabs to line things up. No line should be longer than 69 characters, or it may wrap in funny places on the recipient's screen.

To save your ASCII resume, chose File | Save As from your word processor's menu. Then look for one of the following options: DOS Text, Text Only, or ASCII. Select the option and save your file.

QUICK TIP

Before shipping your resume off to a potential employer, e-mail it to yourself and see what shape it arrives in.

Another request you may encounter is one for a scannable resume. The employer will feed your resume through a scanner and convert it using OCR (optical character recognition) software into a text file for storage in a database. Although any resume can be scanned, results vary widely and illegible results are common. If you design your resume with scanning in mind, you can maximize the chances that yours will scan beautifully. To make your resume scanner friendly, follow these guidelines:

* Keep the format simple, standard, and free of borders
* Avoid graphics
* Use basic, sans serif fonts (such as Arial) that will not confuse scanning software
* Select a font size between 10 and 14 point
* Use light colored paper; white is best
* Send an original; photocopies may not be high enough quality
* Send it in a flat 9 × 12 envelope so it arrives without folds or creases.

As you can see, you may need to create more than one version of your resume to meet employer requirements. Because the differences will be in formatting rather than in content, doing so should not be excessively time consuming. The beauty of electronic resumes lies in their accessibility. They can be searched and called up anytime from anywhere.

QUICK TIP

Rebecca Smith's eResumes & Resources (**www.eresumes.com**) is the only site you will need to find out everything about electronic resumes. This wonderful resource covers everything from how to put your resume into formats that computers can handle to creating an online resume and finding places to post it. You can also browse a gallery of resumes that show how others are marketing themselves online, read loads of useful articles, and even grab a few laughs.

Keeping It Hush-Hush

There are many reasons why you might wish to keep your job search plans to yourself, the foremost being if your search ends without turning up a superior offer, the relationship with your current employer has not been damaged. But discretion has its price; you will not be able to network as extensively for fear of word getting back to your employer. Word of mouth can be a powerful job search tool, and giving it up can cramp your style considerably. You will have to weigh the factors on both sides to decide whether a clandestine job search or a public one will serve you best.

If you do want to keep your plans to yourself, or at least be reasonably discreet, employ the following practices:

✳ Put only your home phone number on your resume, not your work number. Install an answering machine and check it daily to make sure it is operating properly. Call it throughout the day to check for messages so you can respond promptly.

✳ Don't return calls from your desk. Return calls from an empty conference room or, better yet, a phone away from your place of work.

✳ Don't use your employer's materials in your job search. Supply your own paper, and get your copies made at a copy shop.

* If you require the use of a fax machine, a public one (or one that belongs to a friend). Some libraries have a fax machine available, as do copy shops.
* Don't use your business e-mail address for job search communications. Whether it is morally acceptable or not, it is legal for your boss to read your electronic mail.
* Make every effort to conduct your job search without impinging on your work hours. Utilize breaks, your lunch hour, and before- and after-hours options as frequently as possible.

If, despite your efforts, your boss does discover your job search, make the best of it. Explain why you were looking and that you were doing so on your own time. Reassure your employer that you will not leave him in the lurch and even offer to help find/train your replacement.

What if your current employer offers incentives to keep you from leaving? Consider carefully before accepting. You have already made up your mind to leave, and now that your boss knows that, the question of your dedication and loyalty will linger throughout your career with this employer. It may be best not to accept the inducements to stay and instead stick with your original plan to land that new job. On the other hand, if you are offered the plum you were looking for, take it.

How to Find Job Openings

A primary activity of the job search is to find suitable job postings. Professionals in the computer field are currently enjoying a bountiful time, with more jobs than there are qualified people to fill them. This gap is projected to continue to widen.

A 1997 study by the Information Technology Association of America (ITAA) warns that the need for IT workers exceeds supply and will continue to do so until growth slows in both IT and non-IT industries.

According to the ITAA, "In a systematic survey of large- and mid-size IT and non-IT companies, ITAA found that a weighted estimate reveals there are approximately 190,000 unfilled IT jobs in America today. This number actually understates the overall demand for such workers, because ITAA did not survey small companies, non-profit organizations, or local, state, and federal government agencies and, therefore, did not include those employers' needs for skilled IT workers in this study."

The study also found that among IT companies, 82 percent expected to increase the number of IT employees in the coming year and only 2 percent anticipated a reduction. Of companies that are outside the IT industry but still use IT workers, 56 percent expected to add to their IT staffing in the coming year, while only 3 percent anticipated reducing it.

All of this indicates an IT worker's market, with plenty of opportunities to choose from. All you have to do is find the right ones. Thanks to the information technology boom, locating potential employment is easier than ever. You can connect with companies searching for skilled technology workers in many different ways, including through:

* The Cisco Web site
* Headhunters and recruiting companies
* Print advertisements in newspapers and magazines
* Job fairs
* Internet and Web job banks
* Networking opportunities.

To find your optimum position, you will want to explore multiple avenues. Don't overlook opportunities to advance at your current place of employment. See Chapter 13 for help and advice on using your certification to get ahead right where you are.

Cisco's Web Site

Although Cisco does not provide employment assistance, you can still use their Web site to find potential employers. The partner locator, in particular, will prove useful in your search. This site, found along with other related resources at **www.cisco.com/warp/public/767/find/**, can be used to identify resellers and partners near you. Figure 14.2 shows this site. All Cisco silver, gold, and premier partners are required to have Cisco certified personnel on staff. Each premier partner must have one CCNA, one CCDA, and one sales expert per country they serve. Silver partners must have two CCIEs, one CCDP, one CCNP, one CCDA, and one Sales Expert; gold partners need four CCIEs, two CCDPs, one CCNP, and a Sales Expert. Although a single individual can fulfill two requirements, this still translates into lots of job opportunities for Cisco certified professionals.

FIGURE 14.2

Identifying Cisco Partners and Resellers

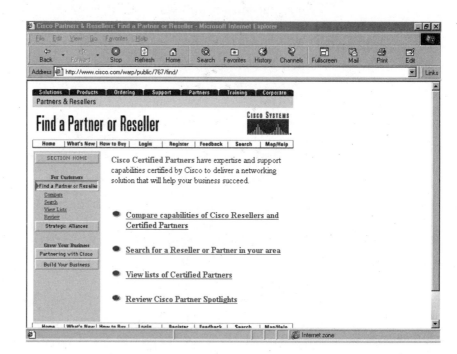

Don't forget to check Cisco's online recruitment page (shown in Figure 14.3) as well. You'll find it at **www.cisco.com/jobs/**.

Headhunters

Headhunters (also known as recruiters) are individuals who find people to fill jobs. Headhunters are hungry. They are always looking for resumes because without resumes they cannot fill positions. They are always looking for positions to fill because they cannot place people without jobs to put them in. Like sharks, they always have to keep moving, on the hunt. Like sharks, they have been known to bite the hand that feeds them.

FIGURE 14.3

Job Openings
at Cisco

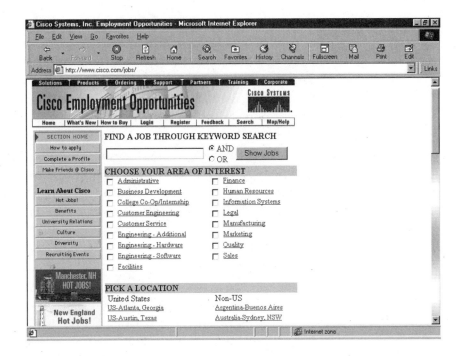

A bad headhunter may send you on as many interviews as possible without performing adequate screening first, with the goal of getting you placed somewhere, anywhere, to get paid the fee. Or he might send a candidate to a position that is a poor match in order to seem to be doing something for the client company. Firms that practice these tactics are sometimes called *body shops*.

Working through a middleman has additional drawbacks. When communication has to pass through an additional layer, it is more likely to get muddled. When you work with a headhunter, communication between you and the potential employer passes through that extra layer.

Sometimes a headhunter will conceal the identity of the company behind a job opening until receiving your resume and interviewing you for fear you will go straight to the company yourself. If you did go to the company yourself, it might not do you much good because, in a large company, you would have no idea of the name of the hiring manger for the position, and your resume might never reach the right person.

Like lawyers, headhunters are much maligned, often with good reason. And like lawyers, a good one can prove very valuable. Headhunters know the jobs available. They have connections at corporations and relationships with hiring managers. Because of their relationships with hiring companies, headhunters are often aware of jobs that have not been advertised. They can put you in for an excellent job you otherwise would not have known about. They can negotiate money for you. That can be a big plus if you find negotiating compensation packages about as appealing as a severe case of stomach flu. The headhunter's payoff is a percentage of your first year's salary, so there is strong incentive to get you the biggest paycheck possible.

Given that headhunters can do so much for you, you may well decide to work with one or more. You will find an extensive array of them on the World Wide Web. There is a huge directory of them on Yahoo! at **yahoo.com/Business_and_Economy/Companies/ Computers/Employment/Recruiting_and_Placement/**. They can also be found by looking for names at the bottom of job postings or using one of the other search engines. Ask friends for referrals; they may be able to point you toward quality recruiters.

Before submitting your resume to a recruiter, find out as much as you can. Inquire about procedures and insist that your resume not be submitted anywhere, for any reason, without your approval. It is a small thing for the recruiter to call you up and say "I've got a position at in ISP in East Oshkosh doing network installation that I want to put you in for. Okay?" Insist on such courtesies.

It is also a good idea to ask other computer professionals what they know of the firm and whether their opinion is good or bad. You can also seek such information online. Post an inquiry in a forum that computer professionals frequent, asking for opinions on the firm you are considering. The computer consultants' forum on CompuServe, for example, would be a suitable place.

Print Advertisements

One of the first places job hunters turn to is the classified section of a nearby newspaper. Because it is such a popular source of job leads, advertisements trigger a large number of responses. Although that means you will face a lot of competition, it is still worthwhile to respond to job announcements that interest you. Just don't be discouraged if you have a lower reply rate from potential employers you contact this way. They may be swamped with candidates and only take time to respond to the top applicants. Your goal, of course, is to be one of those top candidates.

Augment the listings in your local newspaper by picking up copies of (or subscribing to) national newspapers, such as *The Wall Street Journal*, *The New York Times*, and *National Business Employment Weekly*. As an alternative, you can plan an evening at the library browsing these and other national publications, photocopying listings that interest you.

If you are planning a move to a new location, consider obtaining a subscription to the largest newspaper that serves the area. You can have it mailed to your current address.

Trade publications should be key print sources of job postings. Because they focus on the industry in question, you will have fewer irrelevant ads to wade through. Good leads for computer jobs can be found in publications such as *Communications Week*, *InformationWeek*, or *Contract Professional*, among others.

When you come across a job advertisement that interests you, clip it and staple or tape it to a standard sized piece of paper to prevent it from getting mislaid. Each advertisement should have its own page, which will serve as a repository of notes regarding the particular ad. This method also enables easy storage of all your advertisements in a folder or three-ring binder.

The first thing you should record on the page is the name and date of the publication you found the advertisement in. This will spare you the embarrassment of saying, "I don't know" when an employer asks where you encountered the ad, and allows you to mention the ad source in your cover letter.

Next, read the advertisement carefully to identify the company that placed the ad and the qualifications sought. Record what you discover on your notes page. If the advertisement still looks appealing after your second read, it is time to find out something about the company. Some advertisements are blind, meaning they don't mention the employer, but most often the company offering the job is clearly identified. If you are already familiar with it, great. Otherwise, do a bit of research to find out the basics on products, market, and size. A good resource is *Hoover's Handbook of American Companies*, which you can find at your library or access via the Internet at **www.hoovers.com**. Figure 14.4 shows the *Hoover's* Web site.

To respond to the advertisement, you will write a letter. To do that, you will need a name at the company. Human Resources Director is not good enough. Call the company and ask the receptionist for the name and title of the proper person to send your resume to.

FIGURE 14.4
The Hoover's
Web Site

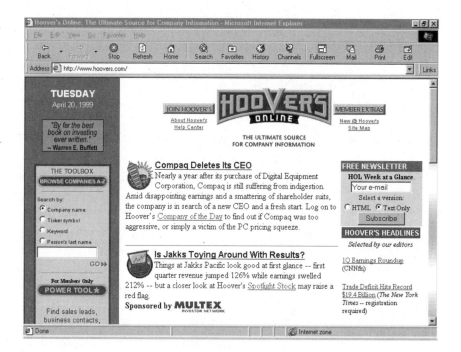

Your cover letter should be succinct, written on quality stationary, and intended to arouse interest in your abilities. As in a good novel, the first sentence is critical. Use it to grab your reader's attention by stating something important to them. One approach is to open with a mention of your strongest qualification for the job. As you continue, don't just mention your strengths, give examples of how you have applied them. Keep the letter short—two pages maximum. One page is better. Whoever is screening the replies will have many to go through and will not appreciate long, rambling letters. Your closing sentence should be compelling, too. Use it to ask for a personal interview to discuss the opportunity.

Staple a copy of your response letter to the page bearing the advertisement and your notes. If you are using more than one version of your resume, attach a copy of the version you sent with your letter as well. Then put everything in your "to follow up" file.

Job Fairs

A job fair offers the opportunity to meet dozens, if not hundreds, of employers in one place over the course of one or two days. It is a chance to do efficient, condensed job hunting.

Job fairs can be intimidating, too. They can feel like meat markets with you as one piece of meat among hundreds. Nonetheless, attending them can prove well worth the temporary discomfort. Besides the obvious opportunity to connect with a specific job, you will also be networking, creating and collecting contacts you can come back to in the future. The job fair is also a great place to learn about new companies, what they are doing, what they plan to do, and the types of jobs they have to fill.

Job fairs are usually advertised in local newspapers, and sometimes you can find them by searching the Internet. Choose one that is geographically compatible with your plans and focuses on technical opportunities. There is no use attending a job fair featuring only local companies if you plan to relocate to the opposite coast.

The advertisement will probably identify the companies that will be in attendance, but if it does not, call the coordinating organization and ask for a list to be sent to you by mail or fax. This gives you a chance to plan hit lists of primary targets and second-choice companies you want to make contact with. Do a little research on companies that interest you.

Your resume should be in tip-top shape, and it won't hurt to bring business cards, too. Make sure your certification is listed prominently on both. Consider preparing a second or third version of your resume that emphasizes different strengths. For example, one version might play up your network management skills while another underscores your expertise with internet-working hardware.

In advance, create a three- to five-minute spiel about yourself and your qualifications. Don't exceed five minutes. The recruiters and hiring managers will speak with hundreds of potential applicants and won't have the patience to listen to rambling, unfocused presentations. You want to say who you are, where your technical strengths lie, and what you have done with them. Include several examples of problems you have solved and how you have solved them. Practice your pitch in front of a mirror.

On the big day, dress as you would for an interview. It is unlikely that you will be hired on the spot, but you need to look your professional best. Bring multiple copies of your resume and plenty of business cards—more than you think you will need. It is also a good idea to bring a notepad for jotting down information on companies that interest you. Of course, bring your list of target companies so you can make sure you visit the booths you have identified as most important.

Start with a company on your B list (or not on your list at all). That way you can fine-tune your spiel before connecting with the companies you are most interested in. When you are introducing yourself to a recruiter, watch his body language and wrap it up if he keeps glancing at his watch or gazing over your shoulder, signs that his interest is not on you.

Collect business cards and company literature and pause between booths to take notes on what you talked about and with whom. Otherwise, it will be difficult to follow up effectively. Speaking of follow-up, do it within a day or so of the fair. Send a letter recapping your conversation, and include a fresh copy of your resume. Then, while you wait for the phone to start ringing with interview calls, continue your job search efforts on other fronts.

QUICK TIP

A job fair is an excellent place to get a feel for which technologies are hot and which skills are in demand. If you notice that many recruiters are searching for people with a particular skill, make a note of it so you can consider adding it to your repertoire.

Online Job Hunting

Job hunting via the Internet is efficient and fun, too. You can browse in all kinds of interesting Web sites and take advantage of the rich supply of job hunting resources. If a particular company interests you, you can visit its Web site. Most will have a job opportunities section. In many cases, you will be able to reply online.

The Web is also a huge repository of job postings. Many sites collect thousands of openings in databases, and you can search them by qualifications, salary, geographic location, or other specifications. Some of these sites will even let you register your preferences and then notify you by e-mail if any postings are added that fit your specifications.

You can also use the Web to bring employers to you. It really is a worker's market in the computer industry, and recruiters are actively looking for bodies to fill open positions. If you post your resume on one of the many sites that allow you to do so, chances are your e-mail box will soon hold inquiries for you to consider.

A Baker's Dozen: Thirteen Places to Find Computer Jobs Online

The Web as a medium is so conducive to job placement functions that the sheer quantity of job sites can, at times, become overwhelming. Although many of the giant job sites post openings in all industries and areas, others focus on particular job markets. The following Web sites cater to the high-tech job hunter. Most are specific to computer professionals. The others are more broadly based, but contain a high percentage of computer-related opportunities.

* **comp.jobs.offered** is a Usenet newsgroup of open computer positions.
* **computerwork.com** is a leading online job board and resume bank, a database of technical jobs and contract opportunities and a potential place to post your resume.
* **www.cio.com/forums/wmf_job_posts.html** is *WebMaster Magazine*'s Webmaster Wanted site containing job postings for

Web-related positions, including Webmasters, Web site managers, intranet managers, and others.

* **www.computerjobs.com** is the home page of The Computer-Jobs Store, which has job listings for Atlanta, Chicago, the Carolinas, and Texas.

* **www.datamation.com/PlugIn/jobs/itjobs.html** is *Datamation*'s site that links to the recruitment pages of leading IT vendors.

* **www.dice.com** sends you to DICE , a monster collection of consulting and permanent computer-related job postings.

* **www.headhunter.net** is Headhunter.Net, and although it is not strictly limited to high-tech jobs, it includes many positions for computer professionals.

* **supersite.net/computercurrentsjobbank** is the Computer Currents Professional Job Bank.

* **www.monster.com** is an online career center with a huge database of jobs from top companies. You can search by industry and geographic area or just browse the latest postings.

* **www.prgjobs.com** is the Jobs For Programmers site, an extensive job resource with full-time, contract, and telecommuting job listings. You can also post your qualifications blind (without your name) and have replies forwarded to you via e-mail.

* **www.softwarejobs.com** is The Software Jobs home page. It lists positions available across the country and can be searched by keyword.

* **www.careerbuilder.com** allows you to search and apply for a job online. This site will e-mail you when opportunities that meet your specifications are posted.

* **www.selectjobs.com** is the home page of the Select Jobs Web site. You can search job openings by skills, location, title, or keywords of your choice. You can also register to be notified of new openings that meet your qualifications.

When responding to an electronic job offering, be sure to follow the instructions mentioned in the posting. If a position identification number is mentioned, be sure to include it in your reply. If you are responding via e-mail, be certain to spell check your message before sending it. E-mail is not an excuse for poor grammar and spelling.

If your electronic mail program does not incorporate spell checking, compose your message using your word processor instead. After you confirm that it is free from spelling errors, select the text of your message and cut and paste it into the body of a new e-mail message.

Networking

Don't underestimate the power of your connections to land your dream job. Tell relatives, coworkers, and friends that you are looking. If you are attempting to be covert, tell only those you can trust to be discreet. Keeping your job search confidential comes with a price because it will limit your options to some degree.

Successful networking largely consists of being visible. Attend professional functions and mingle. If you know someone who knows someone with connections to a place you want to work, don't be afraid to ask for an introduction. The worst you will hear is no, and you will probably hear yes. Seek out professional associations related to your area of expertise. They may have referral services, and if not, are still a good way to meet others who work in (and hire for) your profession.

Follow Up

Whichever route you use to locate job listings, remember to follow up on opportunities you respond to. It is a basic task that's been stressed in every job hunting guide ever published but it is often overlooked. Send that thank-you letter after an interview, and you could distinguish yourself from all the other candidates who never get around to it. Make that follow-up phone call you promised in your cover letter, and you will be demonstrating your ability to follow through. Yes, these are somewhat mundane tasks and they take up your time. But they could be just the step that clinches the interview, or the job that you would really like to call your own.

Going Independent

If you have been on the brink of a career as an independent consultant, your certification may provide the impetus to make the move.

Look carefully before you leap. The benefits of self employment are potentially limitless, but there are plenty of drawbacks, too.

The independent contractor/consultant needs to be tenacious and organized. You will have to find your own work, create and adhere to your own schedule, and perform the functions that accompany running your own business. Table 14.1 summarizes many of the pros and cons you will encounter if you go independent.

Pros	Cons
Manage your own career direction	Will have to manage fluctuations in income
Freedom from office politics and red tape	Work and leisure boundaries blur
Potential tax benefits via business tax deductions	Must wear all the hats: accounting, sales, marketing, production, administration
More control over work/life balance	No externally imposed structure to guide you
Direct responsibility for your income level and success	No corporate benefits

Drake Beam Morin, Inc., an outplacement and career management firm, has devoted a section of its Web site to information for people considering self employment. Visit **www.dbm.com/career/employment/reality.html** (shown in Figure 14.5) to explore your motivations for self employment and the realities you're likely to face.

To form a solid picture of the consulting life, there is no substitute for reports from the field. Seek out friends or coworkers who are self employed or who have been in the past, and take them to lunch so you can get the firsthand scoop. Visit forums and Web sites dedicated to computer contractors, and read, read, read. Professionals who frequent these sites are usually willing to share their advice and experiences and can be very helpful to the new consultant, and you will find many articles to advise you. Some of the more helpful sites include:

FIGURE 14.5
Self-employment
Reality Check

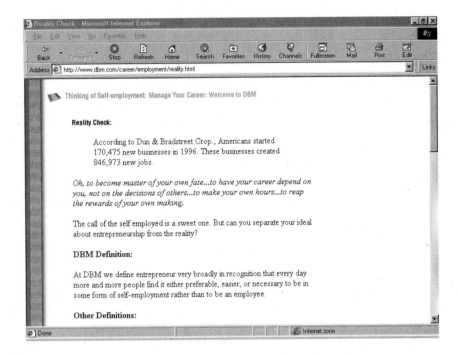

* Janet Ruhl's Computer Consultant's Resource Page (**www.realrates.com**), which is shown in Figure 14.6, is a must-see site for anyone considering going independent. You will find advice on the ins and outs of the consulting life, current billing rates around the country for various skill sets, suggestions on how to negotiate contracts, and much more – including contract job opportunities.
* The discussion forums on the Web site of Contract Professional Forum (**www.cpuniverse.com**) are good ways to seek advice and interact with experienced contractors and consultants.

If you decide to become an independent consultant, don't neglect to capitalize on your certification(s). They are credentials that will add to your credibility with potential clients, which will be especially useful when you're just starting out.

Don't overlook Cisco's consultant program if you decide to go independent. You will get help with sales-related questions and materials, as well as access to the Cisco Consultant Web site at **www.cisco.com/warp/public/792/index.html** (see Figure 14.7).

FIGURE 14.6
Janet Ruhl's
Computer
Consultant's Page

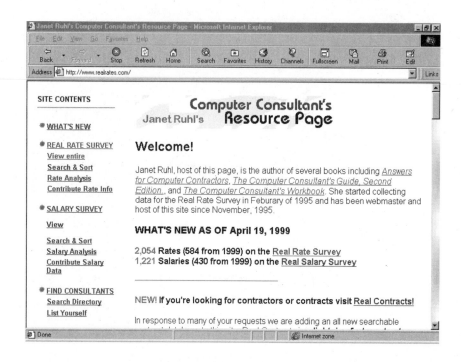

FIGURE 14.7
Cisco Consultants
Web Site

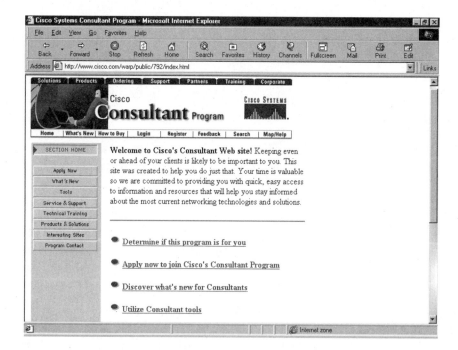

Spare Those Bridges

No matter how aggravating a position you are leaving has been, be careful of how you represent it. Don't criticize your previous employer during interviews or to your new employer. Even if every word you say is true, you are conveying an image of yourself as a complainer and possibly even a backstabber. Those are not good traits to be associated with. If you have done it to a past employer, what is to keep you from badmouthing this one a year down the line?

Along the same lines, be wary of exit interviews. While it can be very satisfying to answer a question like: "Is there anything the company could have done to keep you from leaving?" with a retort like "Yes, treat me decently," don't do it. The future is unpredictable, and the day may come when you encounter your boss somewhere down the road. Such comments, however honest, may come back to haunt you. Although confidentiality may be promised during the exit interview process, don't count on it. It is probably not that hard for a manager to tie a particular exit interview with the individual who gave it, even without your name gracing the page.

Finally, throughout your job search, keep records of all your expenditures. You may be able to deduct some of your job search expenses on your tax return at the end of the year. Items such as resume printing, postage, unreimbursed travel for job-seeking purposes, and placement agency fees, are generally deductible as miscellaneous itemized deductions on Schedule A (Form 1040). As such, they are subject to the 2 percent limit, which means that they are deductible only to the extent that they exceed 2 percent of your adjusted gross income (AGI). Various and sundry other restrictions also apply. Consult a tax professional if your job search expenses are significant.

Although few people, if any, would consider a job hunt enjoyable, the results can certainly justify the effort. By moving on to a new position, you may be able to boost your salary, increase your personal satisfaction, and land a job that offers an optimum blend of challenge, reward, and professional growth—the type of job you can look forward to undertaking each day.

CHAPTER 15

Keeping Current

Once you have obtained your Cisco certification, it is important to pay attention to the currency of your skills. However you look at it, continuing professional education is a critical component of any successful career, especially in the computer professions. As this book went to press, only the CCIE designations required continuing professional education as a condition of retaining certified status. However, even if Cisco does not currently insist on continuing requirements for the other certifications, the value of your certification will be enhanced by the fact that you have taken steps to update your skills to keep pace with technological changes.

Professional development efforts prove most valuable when undertaken in a planned, intentional manner. The requirements set forth by the Cisco certification program outline a minimum path for you to follow. Use it as a starting point, but keep in mind that as a certification sponsor, Cisco's requirements are geared to support the individual certification; if your certification is in a narrow area, they won't provide an adequate continuing education plan on their own. Choose courses and training events that will serve a particular purpose and add to your skills and/or knowledge in a meaningful way.

Your first step should be to determine what requirements, if any, have been set in place by Cisco for your certification. You can do this by checking through the literature you have on hand and by visiting the page for your certification on Cisco's Web site. The Web site is likely to be more current than the printed materials, but don't count on either of these sources to supply complete and timely information. Continuing requirements are subject to change and can suddenly appear in programs where before there were none. This is not always a bad thing, as it actually adds value to your certification in the eyes of those who might hire you.

Vendor-specific certifications are often version specific. This is less true of Cisco certifications than of some others, but IOS versions and hardware specifications do change. Cisco does not require you to recertify with each new version, but be alert in case that changes. When version updates are required, all it usually takes is passing an upgrade exam. You may or may not receive notice that a new version is imminent, but by keeping your eye on trade magazines and industry publications such as *Cisco World*, you should catch wind of new releases before they hit the market. You can then inquire about certification upgrade requirements and be current and ready to go as the new release hits the streets. This is also a good way to be one of the first to have a complete understanding of the strengths and weaknesses of new versions of equipment and software.

Tracking continuing requirements is entirely your responsibility, and there is no guarantee that you will receive any reminders from Cisco. It is also up to you to remember that following the guidelines is not enough—if you don't submit acceptable evidence that you have done so, your efforts will not count. There is an online Cisco certification tracking system you can use once you become a certification candidate. This system (see Figure 15.1) stores details of every Cisco test you have taken and you should use it to verify that your efforts have been properly recorded. You will find it at **www.galton.com/~cisco/**. The tracking system is hosted by Galton Technologies. You can also reach it from most of Cisco's certification Web pages. Your scores will not appear until 4 days after you have taken the test. According to several reports, exams you don't pass are recorded too, although such information is not released to anyone other than you and Cisco.

FIGURE 15.1
Cisco Certification
Tracking System

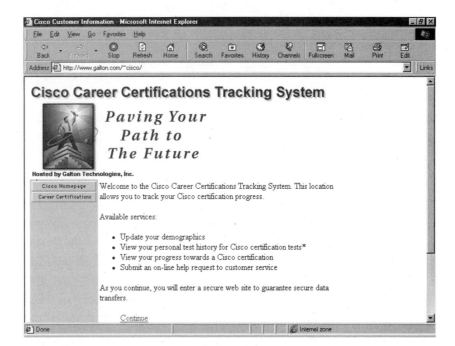

CCIE recertification requirements follow a two-year cycle. The deadline is 24 months following your certification date. By this deadline you must:

* Attend five CCIE designated technical training sessions at one of Cisco's Networker conferences
* Pass a recertification exam.

You can complete these requirements in any order. You can find out where Networker conferences will be held by checking CCIE Central at **www.cisco.com/warp/public/625/ccie/ccie_central.html**. Cisco also runs a conference Web site at **www.cisco.com/networkers/** (shown in Figure 15.2).

FIGURE 15.2

Networkers Conference Information on the Web

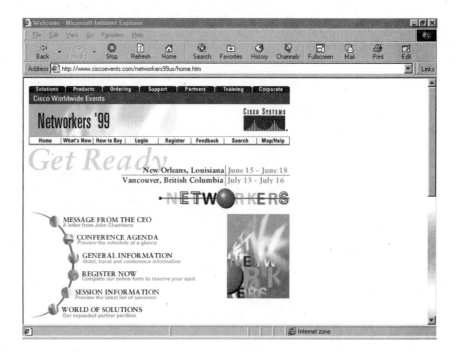

By attending this conference you will also get a chance to hobnob with other experts about the ins, outs, and job outlook of your field. The conference is held at numerous locations and on various dates each year. For example, 1999 conferences were scheduled in Australia, Japan, the United States, Canada, Singapore, China, and Austria. Registration fees vary. In 1999, the registration for the Networkers conference in the United States was US $1395.

A current list of recertification exams can be found at **http://www.cisco.com/warp/public/625/ccie/exam_index.html** (see Figure 15.3). Recertification exams are computer administered through Sylvan Prometric. Over time individual exams may be updated, retired, or changed. Additional recertification exam options are in the works.

FIGURE 15.3
Cisco
Recertification
Exam List
on the Web

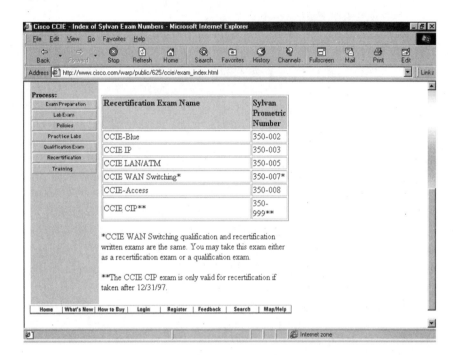

Recertification Exam Name	Sylvan Prometric Number
CCIE-Blue	350-002
CCIE IP	350-003
CCIE LAN/ATM	350-005
CCIE WAN Switching*	350-007*
CCIE-Access	350-008
CCIE CIP**	350-999**

*CCIE WAN Switching qualification and recertification written exams are the same. You may take this exam either as a recertification exam or a qualification exam.

**The CCIE CIP exam is only valid for recertification if taken after 12/31/97.

QUICK TIP

If you fail to recertify, you *do not* have to stop using the CCIE designation. However, Cisco will not list you as a current CCIE and you will not receive any of the ongoing perks and benefits accorded to current CCIEs.

Calculate the deadlines for your certification and incorporate them into your schedule. Because these dates can be far into the future, it will help to circle them in red or flag them in some other prominent way. Remember that these dates are deadlines for completing the requirements, not for signing up for the necessary classes. If you are a procrastinator, consider moving your deadlines up several months to give yourself some breathing room if circumstances interfere with your plans.

Staying current involves more than meeting recertification requirements; it means keeping your skills up to date and staying a the top of your field. To do this you should invest in periodic training, whether or not it is specifically geared toward recertification requirements.

Training Offered by Cisco

The Networkers conference is not the only avenue of training offered by Cisco. You will find numerous other resources, including online seminars, white papers, and self-study software, through Cisco's Web site. Visit periodically to locate the latest resources and learning opportunities.

Company Training

Sometimes organizations provide training to employees by bringing in outside trainers to provide instruction to a whole department. If there is a particular technology you want to learn about and you think it would also prove valuable to other members of your company, consider mounting a campaign to persuade your employer to provide the training. In a written proposal, explain exactly what training you are recommending and how it would benefit the company (for example: through increased productivity, less down time, better product support, increased employee retention, or enhanced Cisco reseller status). Your document should include a cost-benefit analysis showing how the training will benefit the company's bottom line. You should also do preliminary research exploring who might teach the course and how much it would cost, and include those results in your report. In addition to getting training for yourself, this route has the added benefit of demonstrating that you are concerned with ways the company can maintain or improve its competitive edge; this will benefit how the higher-ups view you.

Free Training for Contractors

As certification becomes more widespread, information technology professionals are increasingly eager to become and stay certified. This is true of contractors, consultants, and traditional employees. Often continuing education is facilitated or provided by a corporate employer, but now contractors can receive that benefit too. Although contractors and consultants do not usually have a single employer, they often deal with recruiting and placement firms. In order to attract and keep top talent, some of these firms have begun to offer free training (mostly through CBT) to attract contractors. In some cases, you don't even have to work for the firm, just register with them for potential future assignments. They get another contractor to call on and you get free training, and maybe even a placement that is just what you have been looking for. One such firm is Aquent Partners (**www.aquentpartners.com**).

Do-It-Yourself Options

One of the most cost-effective routes to continuing education is self study. In addition to affordability, this option has the advantages of being self paced, widely available, and obtainable in a variety of formats. Though you cannot do this with instructor-led options, you can also return to the material again for reference or review. Self-study options include:

* Books, manuals, and workbooks
* Video instruction
* Computer-based training (CBT) software
* Internet-based courses
* Hands-on exploration.

You can find products in all of these categories by browsing the Internet using one of the popular search engines. Videos, books, and software can also be found in the computer sections of major book stores or through advertisements in computer trade publications. The quality of self-study materials varies widely, so make every effort to try before you buy. You will often be able to accomplish this by sampling trial versions of software or browsing through printed materials before purchasing. If sampling is not possible, verify that a return policy exists so you can get your money back if the materials do not meet your expectations. Ask friends and coworkers who have experience with self-study materials which vendors they recommend and if they have had any bad experiences with particular products or companies.

When evaluating self-study options, keep in mind that individual learning styles vary, so what works for someone else may be less effective for you, and vice versa. If necessary, revisit Chapter 10, which explains how to analyze your personal learning style and determine which kind of training formats will suit you best.

Many certified professionals find that the best way to keep current with particular technologies is to obtain regular hands-on access to the software and/or hardware. You will find it worthwhile to uncover a way to get your hands on Cisco routers and switches (in addition to the equipment you use daily) on a regular, ongoing basis. This is easiest for those who have equipment at their place of employment and can work with it during breaks, lunch time, or after hours. Individuals who do not have suitable access through an employer sometimes set up the platform and/or software at home—i.e. a home lab. Doing so makes it possible to experiment with new options and technologies at your leisure without the risk of compromising a critical business computer system. You may already have a home lab setup that you used to earn certification in the first place. Instead of dismantling it, add to it over time and use it to keep your skills sharp.

Training Directories

As the need for continuing technical education has become more pronounced, a number of training resource clearinghouses, which connect students with learning resources, have appeared on the Web. These contain contact information and links to vendors that offer courses and training products. They are a good starting place when you are researching learning options for a particular topic. Yahoo!'s directory pages will also prove valuable in your search. Useful pages include:

* **www.1800training.com/traintest.html** is a searchable index of training companies. Just type in your zip code to find centers near you.
* **www.trainingnet.com** includes computer and noncomputer training resources and covers a variety of training formats. Figure 15.4 shows the site's home page.

✴ **www.yahoo.com/Business_and_Economy/Companies/
Computers/Software/Training/** is Yahoo!'s index of comput-
er-training software vendors.

Professional books can be purchased in traditional bookstores or
through online outlets such as Amazon.com (**www.amazon.com**) or
Fatbrain.com (**www.fatbrain.com**).

QUICK TIP

Don't forget to take advantage of any discounts that you received as perks of your
certification program to reduce the price of publications or training you purchase.

FIGURE 15.4
TrainingNet

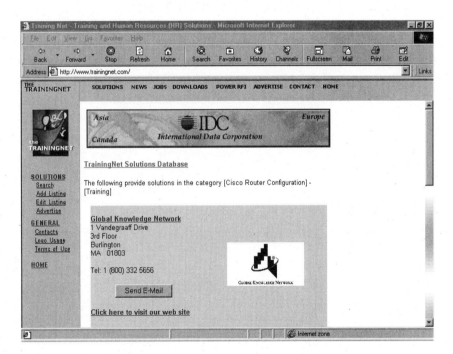

Bonus Benefits

Besides maintaining your status as a certified professional, keeping up with recertification requirements provides other potential
benefits. Completing continuing education requirements will
often serve double duty by providing additional career boosting
benefits not directly related to the certification.

Training venues are a prime networking opportunity. Through them you will connect with other professionals in your field. By establishing relationships with these people, you will build connections that can help you in many ways. When you meet another particularly competent professional (whether online or in person), obtain contact information and take note of the operating environment and other areas of expertise. Offer your information in return. When either of you encounters a technical dilemma, you will be able to call on each other as problem-solving resources.

Connections you make through training forums will also build your career network in another important way: by extending your circle of professional acquaintances you will build a web of personal connections you may wish to draw on when seeking employment in the future. Word of mouth is an often underestimated force when it comes to finding excellent job opportunities, and it is one you will be able to use to great advantage if you know many other individuals in your field.

Continuing education courses can also serve double duty in other ways. If you decide to pursue an academic degree in the future, you may be able to parlay the same courses that earned you recertification into credits applied toward your degree. This has the potential to save you a great deal of time and money.

Going after an advanced degree is not the only way to get your training to count twice. You may also be able to choose courses that maintain your current certification and apply toward obtaining another one. This trick, which requires careful planning and coordination, makes recertification especially painless.

Don't forget to incorporate significant training into your professional resume. It is an easy way to illustrate your abilities and the initiative you have taken to stay current in the industry, traits that employers consider desirable. A good way to include this information is to add a continuing education/continuing professional development heading under the education section of your resume and list the course or seminar titles there, along with the dates you completed them.

Record Keeping

When you investigate the details of the continuing education requirements for your certification, be sure to inquire about the details of submitting evidence that you have met them. The Cisco certification tracking system mentioned above is the key resource you will use to verify that your recertification information has been correctly recorded. You should also keep test fee receipts and test score reports just in case your records go awry—as evidence to back up your assertions. Make sure all your course documentation includes dates and descriptions. If you receive a simple, terse receipt, write the details on it yourself before filing it away.

Besides providing evidence that you have met recertification requirements, there is another reason to be scrupulous about saving your receipts: tax time. Because this training is undertaken to further your skills in your current career, you may be able to deduct the costs as employee expenses (or, if you are self-employed, as business expenses).

To obtain any deductions you are entitled to, record every expense associated with your educational pursuits, including study materials, tuition charges, and even travel and lodging. If you drive to and from a course, record the mileage and dates, too. If you complete your own tax return, you will need the information on file to support your claims. If you use a professional tax preparer you will need to provide this information so the deductions can be claimed for you. Tax preparers do not always remember to ask every question they should, so be sure to bring up your education expenses yourself.

Completing recertification requirements is typically a simple process. These requirements provide a preplanned route for your continued professional development; all you have to do is follow it. If you do, your trip will pay off in numerous ways, including bringing networking opportunities and adding to your sheaf of credentials. On the other hand, if you let your certification lapse because of inattention, you will pay the price with increased hassle and costs.

CHAPTER 16

Taking Advantage
of Perks
and Privileges

Besides adding a credential to boost your marketing advantage, Cisco certifications come with an array of benefits that can help you work more effectively. By taking advantage of your special status, you can gain access to resources that will make it possible to do your job more effectively and efficiently.

Before you can benefit from the perks associated with your certification, you have to know what they are. Don't count on what you read in printed materials you received at the outset; programs are revised frequently, and defined benefits can change. Cisco will probably notify you of such changes, but you can make sure not to miss out by checking the Cisco Web site regularly. Additions and modifications will often appear online before landing in your mailbox. For example, in 1999 Cisco changed the recertification cycle for CCIEs, an important cycle to be aware of.

Cisco Certification Benefits

You can expect to receive a welcome kit explaining your benefits four to six weeks after completing your certification requirements, including the certification agreement. Benefits for each Cisco certification as this book went to press were:

CCNA/CCDA

* Graduation letter
* Certificate
* Wallet card
* T-shirt (while supplies last)
* Use of logo (pending)

CCNP/CCDP

* Graduation letter
* Certificate
* Wallet card
* T-shirt (while supplies last)
* Access to video-on-demand training (limited time offer)
* Use of logo (pending)

CCIE

* Graduation letter
* Certificate
* Framed CCIE medallion
* Priority tech support
* Access to CCIE forum
* Use of CCIE logo
* Advanced training opportunities devised specifically for CCIEs

CCSI

* Authorization to teach official Cisco courses under the sponsorship of a Cisco Training Partner
* Instructor tools, including instructor guide, student course materials, and overhead presentations
* Free update training and materials
* Instructor technical support.

Cisco maintains special news pages detailing certification program changes. There's one for the CCIE at **www.cisco.com/warp/public/625/ccie/whatsnew.html**. Figure 16.1 shows a Cisco's CCIE What's New page. CCIEs should also read the quarterly CCIE Central newsletter at **www.cisco.com/warp/public/625/ccie/ccie_central.html**.

As this book went to press, there was no similar page for the career certifications, but if one appears it will be reachable through the career certifications home page at **www.cisco.com/warp/public/ 10/wwtraining/certprog/**.

These pages list testing changes, program alterations, and other news and announcements that may prove of interest to you. It is also a good idea to check the news pages for other certifications, to keep up on the latest news in the certification marketplace. News pages to visit include:

* CompTIA: **www.comptia.org/ct_news/index.htm**
* IBM: **www.ibm.com/Education/certify/news/**
* ICCP: **www.iccp.org/whatsnew.html**

✱ Lotus: **www.lotus.com/home.nsf/tabs/education** (look under certification)
✱ Microsoft: **www.microsoft.com/mcp/**
✱ Novell: **education.novell.com/certinfo/certnews.htm**.

FIGURE 16.1
CCIE Program
News

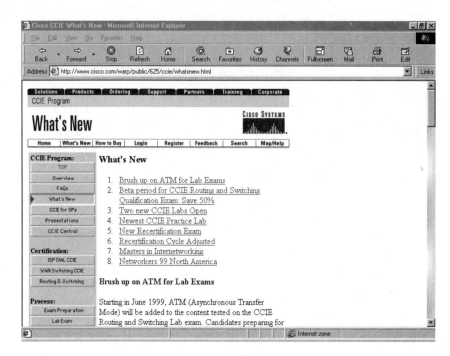

You can also read general certification news at **gocertify.com/ certnews.html**.

Perks may arrive in the form of print or electronic subscriptions, admittance to focused technical forums, access to priority technical support, participation in referral programs that will funnel work your way, use of marketing aids, and other training and product money savers. Once you have identified the benefits specific to your certification, you should put them to work.

Getting the Most from Restricted Forums

Another certification benefit that is becoming more common is the specialized, restricted-access forum. Cisco has one for CCIEs that is part of CCO (Cisco Connection Online). Access to this forum is not restricted to CCIEs, but they are the only ones who can post and answer questions. Other Cisco customers can browse the forum but not post. The CCIE forum can be accessed via the Internet; but only by registered Cisco customers and CCIEs. The registration page is shown in Figure 16.2.

FIGURE 16.2
CCO Restricted
Web Site

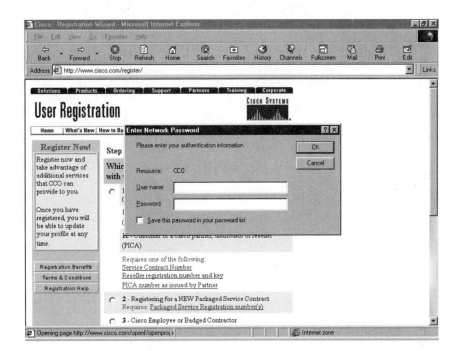

The utility of such forums varies widely, depending on the sponsor's commitment to them and the composition of the professionals who participate. Some forums will be closely monitored by the sponsoring organization's staff, which means they can personally respond to queries and participate in conversations. In other cases, participation is by the certified individuals, and the sponsor does little more than host the site. This is the format reported by users of CCO forums.

These forums provide a number of opportunities for the certified professional. You can use them to problem solve, to network, and to identify ways to better perform common (and even unusual) tasks.

As problem resolution tools, restricted forums have advantages over both tech-support lines and unrestricted forums. First of all, you will not have to spend an extended period on hold, waiting your turn in a tech-support phone queue. When your need is not urgent, you can post your question, go on to something else, and return a few hours (or a day or two) later and probably find several responses awaiting you. In addition, the forum participants will be other Cisco-certified professionals like yourself. As such, they will be handling the technology in question in live environments on a daily basis. Although telephone technical support people may have many data and incident reports collected in a searchable database at their fingertips, when it comes to efficient and effective troubleshooting, there is nothing like interacting with a person who has actually handled the task you are facing. Because the forum is restricted to individuals certified through the same program as yourself, you are likely to get accurate advice from a well-trained, experienced person who has kept up with the latest changes in the field.

You might wonder whether busy professionals are really likely to take the time to assist you with your queries. The answer is yes, and the reason is simple: on these types of forums, the culture is one of information sharing and assistance. Someone helps you today, you help them tomorrow, and everyone is able to do his job better. That is one reason it is important for you to give advice in the forum setting, as well as to seek it. A particular forum will only be as valuable as the participants make it. By doing what you can to create a quality professional environment, you will encourage others to do the same.

When you post a question to the forum, make it as specific as possible. Provide as many relevant details as you can manage, starting with a succinct description of the information you are seeking. Include version numbers of the products/software in question and the hardware platform(s) in your operating environment. Include a brief summary of what you have already tried and the results you obtained. If error messages are involved, reproduce them exactly. The reason for including these details is expediency. If you leave them out, you may return to the forum only to find more questions (for example, "Which IOS version are you running?") rather than solutions to your problem. Then you will have to respond and wait again before finding out what you really wanted to know.

Although it probably will not be your primary purpose for visiting restricted certification forums, they are also a reasonable place to do professional networking. Every time you intervene to solve someone else's technical dilemma, you are advertising your own expertise. Over time, the repetition of your name at the end of your postings will become familiar to others who frequent the forum. This may come in handy if you choose to seek out a new position, when you might decide to ask others in the forum for referrals and job leads. If you have been posting regularly, they will know who you are and as a result will be more likely to share information about employment opportunities.

Don't participate in the more heated discussions (called flame wars) that break out from time to time on such forums. Online arguments tend to deteriorate quickly into emotional mudslinging events, and participating will only detract from your professional image.

QUICK TIP

There is a fail-safe way to prevent yourself from falling into a flame war in the heat of the moment: if you really want to reply, go ahead and compose your response, but don't send it right away. Instead, store it in your outbox for a few hours or overnight. When you come back later, after you have achieved some distance from the incident that initially inflamed you, you will be better able to decide if posting your reply is in your best interest.

Keep in mind that Cisco-operated restricted forums are not the only places you can seek out advice. Don't hesitate to turn to independent forums as well, where it is likely that more people (although possibly fewer experts) will read your postings. Wherever you post, take care to understand how the particular forum works, and follow the protocol. Doing so demonstrates respect for the other individuals who frequent the site.

How to Benefit from Priority Tech Support

As anyone who has been in a computer business for long knows firsthand, obtaining technical support from a vendor can be a frustrating experience. Often, significant wait time is involved while your call is put on hold and a synthesized voice promises it will be handled "in the order it was received." At peak times, and especially after product upgrades, hold time can run up to an hour. Because vendor use of toll-free support phone numbers is dwindling, you (or your company) will be paying at peak phone rates for the privilege of listening to music or recorded messages until you make it to the front of the queue. Some product vendors, including Cisco, charge for technical support on a per instance basis. All of this translates into stress and inconvenience. Priority technical-support privileges can significantly cut this aggravation.

Priority technical-support privileges from Cisco can come in several forms, including:

* Access to a restricted technical support system—You will be able to use a support venue that has fewer people vying for access, which means a quicker response time. The venue is also likely to offer a higher level of support based on the assumption that you (and others with access) are more technically able than the typical tech support line caller and will not be calling for low-level help. Cisco's CCO forum offers some of this type of access.

* Automatic escalation to senior support staff—Support staffing is often organized in levels, with the first line (those who answer the calls) having the least expertise. The first-line staff can pass you on to more technically advanced support if needed. Because you have qualified for certification, you are likely to be able to solve minor product conflicts on your own. Cisco recognizes this by providing a means for you to route your support call directly to a senior person, rather than having to pass through a vendor's first-line support analyst (who will likely have to escalate your call to a senior support person anyway). Your calls to Cisco's TAC (Technical Assistance Center) can be tagged as originating from a CCIE so that they will be boosted to a higher level of support.

These priority-support benefits can translate into significant time savings, and have the potential to save money—especially when time = money is worked into the equation. To make the best use of your priority technical support benefits, it is important to clarify what they are and how to use them. It is also critical to determine whether your priority privileges cover unlimited use or are only valid for a certain number of instances. You should find out the details before you need to make your first call. If this information is not included in your certification welcome kit, call Cisco and ask to have it faxed or mailed (so you will have it in writing).

QUICKTIP

You are a certified professional and the priority technical support privileges are assigned to you, not to your employer. If your employer already has a support agreement/contract with Cisco, you will probably want to use it most of the time, saving your own privileged access for special instances not otherwise covered. When you do need to use your special privileges, you can earn a few brownie points by mentioning to your employer that you did so, along with how it saved the company time and/or money. In cases where the number of incidents you can use your access for is limited, save them for a time when you really need them. That might be while working from home or on a project for a different client.

Putting Priority to Work

Priority technical support privileges will only prove useful if your problem is clearly related to a Cisco product. It can be tempting to use the priority access that you know will not keep you waiting as long, even if you are not certain your difficulty originates with a Cisco product. This is especially true when products from two separate vendors (such as a 3Com router and a Cisco router) interact. In such cases, it is not always obvious which is at the root of the difficulties. If you give in to this temptation, you are likely to run into the "not our product" syndrome. For example, 3Com may claim it is a Cisco problem, while Cisco assures you it is a 3Com problem. To avoid wasting your time, and possibly your priority benefits, be prepared for this potential response and be ready to tell them why your situation should be handled by the technical support line you are calling.

When you place the call, have the following information at hand:

* Your certification identification number, which will probably be required to obtain priority support. You may also be asked for your date of certification or certification renewal.

* A description of the problem, including the exact wording of any error messages, the steps necessary for the support person to reproduce the problem, and what you have already tried.

* Names and version numbers of all software, firmware, and hardware involved.

Record the name and direct phone number (or extension) of the person who handles your call. If you have to call back, you will quickly be able to reach the individual who is already familiar with your problem and assure that your follow-up call is recognized as a continuation of the same incident, rather than an additional occurrence.

You can also submit cases to TAC online, through the CCO (Cisco Connection Online) Web site and via e-mail. Use the same guidelines whether you are using TAC via the Internet or the telephone.

If the number of support incidents is limited, keep a list of what you called about and when you called so you will know exactly how many covered calls you have remaining. A good place to record certification-related technical support calls is in a simple text or word processing file on your computer. Give it an easily recognizable name, such as Cisco incidents.doc.

Landing in the Spotlight

Cisco includes a professional profile as a regular component of the quarterly CCIE Central newsletter. These short articles summarize the qualifications and background individuals and are placed prominently in the newsletter. Anyone who views the page also views the profile, which demonstrates how the certification is being used for professional success, while at the same time promoting the services of the individual being profiled. Figure 16.3 shows a featured professional.

CCIEs who want to be considered for a CCIE Central profile should e-mail **cciecentral@cisco.com** and describe how CCIE certification has made a difference to themselves, their company, or their customers.

FIGURE 16.3

Profile of a
Featured CCIE

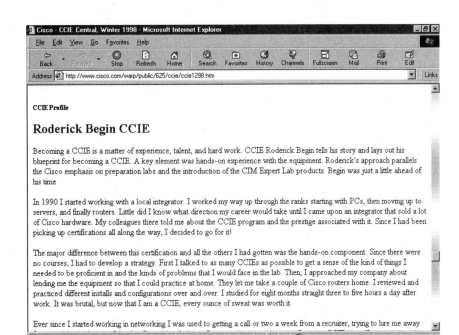

CCIE Profile

Roderick Begin CCIE

Becoming a CCIE is a matter of experience, talent, and hard work. CCIE Roderick Begin tells his story and lays out his blueprint for becoming a CCIE. A key element was hands-on experience with the equipment. Roderick's approach parallels the Cisco emphasis on preparation labs and the introduction of the CIM Expert Lab products. Begin was just a little ahead of his time

In 1990 I started working with a local integrator. I worked my way up through the ranks starting with PCs, then moving up to servers, and finally routers. Little did I know what direction my career would take until I came upon an integrator that sold a lot of Cisco hardware. My colleagues there told me about the CCIE program and the prestige associated with it. Since I had been picking up certifications all along the way, I decided to go for it!

The major difference between this certification and all the others I had gotten was the hands-on component. Since there were no courses, I had to develop a strategy. First I talked to as many CCIEs as possible to get a sense of the kind of things I needed to be proficient in and the kinds of problems that I would face in the lab. Then, I approached my company about lending me the equipment so that I could practice at home. They let me take a couple of Cisco routers home. I reviewed and practiced different installs and configurations over and over. I studied for eight months straight three to five hours a day after work. It was brutal, but now that I am a CCIE, every ounce of sweat was worth it.

Ever since I started working in networking I was used to getting a call or two a week from a recruiter, trying to lure me away

CHAPTER 17

Another Certification?

Now that you have completed the journey to certification, you face another important career decision: Are you going to do it again? Just as some people obtain multiple academic degrees in the course of climbing the career ladder, you can combine various certifications for further boosts to your career. And earning certifications is typically faster and less expensive than obtaining academic degrees.

As part of a 1997 Gartner Group study sponsored by Sylvan Prometric, IBM, Microsoft, Novell, and Sybase, more than 7,000 certification candidates were asked about professional designations they already held. Two thirds of respondents reported already holding one or more certifications prior to the one they were currently pursuing. Less than one third (31%) were earning their first certification. In contrast, when the same question was asked back in 1994, more than half the respondents (56%) were in the process of earning their first certification. These data (illustrated in Figure 17.1) indicate a trend toward earning multiple certifications.

FIGURE 17.1
A Trend toward
Multiple
Certifications

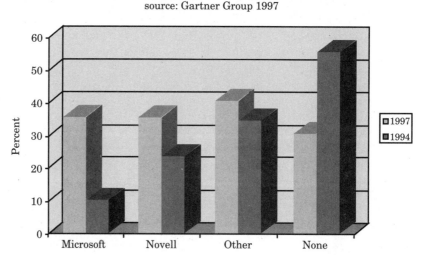

Other Certification Held by Exam Takers
source: Gartner Group 1997

More Can Be Better

There are several reasons you might want to consider going after additional professional certifications. They include:

* Staying abreast of technological change
* Broadening your market
* Increasing your technical level
* Personal pride and a desire to excel.

A few technologies endure for long periods, such as the COBOL programming language, but most fade almost as quickly as they become popular when, inevitably, something newer and better comes along. Professional certification programs can be used as tools for technical excellence. Although many in the computer field are skilled at self-instruction, it is difficult to know what you need to learn about a technology new to you. A certification program for that technology will outline the path to expertise; all you have to do is follow it.

The Cisco career certifications are a natural for this process. There is a clearly defined path for individuals to follow after the first Cisco certification. CCNAs will want to consider stepping up to CCNP, or perhaps over to CCDA. CCNPs and CCDPs should consider CCIE certification as a possible next step. CCIEs should look at the other CCIE designations as a way to expand their technical expertise—i.e. routing and switching CCIEs might go after the WAN switching or ISP dial designation.

Don't limit yourself to Cisco certification alone; adding additional certifications to your professional portfolio can significantly broaden your base of potential clients and employers. You will be qualified for and able to choose from a wider range of positions and employers. Multiple certifications also tag you as a professional who takes initiative and someone who is a "go-getter." These traits are looked upon favorably by many potential clients and employers.

Some certifications are especially complementary. For example, people who are both Netware and NT certified will find plenty of employment opportunities. That is because computer environments today are as blended as they are, more often than not incorporating multiple vendors, products, and platforms. Individuals able to integrate the components of these environments have an additional edge in the marketplace.

Benefiting From Multiple Certifications

I had multiple certifications before I started teaching—partly because I gained a reputation for it and I wanted to open a business. Developers can certainly benefit from learning the other side of the business—the administration and engineering side. And those engineers or administrators that have an aptitude for programming can certainly benefit from learning the developer side of the business. A Microsoft person can benefit from knowing and certifying on Netware. They'll know better how to migrate people from Netware, for instance. Anybody involved with Microsoft or Netware at a high level could benefit from a Cisco certification, because there is more knowledge that they will gain—knowing more of the technical environment they're likely to be working in. With Microsoft, Netware, and/or Cisco certifications, you're more likely to be able to work in a high level environment.

Herb Martin, MCSD, MCT, MCSEx2, and founder of LearnQuick.com

In addition to the more tangible benefits already mentioned, there is another reason people decide to earn numerous professional certifications: personal fulfillment. Holding professional certifications in more than one area can be a source of pride. It also feeds the appetite for excellence and urge to learn that many computer people possess. Figure 17.2 shows a Web page where certified pros boast of their accomplishments.

Drawbacks

Although adding more certifications to your professional credentials is largely a positive move, there are a few drawbacks you should be aware of. The most commonly encountered complication concerns logistics. Once you progress beyond your second certification, tracking the continuing education requirements requires more careful attention. You will have more forms to complete and submit on time, more requirements to comply with.

Individuals who hold multiple certifications may be able to get the education they complete to count double, or more, if it meets the qualifications for several of the programs. There are no rules that limit you to applying continuing education activity toward only one certification.

FIGURE 17.2
Bragging Rights at
Victor Dubin's
Certification
Web Site

VICTOR DUBIN'S CERTIFICATION & NETWORKING PAGE

Certification Wall of Fame

And Current Champs Are:

Anders Gustafsson   6 (SIX) Novell tests a day

Ed Erichson   3 (I&C, D&I, AA) Novell tests a day

Pasha Pergamenchik   Possibly world's youngest CNE & MCPS (14 years old)

Riley K. Fowle   Possibly world's youngest MCSD (19 years old), all four tests in a month.
Herb Martin   All 6 MCSE tests in 11 days. Second place.
Michael Swisher   All 6 MCSE tests in one month, inc one beta

Undell Williams   4 tests in one day - 4.1 Admin, 4.1 I&C, NTS 3.51, NTW 3.51
6 more in three days - S&S, Access 95, D&I, SQL 6 IMP, TCPIP 3.51, Win95

Mark Spain   3 Novell tests in 20 (!!!) minutes - Can you beat it?

Jon Spencer   3 Novell tests(D&I, 3I&C, 3AA in 2 hours 15 minutes,

Pamela Forsyth   (Second) Largest number of certifications from different vendors (5): MCNE, CNX, CLP, CCIE, former CBS

Jens Stark   Fastest single test - Novell NT (200) in 7 (seven) minutes.

Cameron Brendon   **Absolute** record so far: CNE, MCSE, A+ in FIVE!!! months.
The guy claims he has personal life too. (G)

Adrian Roni Havas   **All seven (7)** CNE tests in one hour and 15 minutes, inc 15 minutes brake. Unbeatable
Adrian Roni Havas   since 1993. It seems Rony was really in a hurry.
(There were nice old days when sugar was more sweat, water more wet and tests more easy)

Duane D Thilmony of Minneapolis   Six CNE4 tests (525, 605, 801, 804, 532, 200) in 32 days.

Avery Robert   **MS Win95 best score** so far (957 of 1000 in 18 minutes).
Largest number of records here - all that in 2.5 years!!!
1. **Largest** number of different vendor certs - MCNE(Novell), MCSE(MS), CCIE(Cisco),
CNX(NGC), Lan Server engineer(IBM), Bay Networks Optivity, 3Com Wizard

David Yarashus   2. **MCSE in FOUR (4)** days.
3. **Cheapest** way to CNE (two of seven tests paid, the rest free beta)
4. **Largest** space occupied here (VBG)

My sincere and to them

Your wanna be listed here too? Email me: 71660.117@compuserve.com

Best viewed with

Broken links? Misprints? Wrong info? Questions? Please feel free to email me at
71660.117@compuserve.com

Because of the added complexity of managing several certifications on an ongoing basis, it becomes especially important to use a calendar to track and comply with continuing education deadlines.

Earning and maintaining multiple certifications will also add to your professional expenses. It is likely that at least some of the training options you employ to obtain and maintain the certifications will involve significant expense. Don't forget to apply the money-saving advice in Chapter 5 to earning additional certifications just as you did to earning the first one. That includes going after outside funding and remembering to take any tax deductions you are due.

A final potential drawback you should be aware of applies only when you top three certifications. It is the possibility that some people will look at your list of certifications and think that it is not possible for you to be technically competent in all of the areas you hold certifications for, and then to suspect that the certifications represent an ability to pass tests more than professional expertise. You can counteract this potential backlash by finding additional ways to demonstrate that your broad competencies are genuine. If you have plenty of diverse experience included on your resume, that should take care of it. Otherwise, you may have to do some additional convincing of potential clients.

One way around this potential image problem is to mention only those certifications which are especially relevant when applying for a particular job or contract. You don't have to list every one you hold if you think it will work against you. On the other hand, if you are after a senior position, having multiple certifications on your resume is likely to work in your favor rather than against you.

QUOTE

Maintaining Multiple Certifications

When you hold multiple certifications, employers expect you will be able to deliver on the promise of expertise that multiple certifications imply, which can be a good thing if you can manage it properly. I am finding that maintaining multiple certifications is difficult. Just keeping up with the continuing certification requirements takes a lot of effort. I lose my edge when I don't work with a technology for a certain period of time, so I'm rusty on a lot of specific knowledge that I used to have but don't use every day now.

I let the CBS [Certified Banyan Specialist] lapse because of Banyan's diminishing presence in the market and because of the stringent continuing certification requirement. I would have had to spend about $2500 on additional Banyan training by the end of 1995, plus take a week of vacation, because my employer did not see a business need for me to maintain that certification. I spent the money on Network General training instead, which proved to be a good move.

I allowed the CNP to lapse because there wasn't any interest or recognition amongst prospective employers. One of my technical friends ridiculed me because CNP also stands for Certified Nurse Practitioner. Also, I am chronically bad at keeping track of paper (tree-bark and berry-juice, as one of my friends disparagingly calls it), so when it came time to recertify I wasn't able to put my hands on the documentation I needed in order to prove that I'd been to enough training over the preceding year. I will probably allow the LCCS certification to lapse when the recertification requirement comes up because I don't want to work with applications any more. On the other hand, people are really impressed when the list takes up half a page on your resume!

—Pamela Forsyth, CCSI, ECNE, MCSE, and other certifications

Selecting Additional Certifications

When choosing additional certifications to pursue, follow the same process that helped you decide which certification to make your first. You will also need to decide on a strategy—to obtain an array of complementary certifications or go for diversity. Each option has its benefits. Complementary certifications are those directly related to and likely to prove useful within a single work site. For example, holding several networking certifications will make you attractive to the many organizations that operate heterogeneous networking environments. You can think of this as deepening your marketing options with in a particular market segment. Multiple complementary certifications often increases your level of expertise in a particular area to the extent that you can command premium rates as a senior person.

Choosing to go with a strategy of diversity, on the other hand, widens your customer base to include additional market segments. For example, if you hold a CCNP certification, and decide to add a security-related certification, you will be increasing your access to additional segments of the computer job market. An added benefit of the diversity strategy is that it facilitates more variety in your work, so you can choose different types of assignments that you find interesting.

Once you have settled on an overall strategy, start browsing through the available programs to determine which ones meet your qualifications and appeal to you in terms of cost and time factors. Places to check include:

* The resource listings included with this book
* Certification information on Cisco's Web site. As mentioned earlier, you may find your next certification goal comes from Cisco too.
* Certification news pages for other sponsors. New certifications are being developed at a fairly fast rate, and if you want to be aware of all your options, you will need to do your homework and keep up to date with certification news.
* If you have professional acquaintances who hold certifications, ask them for opinions of the programs they have participated in.
* Visit one or more of the certification discussion forums mentioned elsewhere in this book, post a message mentioning your current certification(s) and goals, and seeking advice and suggestions about which program to look into next.

When you have settled on a certification that will enhance your portfolio of professional qualifications, remember to pursue it using the skills you have already learned. Choose learning options that cater to your learning styles and budget. Having already been through the process once, you should know what those are. Do a quick review of the study tips and advice contained in Chapter 10 to refresh your memory on efficient study habits.

The Bottom Line

Cisco certification and other certifications can be a valuable career-boosting tool, or more accurately, set of tools. Like any other tools, certifications can be used properly or improperly. Using an adjustable wrench to pound in a nail may be somewhat effective, but using it to tighten a bolt will be infinitely more so. As with tools, the key to successful use of certifications is to match the tool to the job. This is true whether selecting your first certification or your fifth.

QUOTE

To Stay Ahead, Keep On Learning

If you see certification as a means to an end, once you achieve the certification you must set new goals. If you stand still, your technical skills will stagnate and you may retain your position for the time being, but when an employer needs someone with the latest skills, you may find your position has evaporated. I routinely scan the help wanted ads in the newspapers to get a feel for the latest skills that seem to be most in demand. If they match my personal interests, I will work to sharpen my skills. Technology has forced a rapid pace on change upon us and I feel that the most successful "technocrats" will be those who love technology for its own sake and have a chameleon-like adaptability to the current tools and innovations.

Eric Charbonneau, holder of MCSE + Internet,
IBM Professional Server Expert, and other certifications

When you take the time to select and earn appropriate certifications, you are already advancing yourself toward the front of the pack. If you stop there you are not getting all you can out of the credentials. Take those certifications and put them to work for you. Advertise your professional status. Use them to land jobs. Employ them to keep your professional edge. And exploit them to launch your career to new heights.

PART 4

Resources

APPENDIX A

Certification
Fact Sheets

Cisco Headquarters Contact Information

Cisco Systems
170 West Tasman Drive
San Jose, CA 95134-170
URL: www.cisco.com
Phone: 800-553-6387   **Fax:** 408-526-7117
Email: cs-rep@cisco.com

Cisco Certified Network Associate (CCNA)
Value Rating: 2 (out of 5)

Date Initiated: 1998   **# Granted:** 4,000

Primary URL: www.cisco.com/warp/public/10/wwtraining/certprog/
lan/programs/ccna.html

Summary: For individuals who install, configure, and operate
simple-routed LAN, routed WAN, and switched LAN and ATM
LANE networks that utilize Cisco routers and switches. This is
Cisco's entry-level certification.

Initial Requirements: There are two tracks: Routing & Switching and WAN Switching. To achieve either you will have to pass
one exam. For routing and switching, that is CCNA Exam 640-
407. For WAN Switching, it's CCNA-WAN-Sw Exam 640-410.
Exams cost $100.

Continuing Requirements: None as this book went to press.

Perks:
* Certificate
* Graduation letter
* Wallet card
  A logo is in the works.

Online Resources: Details of the WAN Switching track can be
found at: www.cisco.com/warp/public/10/wwtraining/certprog/
wan/course.html

The Cisco Certification FAQ can be found at: www.cisco.com/
warp/public/10/wwtraining/certprog/faq1.html

Exam information can be found at: www.cisco.com/warp/public/10/wwtraining/certprog/testing/exam_info.htm.

Cisco Certified Network Professional (CCNP)
Value Rating: 3 (out of 5)

Date Initiated: 1998   **# Granted:** 200

Primary URL: www.cisco.com/warp/public/10/wwtraining/certprog/lan/programs/ccnp.html

Summary: For individuals who install, configure, operate, and troubleshoot complex routed LAN, routed WAN, switched LAN networks, and dial access services that utilize Cisco routers and switches. This is the next step after CCNA certification.

Initial Requirements: There are two Routing and Switching, and WAN Switching CCNP tracks. To earn the CCNP–Routing and Switching you must pass the CCNA–Routing and Switching exam, plus four more: Advanced Cisco Router Configuration (ACRC) exam #640-403, Cisco LAN Switch Configuration (CLSC) exam #640-404, Configuring, Monitoring, Troubleshooting, and Dial-up Services (CMTD) exam #640-405, and Cisco Internetworking Troubleshooting (CIT) exam #640-406. You can elect to take the Foundation R/S exam in place of the ACRC, CLSC, and CMTD exams.

To become a CCNP–WAN Switching, you will have to pass the CCNA–WAN Switching exam plus three or four additional exams, depending on which training and testing path you choose to follow. The exams are: Multiband Switch and Service Configuration (MSSC) exam #640-419, BPX Switch and Service Configuration (BSSC) exam #640-425, MGX ATM Concentrator Configuration (MACC) exam #640-411, and EITHER StrataView Installation and Operation (SVIO) exam #640-451 or exam #640-422 Cisco Strata View Plus (CSVP). Exams cost $100–$200.

Continuing Requirements: None as this book went to press; expect them to appear in the future.

Perks:
* Certificate

* Graduation letter
* Wallet card

Cisco Certified Design Associate (CCDA)

Value Rating: 2 (out of 5)

Date Initiated: 1998   **# Granted:** 4,000

Primary URL: www.cisco.com/univercd/cc/td/doc/pcat/179.htm

Summary: For individuals who design simple routed LAN, routed WAN, and switched LAN networks that utilize Cisco routers and switches. Assumes prerequisite knowledge and skills to install, configure, and operate these. Associate level status is required as a base level of knowledge for the Professional level (CCDP) status.

Initial Requirements: You must pass Designing Cisco Networks (DCN) exam #640-441. You must also sign the Cisco Career Certifications Agreement. Tests cost $100–$200.

Continuing Requirements: None as this book went to press; expect them to appear in the future.

Perks:
* Certificate
* Graduation letter
* Wallet card
  A logo is in the works.

Online Resources: The Cisco Certification FAQ can be found at: www.cisco.com/warp/public/10/wwtraining/certprog/faq1.html Exam information can be found at: www.cisco.com/warp/public/10/wwtraining/certprog/testing/exam_info.htm.

Cisco Certified Design Professional (CCDP)

Value Rating: 3 (out of 5)

Date Initiated: 1998   **# Granted:** 100

Primary URL: www.cisco.com/warp/public/10/wwtraining/certprog/lan/programs/ccdp.html

Summary: For individuals who design complex routed LAN, routed WAN, and switched LAN networks that utilize Cisco routers and switches. Assumes prerequisite knowledge and skills to install, configure, and operate these.

Initial Requirements: There are two tracks for this certification: the standard Routing & Switching, and WAN Switching. To earn the CCDP (routing and switching), you must first earn the CCDA and CCNA certifications. You must then pass Advanced Cisco Router Configuration (ACRC) exam #640-403, Cisco LAN Switch Configuration (CLSC) exam #640-404, Configuring, Monitoring, Troubleshooting, and Dial up Services (CMTD) exam #640-405, and Cisco Internetwork Design (CID) exam #640-025. You have the option of taking a single, composite exam called the Foundation R/S exam (#640-409) in place of the ACRC, CLSC, and CMTD exams.

To earn the WAN Switching CCDP, you must hold the CCNP-WAN Switching Certification and pass DSWVS Exam 640-413.

Continuing Requirements: None as this book went to press; expect them to appear in the future.

Perks:
* Certificate
* Graduation letter
* Wallet card
  A logo is in the works. Access to video-on-demand training was being provided as this book went to press, but was identified as "a limited time offer."

Online Resources: Details of the WAN Switching track can be found at: www.cisco.com/warp/public/10/wwtraining/certprog/wan/course.html

The Cisco Certification FAQ can be found at: www.cisco.com/warp/public/10/wwtraining/certprog/faq1.html

Exam information can be found at: www.cisco.com/warp/public/10/wwtraining/certprog/testing/exam_info.htm.

Cisco Certified Internetwork Expert (CCIE)

Value Rating: 5 (out of 5)

Date Initiated: 1993   **# Granted:** 3217

Primary URL: www.cisco.com/warp/public/625/ccie/ccie4_pl.htm

Summary: The program is designed to identify computer professionals with internetworking expertise. This top-of-the-line certification is for individuals who work specifically with Cisco products. It is currently one of the premier IT certifications.

Initial Requirements: There are actually three versions of this certification: Routing and Switching, WAN Switching, and ISP Dial. Achieving any of them requires passing a written test ($200), as well as a two-day practical lab ($1000).

Continuing Requirements: Every two years after becoming certified, CCIEs must attend a requisite number of CCIE technical seminar sessions and also pass a written exam in one specialty area (IP, LAN/ATM, Dial, WAN Switching).

Perks:
* Graduation letter
* Certificate
* Framed CCIE medallion
* Priority tech support
* Access to CCIE forum
* Use of CCIE logo
* Advanced training opportunities devised specifically for CCIEs

Online Resources: The CCIE Web site contains links to exam objectives and preparation guides for both written and lab exams.

The CCIE newsletter is at: www.cisco.com/warp/public/625/ccie/ccie_central.html.

A logo is in the works. Access to video-on-demand training was being provided as this book went to press, but was identified as "a limited time offer."

Online Resources: Details on CCNP WAN Sw can be found at: www.cisco.com/warp/public/10/wwtraining/certprog/wan/programs/ccnp.html

The Cisco Certification FAQ can be found at: www.cisco.com/warp/public/10/wwtraining/certprog/faq1.html

Exam information can be found at: www.cisco.com/warp/public/10/wwtraining/certprog/testing/exam_info.htm.

Certified Cisco Systems Instructor (CCSI)
Value Rating: 4 (out of 5)

 # Granted: fluctuates

Primary URL: www.cisco.com/warp/public/10/wwtraining/tpprgde2.html

Summary: This certification is for individuals who want to teach authorized Cisco courses.

Initial Requirements: You must have hands-on technical experience in bridging and routing, switching, and/or WAN environments, plus at least a year of technical teaching experience. You must be sponsored by (or yourself become) a Cisco Training Partner. In addition to meeting those conditions, you must attend the course you wish to teach, and then pass the related exam. Afterwards, you must attend and pass a two-day Instructor Certification Process (ICP) at Cisco. Your sponsoring Cisco Training Partner pays the ICP fee.

To extend the certification to additional courses, you will have to attend the course, pass the related exam, and submit a request to extend the certification to include the new course.

Continuing Requirements:
You must maintain a 4.0 out of 5.0 on student critiques. You must maintain a relationship with a Cisco Training Partner or your certification lapses. You must meet administrative deadlines—such as submitting student critiques within 10 days. You must comply with other requirements, such as always using original Cisco materials (no photocopies).

Perks:
* ✳ Electronic version of course materials including overheads
* ✳ An instructor guide
* ✳ Complete set of student materials for the authorized course.

CCSIs also have access to update training materials and instructor support from Cisco.

Online Resources: To register for the ICP call 1-408- 526-7290.

Offline Resources: To register for the ICP by email contact training-registration@cisco.com.

Cisco Router Certification

Value Rating: 2 (out of 5)

Learning Tree International
1805 Library Street
Renton, VA 20190-563
Phone: 800-843-8733   **Fax:** 613-748-0479
Email: cncourses@learningtree.com
URL: www.learningtree.com

Date Initiated: 1997   **# Granted:** unknown

Primary URL: www.learningtree.com/us/cert/progs/785.htm

Summary: For individuals who design, configure, troubleshoot or manage internetworks with Cisco routers, including network managers, technicians, consultants and designers.

Initial Requirements: You must succesfully complete four core courses and one elective course, along with their associated examinations. Core courses are: Introduction to Internetworking: Bridges, Switches and Routers (4 days/$2195); Cisco Routers: A Comprehensive Hands-On Introduction (4 days/$1755); Configuring Cisco Routers: Advanced Hands-On Workshop (4 days/$1755); and IP Routing With OSPF and BGP: Hands-On (4 days/$1755). Electives include: Hands-On Internetworking With TCP/IP (4 days/$1755); Migrating to IPv6: Hands-On (4 days/$1755); Hands-On SNMP: From Workgroup to Enterprise Networks (4 days/$1755); Hands-On Introduction to TCP/IP (4 days/$1755);

Data Network Design and Performance Optimization (4 days/$1755) Deploying Internet and Intranet Firewalls: Hands-On (4 days/$1755); Internet and System Security: Attacks and Countermeasures (4 days/$1755); Fast LAN Technologies (4 days/$1755); Hands-On High-Performance Ethernet: Switched, Fast and Traditional (4 days/$1755).

Continuing Requirements: None

Perks:
* Certificate

Learning Tree has a program affiliation with the American Council on Education (ACE) through which Learning Tree's certification programs are recommended for as many as 10 semester hours of college credit at many colleges and universities.

Online Resources: Detailed course outlines are available on the certification's Web site.

Information on the college credit program can be found at: www.learningtree.com/us/cert/uscolcrd.htm.

APPENDIX B

Cisco Certification Resources

Publications

Cisco World

P.O. Box 399
Cedar Park, TX 78630-0399
(512) 250-9023
E-mail: Cisco@pcinews.com
URL: www.pcinews.com/cisco
This monthly newsprint publication contains news of Cisco Systems
and its products, as well as coverage of internetworking in general.
It is published independently—not by Cisco itself.

Cisco Consultant Newsletter

URL: cco.cisco.com/warp/public/792/news_index.html
Summary: Monthly online newsletter containing information
from Cisco of interest to Cisco consultants.

Packet Magazine

Phone: 408 526-4000
E-mail: packet@cisco.com
URL: cio.cisco.com/warp/public/784/packet/
Summary: Cisco Systems' quarterly Users magazine—available
in online and paper versions. Contains technical articles, case
studies, new product information.

Cisco Press Online

URL: www.ciscopress.com
Summary: This imprint is a partnership between Cisco Systems
and Macmillan Computer Publishing and sells many books
geared toward specific certification exams. Although all titles are
listed here, books must be purchased through traditional and
online bookstores.

Fatbrain.com Cisco Systems online resource center

URL: www.fatbrain.com/partners/cisco
Summary: This section of the online bookstore fatbrain.com is a
great place to find Cisco titles from all of the computer book pub-
lishers in one place.

Self-study Vendors (see also Web sites)

Bad Dog Computer and Internet Services

Phone: 888-567-2496
Email: training@baddogcomputer.com
URL: www.baddogcomputer.com/cisco_training/cisco_training.html
Summary: Vendor of numerous self-study titles including videos, CBT, and training bundles.

Beach Front Quizzer

Phone: 888-992-3131
E-mail: info@bfq.com
URL: www.bfq.com
Summary: Sells practice tests for CCNA and other Cisco certification exams.

CBT Systems

Phone: 888-395-0014
Fax: 800-817-5902
E-mail: salesinfo@cbtsys.com
URL: www.cbtsys.com
Summary: Sells CBT software for CCNA, CCNP, and CCDP self-study.

CDi Communications

Phone: 800-617-5586
Fax: 914-368-2472
E-mail: sales@netwind.com
URL: www.netwind.com
Summary: Sells third-party Cisco certification training packages, including books and software, for CCNA preparation.

Forefront Direct

Phone: (800) 475-5831
URL: www.ffg.com/products/default.htm
Summary: Sells CBT Systems preparation materials.

GlobalNet System Solutions

E-mail: globalnetsys@earthlink.net
URL: www.lammle.com
Summary: Sells training practice questions and instructor-led training for Cisco's career certifications. Operated by the author of several well-respected certification books.

LearnKey

Phone: 800-865-0165
E-mail: sales@learnkey.com
URL: www.learnkey.com
Summary: Sells CCNA self-study video.

MaxIT

Phone: 800-868-8039
Fax: 904-998-0221
URL: www.maxit.com
Summary: Sells CCIE preparation curriculum.

MeasureUp!

Phone: 800-649-1MUP
Fax: 770-649-9149
E-mail: info@measureup.com
URL:www.measureup.com
Summary: Online and offline practice tests for CCNA candidates. You can also purchase access to written study material.

NETg

Phone: 800-265-1900
URL: www.netg.com/catalog1.htm
Summary: Sells certification curriculums for the CCNA and CCNP. Curriculums still under development as this book went to press.

TCT Technical Training

Phone: 800-743-9990
Fax: 510-492-6618
URL: www.tcttech.com

Summary: Offers training packages by subscription to corporations—not priced for individuals. Includes complete internetworking training curriculums.

Training Companies (not Cisco partners)

Athena Computer Learning Centers

URL: www.athenaclc.com/
Summary: Through partnership with authorized Cisco Partner CCTI, offers training for all Cisco certifications. Locations in Tennessee, Mississippi, and Alabama.

Babbage Simmel

Phone: (800) 288-5937
Fax: (614) 764-9049
E-mail: info@babsim.com
URL: www.babsim.com
Summary: Through partnership with authorized Cisco Partner CCTI, offers training for all Cisco certifications. Located in Dublin, Ohio.

Hello Computers Inc.

Phone: 510-795-6815
Fax: 510-291-2250
E-mail: info@hellocomputers.com
URL: www.hellocomputers.com/
Summary: Offers boot camp and instructor-led training for CCNA. Located in Fremont, CA.

MicroHard Technologies

Phone: 800-266-7648
E-mail: info@microhard.com
URL: www.microhard.com
Summary: Offers CCNA and CCNP hands-on curriculums.

Web Sites

Atlanta Cisco Certification Self-study Group (ACCSG)

E-mail: cnebody@mindspring.com
URL: cnebody.home.mindspring.com/ciscofaq.htm
Summary: Cisco certification study group facilitated by Joel Barrett. Meets every two weeks. Web site contains study notes and resources.

CCIE Study 12 Step Plan

URL: www.dimension.net/~tbaldwin/ccie-track.html
Summary: CCIE Todd Baldwin's 12-step plan for achieving CCIE certification.

CCIE Self-study Web Site

E-mail: knight@lebanon1.com
URL: www.lebanon1.com/ccie/
Summary: This site contains study tools, a forum, and a CCIE practice test to help you prepare for certification exams.

CCPrep.com

Phone: 877-CCIE123 (US)/904-394-0051 (Out of US)
Fax: 904-394-0051
E-mail: lrossisr@ccprep.com
URL: www.ccprep.com
Summary: This is a subscription Web site. Subscribers gain access to lab scenarios, practice questions (which are posted monthly), and detailed explanations. Site is hosted by Certified Cisco Systems instructors. This site also offers free Internet Radio broadcasts on topics related to Cisco certification. Single-issue subscription $19.95US, one-year subscription $169 US. CCNA subscriptions cost $129 US per year. Also runs 5 day CCNA bootcamp.

Cisco Certified

E-mail: support@ciscocertified.com
URL: www.ciscocertified.com
Summary: This subscription Web site is for CCNA candidates. Content includes lab exercises, online exam, forum, and access to study guides. One-year subscription costs $69US.

Cisco Networking FAQ

URL: www.cis.ohio-state.edu/hypertext/faq/usenet/cisco-networking-faq/faq.html

Cisco Router FAQ

URL: web.syr.edu/~jmwobus/comfaqs/faq-comp.dcom.sys.cisco

CyberState University

Phone: 888-438-3382
URL: www.cyberstateu.com/text/CATALOG/CISCO_CCNA.HTM
Summary: Offers online CCNA training—two tracks based on student background. Includes access to Cisco routers via telnet along with course materials, courseware, and instructor access. Prices are $1795 US or $2195 US depending on track.

Digital Concepts

E-mail: info@networkstudyguides.com
URL: www.networkstudyguides.com/
Summary: Subscription Web site for CCNA, CCNP, and CCIE candidates. Membership includes extensive study guide, forum, and exam simulations. One year subscription is $75 (for a specific certification area).

Gocertify.com

E-mail: author@gocertify.com
URL: gocertify.com
Summary: This is a gathering place and resource center for people interested in computer professional certification. Includes information on Cisco certifications and discussion/study area.

Groupstudy.com

E-mail: pborghese@groupstudy.com
URL: www.groupstudy.com
Summary: An excellent resource for CCIE candidates, this site maintains a CCIE study mailing list and archive, study rooms on various CCIE topics, and other resources. Focus is on CCIE, although candidates for other Cisco certifications also frequent the site and mailing list.

Learning The Cisco IOS is Easy!

URL: www.haskins.net/ccie/

Summary: This site is an index of Cisco IOS commands and serves as a good study guide for learning the commands for programming Cisco routers.

Randall Benn's Web site

URL:www.clark.net/pub/rbenn/home.html

Summary: This site contains an extensive and handy index into useful pages of Cisco's Web site. Use it to find article on subnetting, OSPF, and loads of other topics.

Used Cisco Equipment Sources

Remarketing.com's Cisco World

URL: www.remarketing.com/ciscoworld/

Summary: Index of companies that sell used/refurbished Cisco equipment

NetFix

Phone: 210-352-9804
E-mail: lskok@netfix.com
URL: www.netfix.com
Summary: Vendor of new and used Cisco equipment

Network Hardware Resale Inc.

Phone: 800-451-3407
Fax: 805-964-9405
E-mail: sales@networkhardware.com
URL: www.networkhardware.com
Summary: Buys and sells used Cisco equipment

Network Solutions

Phone: 0181 88 44 800 (UK)
Fax: 0181 88 44 030
E-mail: sales@network-sol.com
URL: www.network-sol.com

Summary: Buys and sells used Cisco, 3COM, and Bay Networks equipment.

Warwick Data

Phone: 973-560-3200
Fax: 973-560-1660
E-mail: sales@warwickdata.com
URL: www.warwickdata.com
Summary: Vendor of used/refurbished Cisco equipment

Cisco Users Groups

Central Texas LAN Association (CTLA) Cisco SIG

Phone: 800-505-5333
URL: www.ctla.org/public/ctla/sigs/cisco.htm

Cisco Users Group of Central Iowa

URL: cisco.farmdayta.com/index.html

Colorado Springs Cisco Users Group (CSCUG)

URL: cug.atsgroup.com

Dallas/Fort Worth Cisco Users Group

Phone: 972-364-8700
URL: dfw.cisco-users.org

Denver Cisco Users Group (DCUG)

Phone: (303) 220-6100
URL: www.scd.ucar.edu/nets/Introducing/Staff/siemsen/DCUG/

Eastern Iowa Cisco Users Group (EICUG)

URL: eia.cisco-users.org

East Tennessee Cisco Users Group (ETCUG)

URL: www.etcug.org/news.htm

Kansas Cisco Users Group (KCUG)

URL: www.cugkansas.com/home.cfm

New England Cisco Systems Users Group

URL: www.ciscousers.com/index.htm

Northern California Cisco Users Group

Phone: 916-636-2003
URL: www.csecnet.com/cisco/index.htm

Phoenix Cisco Users Group

Phone: 602-912-1800
E-mail: phx-ciscousers@cisco.com
URL: phx.cisco-users.org/non_js/index.html

On Cisco's Web Site

CCIE Update presentations

URL: www.cisco.com/warp/public/625/ccie/presentations.shtml
Summary: Contains Adobe PDF documents with technology updates—good for boning up on things like LAN and WAN switching, network management, core routing, Voice over IP, and more.

Cisco Self Study Materials

URL: www.cisco.com/warp/public/10/wwtraining/cust/course_selfp_main.shtml
Summary: This page provides descriptions, part numbers, pricing, and ordering information for Cisco's self-study materials.

Cisco Class Locator

URL: www.cisco.com/pcgi-bin/front.x/wwtraining/locator.pl
Summary: Find Cisco classes by location and/or date.

Cisco Product Documentation

URL: www.cisco.com/univercd/cc/td/doc/product/index.htm
Summary: This is the place to read up on specific Cisco products.

Cisco Networking Academies

URL: www.cisco.com/warp/public/779/edu/academy/
Summary: This is the home page for the Networking Academies program. This program is one way to obtain hands-on training.

Cisco University Online

URL: www.cisco.com/warp/public/10/ciscou/cco/welcome2.html
Summary: The "classes" available at this site are online presentations covering various internetworking technologies.

Internetworking Technology Overview

URL: www.cisco.com/univercd/cc/td/doc/cisintwk/ito_doc/55181.htm
Summary: This extensive document covers internetworking basics, LAN and WAN protocols, bridging and switching, networking protocols, routing protocols, and network management.

Internetwork Design Guide

URL: www.cisco.com/univercd/cc/td/doc/cisintwk/idg4/index.htm
Summary: This document was created for CCIE candidates, but will prove useful to other Cisco certification candidates as well.

Internetwork Troubleshooting Guide

URL: www.cisco.com/univercd/cc/td/doc/cisintwk/itg_v1/itg_pref.htm
Summary: This document was written for individuals who manage internetworks that use Cisco products and protocols.

OSPF Design Guide

URL: www.cisco.com/warp/public/104/2.html
Summary: This document explains how the OSPF (Open Shortest Path First) Internet gateway protocol works.

Cisco Certified Training Partners Worldwide

> This list changes from time to time. For the latest information check Cisco's Web site.

Argentina

IT College
Maipu 939 1 Piso, Buenos Aires, Argentina - 1006
Phone: 541-312-2188   **Fax:** 541-312-3311
E-mail: info@itcollege.com.ar
URL: www.itcollege.com.ar/

Softnet SA
Peru 327, Piso 1, Buenos Aires, Argentina - 1067
Phone: 541-343-4990   **Fax:** 541-343-9132
E-mail: capacitacion@softnet.com.ar
URL: www.softnet.com.ar/

Australia

Cisco Systems Australia Pty Ltd
Level 17, 99 Walker Street
North Sydney, NSW, Australia - 2060
Phone: 61 2 9937 4343   **Fax:** 61 2 9957 4350

Com Tech Education Services
10th Floor, Thakral House, 301 George Street
Sydney, NSW, Australia - 2000
Phone: 61 131 201   **Fax:** 61 2 9299 3154
E-mail: training@comtech.com.au
URL: education.comtech.com.au/

GeoTrain Corporation–Asia Pacific
100 Miller St., Level 30
North Sydney, NSW, Australia - 2060
Phone: + 61 2 9923 0888   **Fax:** + 61 2 9956 7846
E-mail: info@geotrain.com.au
URL: www.geotrain.com/

Global Knowledge Network-Australia
Level 12, 1 Castlereagh Street,
Sydney, NSW, Australia - 2000
URL: www.arg.com/

Austria

Global Knowledge Network GmbH-Austria
Gutheil-Schoder-Gasse 11, Vienna, Austria - A-1100
Phone: 43 1 66 55 655   **Fax:** 43 1 66 55 655-6
E-mail: info@globalknowledge.at
URL: www.globalknowledge.at/

Pro In Consulting–Austria
Hietzinger Hauptstrasse 49, Vienna, Austria - A-1130
Phone: 43 1 87860 0   **Fax:** 43 1-87860 60
E-mail: education@proin.via.at
URL: www.proin.via.at/

Pro In Consulting–Europe
Hietzinger Hauptstrasse 49, Vienna, Austria - A-1130
Phone: 43 1 87860 0   **Fax:** 43 1 87860 60
E-mail: education@proin.via.at
URL: www.proin.via.at/

Belgium

Ilion S.A.–Belgium
Tweedekkerstraat 187, Brussels, Belgium - B-1140
Phone: 32 2 245 31 00   **Fax:** 32 2 245 42 10
E-mail: faculty@ilion.be

NetBrain Europe (formerly Comtech)
Rue De La Fusee, 66 Raketstraat, Brussels, Belgium - B-1130
Phone: +32 2 745 04 45   **Fax:** +32 2 705 04 45

Telinfo High-Tech Institute
Geldenaaksebaan 335, Leuven, Belgium - B-3001
Phone: + 32 16 38 28 18   **Fax:** + 32 16 40 02 54
URL: www.thti.telinfo.be/

Brazil

Multirede Informatica Ltda.
Rua Dr. Renato Paes de Barros, 778-50 Andar
Itaim Bibi, Sao Paulo, Brazil - SP-04530-0
Phone: + 55 1 1828 9001   **Fax:** + 55 1 1828 0001
E-mail: info@multirede.com.br
URL: www.multirede.com.br/

Telecon Cons. e Trein. em Telematica Ltda
Av. Joao Dias, 76 - 2. Andar, Sao Paulo – SP, Brazil - 04624-000
Phone: (5511) 524-2624   **Fax:** (5511) 524-2624
E-mail: telecon@telecon.com.br
URL: www.telecon.com.br/

Canada

GeoTrain Corporation–Canada
2430 Don Reid Drive, Ottawa, Ontario, Canada - K1H 1E1
Phone: 800-268-7737   **Fax:** 800-265-0603
E-mail: teachme@geotrain.co
URL: www.geotrain.com/

Global Knowledge Network–Canada
393 University Avenue, Suite 1601, Toronto, Ontario, Canada - M5G 1E6
URL: www.arg.com/

Chile

FACT Ingenieria
Jorge VI 218, Santiago, Chile
Phone: 562 229 2272   **Fax:** 562 212 7753
E-mail: adp@fact.cl
URL: www.fact.cl/

China

Beijing Xiao Tong Electronic Co.
Building 4, No.4 Nan SiJie, Zhong Guan CunBeijing, China - 100080
Phone: 8610 6261 1503   **Fax:** 8610 6261 1513
E-mail: binbing@xiaotong.com.cn

Legend Technology Ltd
No. 10 Ke-Xue-Yuan South Road, Beijing, China - 100080
Phone: 8610 8809 7777   **Fax:** 8610 8809 7514
E-mail: longw@legend.com.cn

ST Computer Systems and Services LTD–China
Beijing New Century Hotel/Office Tower Room 1059, No.6 Capital
Gym South Road, Beijing, China - 100044
Phone: 8610 6849 2618   **Fax:** 8610 6849 2619
E-mail: achowkk@public.bta.net.cn

Tsinghua Network Training and Services
Main Building, Tsinghua University, Beijing, China - 100084
Phone: 8610 6278 5931 or 86   **Fax:** 8610 6278 5933
E-mail: training@moon.bjnet.edu.cn
URL: www.training.cernet.edu.cn/

Colombia

Centro de Transferencia de Tecnologia
Calle 93B No. 18-12, Santa Fe de Bogota, Colombia
Phone: +571 616 3873   **Fax:** +571 616 0098
E-mail: ctt@cttcorp.com
URL: www.cttcorp.com/

Czech Republic

ALEF NULA s.a.
Zirovnicka 1/2389, Praha 10, Czech Republic - 10600
Phone: 420 2 6718 2704   **Fax:** 420 2 6718 2717
E-mail: alef@alef0.cz

ANECT s.a.
Videnska 55, Brno, Czech Republic - 639 00
Phone: 420 5 4352 4352   **Fax:** 420 5 4352 4353
E-mail: anect@anect.cz

Denmark

2T A/S Technology Team-Denmark

Park Alle 295, Brondby, Denmark - 2605
Phone: 45 43 46 07 77
Fax: 45 43 43 44 59
E-mail: training@2t.dk
URL: www.2t.dk

Finland

2T A/S Technology Team–Finland

Park Alle 295
Brondby
Denmark - 2605
Phone: 45 43 46 07 77
Fax: 45 43 43 44 59
E-mail: training@2t.dk
URL: www.2t.dk/

TeleWare Oy

Itakeskuksen Maamerkki, Helsinki, Finland - 00930
Phone: 258 9 343 910   **Fax:** 358 9 343 1321
E-mail: info@teleware.fi

France

Azlan France

25, Quai Gallieni, Suresnes, France - 92150
Phone: 33-1-41 38 15 80   **Fax:** 33 1 40 99 96 39
E-mail: frederic.thollot@azlan.co.uk
URL: www.azlan.fr/

Cisco Systems Europe

Parc Evolic - Batiment L1.2, 16 Avenue du Quebec, Villebon -
BP706, Courtaboeuf Cedex, France - 91961
Phone: 33 1 69 18 61 00   **Fax:** 33 1 69 28 83 26
E-mail: euro-edu-info@cisco.com

Global Knowledge/CATS

Tour Atlantique, Place de la pyramide, La defense 9, Paris,
France - 92911
Phone: 33 1 47 17 44 66   **Fax:** 33 1 49 06 97 93

E-mail: Bienvenue.fr@globalknowledge.net
URL: www.globalknowledge.fr/

Ilion SA (France)
Quai Galliem - Les River de Bagatelle, 7 Allee de l'Ancieu Pont, Suresnes, France - 92154
Phone: 33 41 18 35 00   **Fax:** 33 47 72 91 85
E-mail: jmuselli@toplog.fr

Institute ERIS
2/12 Chemin des Femmes, Batiment D, Immeuble Odyssee, Massy Cedex, France - 91886
Phone: 33 01 64 53 89 00   **Fax:** 33 1 64 53 89 10
E-mail: info@institut-eris.com
URL: www.institut-eris.com/

Germany

Anixter Distribution–Germany
Gottlieb-Daimler-Str. 55, Murr, Germany - D-71711
Phone: 49 7144 2694-0   **Fax:** 49 7144 2694-105
E-mail: thomas.moetz@anixter.com

Azlan GmbH
Inselkammerstr. 10, Unterhaching, Bayern, Germany - D82008
Phone: 49 0 89 61 44 90-137 or 140   **Fax:** 49 0 89 61 44 90 –111
URL: www.azlan.de/

COMPU-SHACK Electronic GmbH
Ringstr. 56-58, Neuwied, Germany - D-56564
Phone: 49 26 31 983 0   **Fax:** 49 26 31 2810 0

Computer 2000 Deutschland GmbH
Baierbrunnerstr. 31, Muenchen, Germany - 83179
Phone: 49 89 7494-0   **Fax:** 49 89 7494 1000
E-mail: computer2000.de
URL: www.computer2000.de/

Deutsche Telekom AG/DeTeLine
Goslarer Ufer 39, Berlin, Germany - D-10589
Phone: 49 30 3 0680 207   **Fax:** 49 30 3 0680 220
E-mail: T-LAN-Schulung@DeTeLine.de

ICON/Global Knowledge

Network Technology GmbH, Gasstrasse 2, Hamburg, Germany - 22761

Phone: 49 40 8996 700 **Fax:** 49 40 898512

E-mail: icon@icon-gmbh.com

URL: www.globalknowledge.de/

NCR GmbH, Germany

Ulmer Strasse 160, Augsburg, Germany - 86135

Phone: 49 821 405 615 **Fax:** 49 821 405 8855

E-mail: bodo.froesch@germany.ncr.com

Siemens AG

Vernetzungssysteme, VS V72 Training Center, Munich, Germany - 81359

Phone: 49 89 722 34050 **Fax:** 49 89 722 24160

E-mail: training@vs.siemens.de

Telemation AG & Co. Netzwerke

Gueterstrasse 5a, Dieburg, Germany - D-64807

Phone: +49 6071 981 0 **Fax:** +49 6071 981 150

E-mail: training@telemation.de

URL: www.telemation.de/

Greece

Pouliadis Associates Corporation

142 Sygron Avenue, Athens, Greece - 176 71

Phone: 30 1 9242072 **Fax:** 30 1 9241066

E-mail: cisco@pouliadis.gr

Hong Kong

Global Knowledge Network Ltd.-Hong Kong

18F CityPlaza 4, 12 Taikoo Wan Road, Hong Kong, Hong Kong

Phone: 85 2 2805 3184 **Fax:** 85 2 2805 4212

URL: www.globalknowledge.com.hk/

Hungary

Walton System House (WSH)

Frangepan u. 8-10, Budapest, Hungary - H-1139

Phone: 36 1 452 5050   **Fax:** 36 1 452 5055
E-mail: wsh@walton.hu

India

MicroUniv

MicroLand House 58, 80 Feet Road, Koramangala Block 7,
Bangalore, India - 560 095
Phone: 91 80 552 1451   **Fax:** 91 80 553 8415
E-mail: train@microland.co.in
URL: www.microuniv.com/

Indonesia

PT Inixindo Persada Rekayasa Komputer

8/F Wisma Bisnis Indonesia, JL. Leijon S. Parman Kav 12,
Jakarta, Indonesia - 11480
Phone: 62 21 530 7253   **Fax:** 62 21 530 4034
E-mail: ifik@inixindo.co.id

Israel

Net Bryce Ltd

5, Jabolinsky Street, Ramal Gan, Israel - 52520
Phone: 972 3 7535815   **Fax:** 972 3 7523906
E-mail: netbryce@johnbryce.co.il

Sivan Training & Systems Company Ltd.

24 Sderot Yehudit St, Tel-Aviv, Israel
Phone: 972 3 6840625   **Fax:** 972 3 5760471
E-mail: yuval@sivan.co.il
URL: www.sivan.co.il/

Italy

ALGOL SPA

Via Feltre 28/6, Milan, Italy - 20132
Phone: 39 2 215 691   **Fax:** 39 2 215 69 444
E-mail: fvincenzi@algol.it
URL: www.algolcollege.com

Anixter Italia srl
Via Walter Toragi 18, Peschiera Borromeo, Milano, Italy - 20068
Phone: 39 02 547491   **Fax:** 3902 55301777
E-mail: infomktg@anixter.com

Azlan s.r.l.
Via M. Gorky, 105, Cinisello Balsamo (MI), Italy - 20092
Phone: 39 02 660601   **Fax:** 39 02 66060333
E-mail: antonio.ierano@azlan.co.uk
URL: www.azlan.it/

Global Knowledge Network Italia s.r.l.
Viale Fulvio Testi 280/6, Milano, Italy - 20146
Phone: 39 2 66182202   **Fax:** 39 2 6610 1958
E-mail: renzo.silvestri@globalknowledge.net

Horizon Technical Services–Italy
C.SO COMO, 15, Milano, Italy - 20154
Phone: 39 02 6599131   **Fax:** 39 02 6598660
E-mail: training.admin@horizon.ie
URL: www.hts.horizon.ie/

PRES s.r.l.
Srada 4 Pal. Q8, Rozzano (MI), Italy - 20089
Phone: 39 2 892141   **Fax:** 39 2 89214200
E-mail: education@pres.it
URL: www.pres.it/formazio.htm

Japan

CSK Corporation
Sumitomo-Bldg 17F, Nishi-Shinjuku 2-6-1, Shinjuku-ku, Tokyo, Japan - 163-0227
Phone: 81 3 5321 3951   **Fax:** 81 3 5321 3952
E-mail: tootakeg@cii.csk.co.jp
URL: www.csk.co.jp/edu

CTC Technology
System Education Group No. 2, 16-7 Komazawa 1-Chome, Setagaya-ku, Tokyo, Japan - 154
Phone: 81 3 3419 9065   **Fax:** 81 3 3419 9069
E-mail: Sumio.Yamada@ctc-g.co.jp

Kokusai Electric System Services Co., LTD

Daihyaku Seimei Bldg, 2-1-9 Shinjuku, Shinjuku-ku Tokyo, Japan - 1600022

Phone: 81 3 3551 5931   **Fax:** 81 3 3551 5665

E-mail: h-ootani@kss.co.jp

NEC Corporation

7-17, Shiba 2-Chome, Minato-ku, Tokyo, Japan - 105-0014

Phone: 81 3 5232 3074   **Fax:** 81 3 5232 3076

E-mail: terai@educ.mt.nec.co.jp

Net One Systems Co., Ltd

Sphere Tower Tennoz, 2-2-8 Higashi-Shingawa, Shingawa-ku, Tokyo, Japan - 140-8621

Phone: 81 3 5462 0877   **Fax:** 81 3 5462 0885

Nihon Cisco Systems KK

Fuji Bldg, 3-2-3, Marunouchi, Chiyoda-ku, Tokyo, Japan - 100

Phone: 011-81-3-5219-6000   **Fax:** 011-81-3-5219-6026

E-mail: kkato@cisco.com

Nihon Unisys

Toyosu 1-1-1, Koutou-ku, Tokyo, Japan - 135

Phone: 81 3 5546 4111   **Fax:** 81 3 5546 7860

E-mail: hideyoshiokawa@unisys.co.jp

SB Networks Corporation

Nihonbashi Hakozaki Bldg, 24-1, Nihonbashi, Hakozakicho, Chuo-ku, Tokyo
Japan - 103-0015

Phone: 81 3 5642 8173   **Fax:** 81 3 5641 3436

E-mail: sdc-education@softbank.co.jp

Latin America

Cisco Systems Latin America

150 West Tasman Drive, SJ-C1 - Building C, San Jose, CA, United States - 95134

Phone: 408 525 8085   **Fax:** 408 526 7117

E-mail: ciscotraining@cisco.com

URL: www.cisco.com/warp/public/10/wwtraining/regform.shtml

Malaysia

IMS ASIA SDN. BHD

(company No: 448949-H) Level 28 Central Plaza, 34 Jalan Sultan
Ismail, Kuala Lumpur, Malaysia - 50250
Phone: 603 247 4619   **Fax:** 603 247 4617
URL: www.imsinc.com/

Mexico

Centro de Estudios Tecnologicos - CENTEC

Consorcio Red Uno, S.A. de C.V., Periferico Sur 4118 3 Floor, Del
Alvaro Obregon, DF, Mexico - cp 01900
Phone: 525-624-4400   **Fax:** 525-624-4298
URL: www.centec.com.mx/

NETEC S.A. de C.V.

Providencia 1000, Colonia Del Valle, Mexico, DF, Mexico - cp
03100
Phone: 525 523 2700   **Fax:** 525 536 1765
E-mail: coseguera@netec.com.mx
URL: www.netec.com.mx/

Netherlands

ACAL Nederland b.v.

Beatrix de Rijkweg 8, Eindhoven, Netherlands - 5657 EG
Phone: 31 40 2502602   **Fax:** 31 40 2510255
E-mail: berryw@acal.nl

Akam/Azlan BV

Poldermolen 4, Papendrecht, Netherlands - 3352
Phone: 31 78 6414 022   **Fax:** 31 78 6413 164
E-mail: info@ronin.nl
URL: www.training.azlan.co.uk/

Getronics Education

Gentronics Software BV, Gyroscoopweg 2, Amsterdam, Netherlands
- 1042 AB
Phone: +31 20 430 6414   **Fax:** +31 20 430 6039
E-mail: getronicseducation.gso@getronics.nl

Landis Group BV

Kobaltweg 58, Utrecht, Netherlands - 3542 CE
Phone: 31 30-2489511   **Fax:** 31 30-2412242
E-mail: jvgoch@landis.nl

VMX Educational Services B.V.

De Brand 36, Amersfoort, Utrecht, Netherlands - 3823 LK
Phone: 31 33 450 6262   **Fax:** 31 33 450 6263
E-mail: info@vmx.nl
URL: hwww.vmx.nl/

Norway

Skrivervik Data AS

Postboks 3885 Ulleval, Hageby, Oslo, Norway - N-0805
Phone: 47 22 18 58 00   **Fax:** 47 22 18 59 98
E-mail: johanna@sdata.no
URL: www.sdata.no/

Pakistan

Comsats

30-Ataturk Avenue, G-6/4, Islamabad, Punjab, Pakistan - 44000
Phone: 92 51 920 4894   **Fax:** 92 51 921 6539
E-mail: comsats@isb.comsats.net.pk
URL: www.comsats.net.pk/

Sysnet Education (Pvt)

79-B, Tipu Sultan Road, Karachi, Pakistan - 75350
Phone: 92 21 453 3366   **Fax:** 92 21 453 3369
E-mail: nasser@sys.net.pk

Poland

Hector SA

Gwiazdzista 19, Warsaw, Poland - 01-651
Phone: 48 22 639 25 00   **Fax:** 48 22 639 2501
E-mail: school@hector.com.pl

Solidex Ltd

ul Juliuza Lea 124, Krakew, Poland - 30-133
Phone: 48 12 636 85 88   **Fax:** 48 12 636 5545
E-mail: solidex@solidex.com.pl

Techmex S.A.

Ul Partyzantow 71, Bielsko-Biata, Poland - 43-316
Phone: 48 33 130 291   **Fax:** 48 33 130 030
E-mail: kmarkowicz@techmex.com.pl

Portugal

Rumos, Formaçao e Communicaçao SA

Rua D. Estefania, 165-D, 1000 Lisboa, Portugal
Phone: 351 1 315 81 77   **Fax:** 351 1 355 55 11
E-mail: susana.godinho@rumos.pt

Russian Federation

Comptek International, Inc.

GUBKINA, 3, Moscow, Russian Federation - 117809
Phone: 7 095 135 4313   **Fax:** 7 095 135 1581
E-mail: igor@comptek.ru
URL: www.comptek.ru/

Hewlett-Packard AO

4/17, Kv. 12 Pokrovsky Blvd., Moscow, Russian Federation - 101000
Phone: 7 095 797 3500   **Fax:** 7 095 797 3501

ISL aka Internetworking Solutions Laboratory

Maliy Znamensky Preulok 8, Stroenie 1, Office 5B 5th Floor, Moscow, Russian Federation - 121019
Phone: 7 095 203 85 15   **Fax:** 7 095 926 51 59
E-mail: info@isl.ru
URL: www.isl.ru/

Microtest

Schors str. 15, Ekaterinburg, Russian Federation - 620142
Phone: +7 (3432) 605-253, 222-155   **Fax:** +7 (3432) 605-175
E-mail: TBykova@microtest.ru
URL: www.microtest.ru/

Redcenter

Computer Science Department, Room 764,
2nd Educational Bldg, Moscow State University,
Moscow, Russian Federation - 119899

Phone: 7 095 939 46 71   **Fax:** 7 0 95 939 25 96
E-mail: info@redcenter.ru

Singapore

ST Computer Systems and Service LTD
Network Communications, 7 Bedok South Road, Singapore, Malaysia- 469272
Phone: 65 240 3769   **Fax:** 65 2403110
E-mail: training@stcs.com.sg

Training Partners Pte Ltd.
6 Shenton Way, #24-11 DBS Tower 2, Singapore, Malaysia - 068809
Phone: 65 3237988   **Fax:** 65 3237933
E-mail: help@training-partners.com
URL: www.training-partners.com/

Slovenia

NIL Limited
Einspielerjeva 6, Ljubljana, Slovenia - SI-1000
Phone: +386 61 1746 500   **Fax:** +386 61 1314 161
URL: www.nil.si/

South Africa

Executrain of South Africa
Suite 317, South Tower, Sandton Square, Sandton, Gauteng, South Africa - 2196
Phone: 27 11 320 7900   **Fax:** 27 11 883 7171
E-mail: info@executrain.co.za

Professional Network Training (Pty) Ltd.
13 Autumn Road, Rivonia, Sandton, Gauteng, South Africa - 2128
Phone: 27 11 807 6783   **Fax:** 27 11 807 8052
E-mail: caryne@connect.co.za

South Korea

DACOM International
DACOM Corp. Bldg. Rm 1403, Hangang-ro 3-Ga, Yongsan-ku, Seoul, South Korea - 140-716
Phone: 82 2 3465 4717   **Fax:** 82 2 3465 4754
E-mail: wingss@chollian.dacom.co.kr

SoftBank Korea Co, Ltd
8F Yongsan B/D, 92 Gaweol-dong Yongsan-ku, Seoul, South Korea - 140-150
Phone: 82 2 3600 091   **Fax:** 82 2 716 5295
E-mail: hkki@softbank.co.kr

Spain

FRINGES Systemas Informaticos S.A.
Av. Aragon, 30, Ed. Europa, 11 Floor, Valencia, Spain - 46185
Phone: 34-6-275-43-21   **Fax:** 34-6-275-41-97
URL: www.fringes.net/

Global Knowledge Network–Spain
Paseo de la Castellana, No. 216 Pl. 2, Madrid, Spain - 28046
Phone: 34 13449649   **Fax:** 34 13449333
URL: www.globalknowledge.es/

Tecnova
Consultores e Ingenieros, de Sistemas de Informacion, Madrid, Spain - 28006
Phone: 34 1 431 9016   **Fax:** 34 1 575 1026
URL: www.tecnova.es/

Sweden

2T A/S Technology Team -2T Sweden
Eurostop, Box 919, Halmstad, Sweden - 30119
Phone: 45 43 46 07 77   **Fax:** 45 43 43 44 59
E-mail: training@2t.dk
URL: www.2t.dk

Azlan Scandinavia AB–Sweden
Parkvagen 2A, Solna, Sweden - 16935
Phone: 46 8544 90600   **Fax:** 46 8 470 2720
E-mail: traning@azlan.se

Enator Dotcom AB
Kronborgsgrand 9, 2tr, Box 71, Kista, Sweden - 164 94
Phone: 46 8 4776722   **Fax:** 46 8 250030
E-mail: edu.academy@enator.se
URL: www.netac.enator.se/

Internetworking University Sweden
Archimedesv. 4, Box 20161, Bromma, Sweden - 161 02
Phone: 46 8 566 232 40   **Fax:** 46 8 566 232 41
E-mail: info@iuab.se
URL: www.iuab.se/

PC LAN AB
Englundavagen 13, Solna, Sweden - 17121
Phone: 46 8 404 1300   **Fax:** 46 8 404 1301
E-mail: info@pclan.se

Switzerland

ABC Systems AG
Ruetistrasse 28, Schlieren, Switzerland - CH-8952
Phone: 41 1 730 6000   **Fax:** 41 1731 0141
E-mail: manuelmaranta@abcsystems.ch

AnyWeb-Osys
Osys Informatik-Schulung, Hofwiesenstrasse 350, Zurich, Switzerland - 8050
Phone: 41 1 317 18 19   **Fax:** 41 1 317 18 20
E-mail: office@osys.ch
URL: www.osys.ch

Datrac AG
Grabenweg, CH-3177, Laupen, Switzerland
Phone: 41 31 740 21 11   **Fax:** 41 31 740 21 21
E-mail: training@datrac.ch
URL: www.datrac.ch/

Taiwan

First International Computer, Inc.
6F. Formosa Plastics Rear Building, 201-24., Tun Hwa N. Rd., Taipei, Taiwan - 105
Phone: 886 2 2717 4500   **Fax:** 886 2 2713 0241
E-mail: nelly-lin@fic.com.tw

Sysage Technology Company Ltd
3F-3, No. 135 Section 4 Pa-Der Road, Taipei, Taiwan - 105
Phone: 886 2 2761 6662   **Fax:** 886 2 27480060
E-mail: sonny@sysage.com.tw
URL: www.sysage.com.tw/

Zero One Technology Co., Ltd
4F, 111, Chung-Shan N. Road Sec 2, Taipei, Taiwan - 10450
Phone: 886 2 2565 2323   **Fax:** 886 2 2571 4698
E-mail: csean@zerone.com.tw
URL: www.techdata.com/content/training/td_train.asp

Thailand

Assumption University
Huamark Bankapi, Bangkok, Thailand - 10240
Phone: 662 300 4553 ext.13   **Fax:** 662 719 0484
E-mail: training@ksc.au.ac.th

Turkey

Armada Bilgisayar A.S.
Abide-i Hurriyet Cad No. 286, Istanbul, Turkey - 80330
Phone: 90 212 230 8980   **Fax:** 90 212 232 2355
E-mail: egitim@mail.armada.com.tr

KocSistem
Unalan Mah. Ayazma Cad, Camlica Is Merkezi B3 Blok 81190,
Iskudar Istanbul, Turkey
Phone: 90 216 454 1300   **Fax:** 90 216 454 13 63
URL: www.kocsistem.com.tr/

United Arab Emirates

Fast Lane Computer Consultancy
White Crown Building 1402, PO Box 53941, Dubai, United Arab
Emirates
Phone: 9714 314302   **Fax:** 9714 314660
E-mail: fastlane@emirates.net.ae
URL: www.flane.com/

Synergy Consulting and Training
Almoosa Tower 2, Suite 202, PO Box 25238, Dubai, United Arab Emirates
Phone: 971 4 316 144   **Fax:** 971 4 323 348
E-mail: synergyt@emirates.net.ae

United Kingdom

Azlan Limited
Azlan House, Mulberry Business Park, Wokingham, Berkshire RG41 2GY, United Kingdom
Phone: 44 1734 894400   **Fax:** 44 1734 894300
URL: www.training.azlan.co.uk/

GeoTrain Corporation–Europe
1 Grenfell Road, Maidenhead, Berkshire SL6 1HN, United Kingdom
Phone: 44 1 628 594700   **Fax:** 44 1 628 776600
E-mail: hqoffice@geotrain-europe.co.uk
URL: www.geotrain.com/

Horizon Technical Services – UK/Ireland
No. 1 Chancery Lane, London WC2A 1AF, United Kingdom
Phone: 44 1 71 632 4000   **Fax:** 44 1 71 632 4001
E-mail: training.admin@hts-europe.com
URL: www.hts-europe.com/

Ilion Faculty – UK
Unit 1, Silverglade Business Park, Leatherhead Road, Chessington, Surrey KT92NQ, United Kingdom
Phone: 44 1371 7404 00   **Fax:** 44 1372 737478
E-mail: jhunter@ilion.com

Managed Training Services Ltd
Mantras House, 37a High Street, Marlow, Bucks SL7 1AU, United Kingdom
Phone: 44 1628 898 121   **Fax:** 44 1628 898 166
E-mail: office@mantras.com
URL: www.mantras.com/

OutSource Group
Westerly Point, Market Street, Bracknell, Berkshire RG 12 1QB,
United Kingdom
Phone: 44 1344 497700   **Fax:** 44 1344 497711
URL: www.outsourcegroup.com/

RBR Networks Limited
Chandlers House, Wilksinson Road, Cirencester GL7 1YT, United
Kingdom
Phone: 44 1285 647001   **Fax:** 44 1285 644905
E-mail: jamess@rbrnet.co.uk

Silverlake International Ltd.
8, Adam Court, Henley on Thames, Oxon RG9 2BJ, United Kingdom
Phone: (44) 1491 577322   **Fax:** (44) 1491 577315
URL: www.silverlake.co.uk/

Tower Education Limited
Cornaways House, Southlands Road, Wokingham, Berkshire
RG402H5, United Kingdom
Phone: 44 1 256 847314   **Fax:** 44 1 256 847991

Wang Global
Mill Court, Featherstone Road, Wolverton Mill, Milton Keynes,
MK12 5RF, United Kingdom
Phone: 44-1-908 203403   **Fax:** 44-1-908 203412
URL: www.wang.com/uk/

United States

ARG/Global Knowledge
9000 Regency Parkway, Suite 500, Cary, NC 27511
Phone: 919-461-8600   **Fax:** 919-461-8646
E-mail: am_info@globalknowledge.com
URL: am.globalknowledge.com

Ascolta Training Company, LLC
2351 McGaw Avenue, Irvine, CA 92614
Phone: 949-477-2000   **Fax:** 949-477-2162
E-mail: training@ascolta.com
URL: www.ascoltatraining.com

Automation Research Systems -ARS
4480 King St., Suite 300, Alexandria, VA 22302
Phone: 703-824-6222   **Fax:** 703-824-6418
E-mail: training@arslimited.com
URL: www.arslimited.com

Chesapeake Computer Consultants, Inc.
275 West Street, Annapolis, MD 21401
Phone: 800-447-5967   **Fax:** 410 280-8859
E-mail: training@ccci.com
URL: www.ccci.com/

Cisco Systems – ESMBU
25 Sundial Avenue, Manchester, NH 03103
Phone: 603-665-3106   **Fax:** 603-437-6352
E-mail: bantos@cisco.com
URL: www.cisco.com/warp/public/10/wwtraining/regform.shtml

Cisco Systems - IBU
3100 Smoketree court, Raleigh, NC 27604
Phone: 919-874-0162
URL: www.cisco.com/warp/public/10/wwtraining/regform.shtml

Cisco-Internals
150 Tasman Drive, Building C SJ-C1, San Jose, CA 95134
Phone: 408-526-4100   **Fax:** 408-526-4000
E-mail: ciscotraining@cisco.com
URL: www.cisco.com

Colorado Computer Training Institute, Inc.
5500 Greenwood Plaza Blvd., #130, Englewood, CO 80111
Phone: 303-741-2284   **Fax:** 303-741-6814
E-mail: cisco@ccti.com
URL: www.ccti.com/

GeoTrain Corporation – US
400 S. El Camino Real, 2nd Floor, San Mateo, CA 94402
Phone: 650-685-6830   **Fax:** 650-685-6838
E-mail: register@geotrain.com
URL: www.geotrain.com/

Information Management Systems –IMS
2470 Cheshire Bridge Road, Atlanta, GA 30324
Phone: 404-329-6260 or 888-812-9028 **Fax:** 404-329-6365
E-mail: register@imsinc.com
URL: www.imsinc.com/

NCR Corporation
1200 Peachtree St. NE, Promenade 1, Atlanta, GA 30309
Phone: 937-436-8522   **Fax:** 937-438-6140
E-mail: Customer.Education@DaytonOH.ncr.com
URL: www.ncr.com/trainus

Sequoia Networks LLC
1702 Meridian Avenue H293, San Jose, CA 95125
Phone: 408-278-9021   **Fax:** 408-278-9022
E-mail: sequoia@sequoia-networks.com
URL: www.sequoia-networks.com/

Skyline Computer Corporation
490 Division Street, Campbell, CA 95008
Phone: 408-370-1200   **Fax:** 408-370-1419

Tech Data Education Inc.
5301 Tech Data Drive, Clearwater, FL 33760
Phone: 800-237-8931   **Fax:** 813-538-7899
E-mail: kseverie@techdata.com
URL: www.techdata.com/content/training/td_train.asp

Telcordia Training and Education Center / Bellcore
6200 Route 53, Lisle, IL 60532-3198
Phone: 1-800-TEACH-ME   **Fax:** 630-960-6160
E-mail: teachme@bing.il.telcordia.com
URL: www.800teachme.com/

Venezuela

CTT Centro de Transferencia de Tecnologia CA
Av. Orinoco, Torre Uno Planta, Commercial, Las Mercedes,
Caracas, Miranda, Venezuela
Phone: 582 993 6544   **Fax:** 582 993 8530
E-mail: ctt@cttcorp.com
URL: www.cttcorp.com/

Glossary of Internetworking Terminology

This glossary is not intended to be an exhaustive resource, but rather to give an idea of the types of ideas and technologies that you will be learning as you pursue Cisco certification.

Application Layer

Layer 7 of the OSI model. This layer interacts with software applications that require communication services.

AppleTalk

A set of networking protocols built into Apple computers.

Address Resolution Protocol (ARP)

A TCP/IP protocol used to translate a logical (IP) address into a physical (MAC) address.

Asynchronous Transfer Mode (ATM)

A high-speed technology for transmitting data over networks in small fixed-size segments called packets or cells.

ATM LAN Emulation (LANE)

A method that allows an ATM network to serve as a LAN backbone.

Bandwidth

The amount of traffic (data) that a network can transfer—i.e. the maximum throughput.

Basic Rate Interface (BRI)

An ISDN interface consisting of two B channels and one D channel. The B channels carry voice and data while the D channel carries control information.

Border Gateway Protocol (BGP)

An interdomain routing protocol.

Cell

A fixed-length unit of data. In its strictest sense, cells are packages of information sent from the data-link layer of one system to the data-link layer of another. All cells are all exactly the same size.

Cisco Discovery Protocol (CDP)

This protocol runs on all Cisco-manufactured equipment. Devices use it to advertise their existence or receive information about other devices connected to the same network.

Classless Inter Domain Routing (CIDR)

A technique for aggregating subnetworks so that a group of subnetworks can appear as a single network to outside entities. This cuts down on the quantity of routing information needed.

Data-Link Layer

Layer 2 of the OSI model. It provides reliable transmission of data across physical links and consists of two sublayers: Logical Link Control (LLC) and Media Access Control (MAC).

Distance-Vector Protocol

Distance vector protocols uses the number of hops in a route to determine the shortest path to a destination. Distance vector routers send routing table updates only to neighboring routers, rather than to all routers on the network. *See also* Link-State Protocol.

Domain Naming System (DNS)

A hierarchical system for translating network names into IP addresses.

Dynamic Host Control Protocol (DHCP)

A protocol for dynamically allocating IP addresses.

Dynamic Routing

Routing that adjusts automatically to changes in network traffic or connectivity.

Enhanced IGRP (EIGRP)

An advanced version of Interior Gateway Routing Protocol (IGRP).

Ethernet

A commonly used networking architecture that uses Carrier Sense Multiple Access with Collision Detection (CSMA/CD) for media access and runs over various media at 10 Mbps.

Exterior Gateway Protocol (EGP)

A protocol used for connecting systems into a larger network—it operates between several autonomous systems.

Fiber Distributed Data Interface (FDDI)

A 100-Mbps network topology that uses fiber optic cable wired in a dual ring.

Frame

A unit of data. Frames are packages of information sent from the data-link layer of one system to the data-link layer of another. Frames are not always the same size.

Frame Relay

A packet switching data-link layer protocol used by some WAN networks.

Gateway Discovery Protocol (GDP)

A Cisco protocol that allows hosts to dynamically detect the appearance of new routers and as well as determine when routers go down.

Integrated Services Digital Network (ISDN)

A communications standard offered by telephone companies. Used for transmitting data over digital telephone lines, it comes in the form of multiple channels. *See also* Basic Rate Interface (BRI) and Primary Rate Interface (PRI).

Interior Gateway Protocol (IGP)

A protocol that operates within a single domain.

Interior Gateway Routing Protocol (IGRP)

A distance-vector routing protocol created by Cisco.

Internetwork

A collection of independent networks joined together by networking devices.

IP Address

A unique 32-bit address assigned to each host on a network. It is written as four decimal octets separated by dots (e.g. 131.220.16.254).

Internetwork Packet Exchange (IPX)

A Netware network-layer protocol similar to IP.

Link-State Protocol

Link-state routers calculate a cost factor to determine which routes to use. Routers send their routing information to all other routers on the network. *See also* Distance Vector Protocol.

Local Area Network (LAN)

A network connecting workstations and other computing equipment. It usually covers a small geographic area such as a single building or department.

Logical Link Control (LLC)

A sublayer of the OSI model data-link layer that manages communications between devices over a single link of a network.

Media Access Control (MAC)

A sublayer of the OSI model data-link layer that manages access to the physical network medium.

Multiplexing

Multiplexing is a process in which multiple data channels are combined into a single data or physical channel at the source.

Network Layer

Layer 3 of the OSI model. This layer handles connectivity, including routing, between two systems.

NVRAM (non volatile RAM)

RAM that retains its contents even when equipment is powered off.

Open Shortest Path First (OSPF)

A link-state routing protocol used with the TCP/IP protocol suite.

Open Systems Interconnect (OSI) Model

A seven-layer conceptual model created by International Organization for Standardization (ISO) in 1984 to describe how data move from a software application through a network to a software application running on another computer. The layers are:

Layer 7 - Application layer
Layer 6 - Presentation layer
Layer 5 - Session layer
Layer 4 - Transport layer
Layer 3 - Network layer
Layer 2 - Data-link layer
Layer 1 - Physical layer

Remember this using the mnemonic "application presentation sessions transport network data physically". An alternative mnemonic, starting from the bottom, is "please do not throw sausage pizza away." Understanding this model is crucial to obtaining Cisco certification.

Packet

A packet is a unit of data. In its strictest sense it is an information unit sent by one network layer of one system to the network layer of another.

Physical Layer

Layer 1 of the OSI model. This layer handles the actual physical transmission of data. It includes cabling, hardware, connectors, voltages, and so on.

Ping

A TCP/IP command commonly used to test the reachability of network devices.

Point to Point Protocol (PPP)

> An industry-standard dial up networking protocol that uses authentication and error control.

Presentation Layer

> Layer 6 of the OSI model. This layer provides coding and conversion functions that assure that data sent by the application layer of one system will be readable by the application layer of a different system.

Primary Rate Interface (PRI)

> An ISDN channel consisting of one 64 Kbps D channel plus 23 B channels (30 in Europe).

Protocol

> A formal set of rules governing how computers or other devices exchange data.

Routed (or Routable) Protocol

> A protocol capable of being routed over an internetwork. Not all networking protocols can be successfully routed. NetBEUI, for example, is NOT a routed protocol. TCP/IP is a routed protocol.

Routing Protocol

> These actually implement routing algorithms. They do the routing of routed protocols.

Router

> A device (hardware and/or software) used to forward and direct information between multiple networks. Routers operate at the network layer of the OSI model.

Routing Information Protocol (RIP)

> A routing protocol commonly used on the Internet.

Service Access Point (SAP)

> A conceptual point in an OSI layer that allows one OSI layer to request the services of another OSI layer.

Session Layer

> Layer 5 of the OSI model. The session layer is responsible for establishing, maintaining, and terminating connections between two applications.

Static Routing

> Routing that uses information that has been manually entered into tables by a network administrator. The tables never change unless the network administrator changes them.

Subnetwork (or Subnet)

> A portion of a larger network. Larger networks are sometimes divided into subnets by network administrators for managerial and technical reasons.

Subnet Address

> The portion of an IP address that identifies the subnetwork.

Subnet Mask

> A mask applied to an IP address to identify which bits of the address are being used as a subnet address.

Switch

> A device that links, filters and forwards data between separate networks. Switches operate at the data-link layer of the OSI model.

System Network Architecture (SNA)

> A set of network protocols developed by IBM in 1974.

T1

> A dedicated leased line consisting of 24 64Kbps channels, it supports data rates of 1.544Mbps.

T2

> A dedicated leased line consisting of 96 64Kbps channels, it supports data rates of 6.313Mbps.

T3

> A dedicated leased line consisting of 672 64Kbps channels, it supports data rates of 44.736Mbps.

T4

> A dedicated leased line consisting of 4032 64Kbps channels, it supports data rates of 274.176Mbps.

Transmission Control Protocol/Internet Protocol (TCP/IP)

> A suite of communications protocols widely used on the Internet.

Transport Layer

> Layer 4 of the OSI model. This layer is responsible for reliable data transport that is transparent to higher layers. Functions include flow control, error checking and recovery, and establishing and terminating virtual circuits.

Virtual LAN (VLAN)

> A group of computers configured to behave as if they were on the same wire even though they are on different segments of a LAN.

Wide Area Network (WAN)

> Larger networks created by connecting several smaller networks (LANs) using telephone lines and other media, they usually cover large geographic areas.

X.25

> An older packet switching communications standard that operates at 64Kbps over public data networks.

APPENDIX D

Cisco and Internetworking Acronyms

ACRC	Advanced Cisco Router Configuration (a Cisco course)
ACL	Access Control List
ATM	Asynchronous Transfer Mode
BGP	Border Gateway Protocol
BRI	Basic Rate Interface
BNOC	Broadband Network Operations Course (a Cisco course)
BSSC	BPX Switch and Service Configuration (a Cisco course)
CATM	Cisco Campus ATM Solutions (a Cisco course)
CCDA	Cisco Certified Design Associate
CCDP	Cisco Certified Design Professional
CCIE	Cisco Certified Internetwork Expert
CCNA	Cisco Certified Network Associate
CCNP	Cisco Certified Network Professional
CCO	Cisco Connection Online (Cisco's Web site)
CID	Cisco Internetwork Design (a Cisco course)
CIDR	Classless Inter Domain Routing
CIT	Cisco Internetwork Troubleshooting (a Cisco course)
CLSC	Cisco LAN Switch Configuration (a Cisco course)
CMTD	Configuring, Monitoring, and Troubleshooting Dial-up Services (a Cisco course)
CSVNO	Cisco StrataView Plus Network Operations (a Cisco course)
CSVIM	Cisco StrataView Plus Installation and Maintenance (a Cisco course)
CTP	Cisco Training Partner
CVOICE	Cisco Voice over Frame Relay, ATM, and IP (a Cisco course)
DLSWP	Data Link Switching Plus (a Cisco course)
DSWVS	Designing Switched WAN and Voice Solutions (a Cisco HTML-based self-study course)

EGP	Exterior Gateway Protocol
FDDI	Fiber Distributed Data Interface
ICRC	Introduction to Cisco Router Configuration (a Cisco course)
ICWS	Installing Cisco WAN Switches (a Cisco course)
IGP	Interior Gateway Protocol
IMCR	Installing and Maintaining Cisco Routers (a Cisco course)
IOS	Internetworking Operating System
IP	Inernet Protocol
ISDN	Integrated Digital Services Network
ISP Dial	Internet Service Provider Dial-up Networking
IPX	Internetwork Packet Exchange
LAN	Local Area Network
LANE	Local Area Network Emulation
LLC	Logical Link Control
MAC	Media Access Control
MCCM	Multiservice Concentrator 3810 Configuration and Monitoring (a Cisco course)
MCNS	Managing Cisco Network Security (a Cisco course)
MCRI	Managing Cisco Routed Internetworks (a Cisco course)
MCSI	Managing Cisco Switched Internetworks (a Cisco course)
MACC	MGX ATM Concentrator Configuration (a Cisco course)
MSSC	Multiband Switch and Service Configuration (a Cisco course)
NNOC	Narrowband Network Operations Course (a Cisco course)
OSPF	Open Shortest Path First
PRI	Primary Rate Interface (PRI)
PPP	Point to Point Protocol
PPTP	Point to Point Tunneling Protocol

PSTN	Public Service Telephone Network
RIP	Routing Information Protocol
SAP	Service Access Point
SNA	System Network Architecture
SNAM	SNA Configuration for Multiprotocol Administrators (a Cisco course)
SVIO	StrataView Installation and Operation (a Cisco course)
TAC	Technical Assistance Center
TCP/IP	Transmission Control Protocol/Internet Protocol
VLAN	Virtual LAN
WQS	WAN Quick Start (a Cisco course)
WSSC	WAN Switch and Services Configuration (a Cisco course)

Index

Note: Boldface numbers indicate illustrations.

About the Author

ANNE MARTINEZ is a respected computing writer and regular contributor to *Contract Professional*. She is the author of *Get Certified and Get Ahead*. Her work has also appeared in *Small Business Builder* and many other publications. She holds a degree in computer science and previously worked in the MIS department of a major corporation.

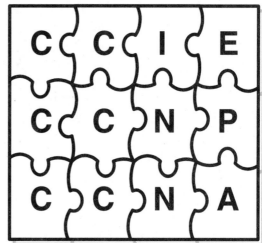